THE

UNION JACK

The Story of the British Flag

NICK GROOM

Atlantic Books
London

This book is dedicated to my grandfather, Pa,
who served under the flag, and to all those
who served with him.

First published in Great Britain in 2006 by Atlantic Books,
an imprint of Grove Atlantic Ltd.

1 2 3 4 5 6 7 8 9

A CIP catalogue record for this book is
available from the British Library.

ISBN 1 84354 336 2

Text design by Lindsay Nash
Printed in Great Britain by MPG Books Ltd, Bodmin, Cornwall

Atlantic Books
An imprint of Grove Atlantic Ltd
Ormond House
26–27 Boswell Street
London WC1N 3JZ

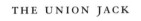

THE UNION JACK

The flag that's braved a thousand years

The battle and the breeze.

(*Traditional*)

CONTENTS

LIST OF ILLUSTRATIONS

1. 'A Young Daughter of the Picts'. Yale Centre for British Art, Paul Mellon Collection, USA / The Bridgeman Art Library.

2. Heraldic tattoo borne by British soldier. Roger-Viollet / Rex Features.

3. The Papal banner (Bayeux Tapestry). Mary Evans Picture Library.

4. The dragon standard of the Saxons (Bayeux Tapestry). Mary Evans Picture Library.

5. Tomb plaque of Geoffrey Plantagenet. Musee de Tesse, Le Mans, France / Lauros / Giraudon / The Bridgeman Art Library.

6. Richard I. The British Library.

7. St George arming Edward III. The Governing Body of Christ Church, Oxford (MS 92, fo.3r).

8. Christ leading a Crusade. The British Library.

9. The Wilton Diptych. The National Gallery, London.

10. The armorial bearings and badges of Henry VI, Richard III, Henry VII, and Edward IV. College of Arms MS. Vincent 152, p.53, and College of Arms MS. Vincent 152, p.54.

11. The Earl of Nottingham's designs for the first Union Flag. The Trustees of the National Library of Scotland.

12. The Grand Union Flag. Private Collection / Archives Charmet / The Bridgeman Art Library.

13. Funeral escutcheon of Oliver Cromwell. Museum of London, UK / The Bridgeman Art Library.

14. 'The Death of General Wolfe'. National Library of Canada, transfer from the Canadian War Memorials, 1921 (Gift of the 2nd Duke of Westminster, Eaton Hall, Cheshire, 1918).

15. Frontispiece to *Visions of the Reformation*. Author's collection.

16. 'The Mary Rose'. Pepys Library, Magdalene College, Cambridge.

17. 'The Fighting Temeraire'. The National Gallery, London.

18. 'Britain's Day' poster. Swim Ink / Corbis.

19. Postcard treating the Union Jack as the flag of British Empire. Rykoff Collection / Corbis

20. Poster for the British Empire Exhibition. Thames & Hudson Ltd. From *The English World: History, Character and People*, ed. Robert Blake, Thames & Hudson Ltd, London.

21. Africans shake hands. Hulton-Deutsch Collection / Corbis.

22. Sewing for victory. Hulton-Deutsch Collection / Corbis.

23. Women working on the layout of coronation banners. Bettmann / Corbis.

24. The Jam. London Features International

25. Sebastian Coe. Sipa Press / Rex Features

26. Ginger Spice at the Brit Awards. Richard Young / Rex Features.

27. Buckingham Palace provides the screen for a gigantic illuminated Union Jack. Tim Graham / Corbis

28. The Black Watch on Operation Bracken, southern Iraq. Giles Penfound / Handout / Reuters / Corbis.

29. Navy Divers at the Royal Oak. Rex Features.

The *Oxford English Dictionary* defines the 'Union Jack' as 'Originally and properly, a small British union flag flown as the jack of a ship; in later and more general use extended to any size or adaptation of the union flag (even when not used as a jack), and regarded as the national ensign'. Many people object to the term Union Jack being applied to the national ensign, arguing that the distinction between Union Jack and Union Flag should be observed because of the specific use of the Jack flag at sea: it is more accurate to say that it is the flag flown from the jackstaff of a ship. In the late nineteenth century there was an attempt to restrict the use of the term 'Union Jack' to such flags flown from the jackstaff of British maritime vessels.

The Union Flag has, however, been known as the Union Jack since the seventeenth century. An Admiralty Circular of 1902 noted that the two names were interchangeable, and Parliament confirmed the terminology by declaring in 1908 that 'the Union Jack should be regarded as the national flag'. It is therefore unnecessarily pedantic to insist on calling the national ensign the 'Union Flag' unless one is distinguishing it from the 'Union Jack' flown by the Royal Navy, and this book follows the current everyday usage.

Likewise, for the sake of clarity, names are given in their most familiar form: hence 'Glendower' for 'Glyndŵr', 'Godwinson' for

'Godwineson' or 'Godwinsson', 'Stuart' for 'Stewart', and so forth, and Old English forms have been modernized. A glossary of specialist terms can be found after the 'Preface' and a chronology of the English, Scottish, and British monarchs is printed at the back of the book.

PREFACE

THE UNION JACK is instantly and universally recognizable: it flies proudly from government buildings, is waved gaily at the Last Night of the Proms, and is draped enthusiastically over the shoulders of victorious British athletes. It is also cheerfully quoted in dozens of contexts – anything from James Bond films to advertisements for cheese, from novelty boxer shorts to punk fashion – and remains synonymous with Great Britain and the 'Empire on which the sun never set'. But what has the Union Jack really stood for in the past, and what – if anything – does it symbolize today?

Everyone in the British Isles and the former British Empire has their own relationship with the flag – as do many more people throughout the world – and the following account is only one of thousands that could be told. In one sense, the story can be summarized in a single sentence: the Union Jack is made up of the crosses of St George, St Andrew, and St Patrick, respectively the patron saints of England, Scotland, and Ireland, and it was first flown on 1 January 1801, when the United Kingdom of Great Britain and Ireland came into being. And yet a long and turbulent history leads to that moment: for almost two centuries there had already been a flag symbolizing the union between Scotland and England (and its principality Wales), and, even before that first Union Flag was raised in 1606, there are over a thousand years of Union Jack prehistory – a strange menagerie of dragons, lions, and ravens. These were the standards of the Dark Ages: of the armies that fought across the Anglo-Saxon kingdoms of Mercia and Wessex, who rallied against the persistent raids of Viking marauders, and who at last fell at the Battle of Hastings to the Norman invaders. Such standards developed into the badges of medieval heraldry – that cryptic science that happily places an armed blue lion ramping in a field of gold against a shower of red hearts – and the laws of heraldry helped to establish both the elements that make up the Union Jack and the ways in which they were put together.

So the Union Jack was conceived on the banners of the ancient Britons and in heraldry, and its birth came under the influence of the cults of certain saints. It was carried across the globe as the ensign of the British Empire, and was a symbol of everything that went with it. Centuries later, the Union Jack has arrived in the present day, where, in addition to leading a tireless life within popular culture, it remains very much alive as a potent political symbol. Indeed, because it is explicitly a flag of *union*, the Union Jack is a perpetual reminder of the unity – and disunity – between the nations of Britain, and of the persistent problems of compromise in defining a British identity.

The Union Jack is, then, the flag of Britain – but where is Britain? Or, one might ask, *what* is Britain? In his essay 'The Lion and the Unicorn', George Orwell apologizes for confusing terms such as 'the nation', 'England', and 'Britain'. He notes that the islands have at least six different names: England, Britain, Great Britain, the British Isles, the United Kingdom, 'and, in very exalted moments, Albion'.[1] Great Britain is actually formed of the kingdoms of England and Scotland and the principality of Wales; the United Kingdom is currently the United Kingdom of Great Britain and Northern Ireland, and the British Isles includes the Republic of Ireland and the Crown Dependencies (the Isle of Man and the Channel Islands). Orwell's aim was to play down the differences and promote a sense of unity during the Second World War (the essay was published on 19 February 1941), but today these differences are being played up.

Recently, there have been suggestions made by such august bodies as the British Council that the term 'British Isles' should be abandoned and replaced with something like 'the North-East Atlantic Archipelago'.[2] This is a ghastly phrase, but it would at least remove the confusion that exists, among the English at least, between England, Britain, and the UK – even in George Orwell's mind. There are serious political implications in confusing the words Britain and England. Making England, a part of the Union, stand for the whole of Great Britain has the potential to be profoundly insulting as it treats Scotland and Wales as if they are minor English provinces, and it has been symptomatic of the history of this group of North European islands that England has been almost perpetually seeking to usurp the title of Britain for itself, if sometimes with the collusion of its partners. So implicit is the imagined identity between England and Britain that many English people cannot perceive that the two words mean entirely different things, and describe significantly different landmasses with their own distinct histories. The confusion persists in Europe and beyond. I was talking to a German recently who was taken aback to learn that the Scots had their own football team: she assumed that 'Eng-er-land' were cheered on by the whole of the British Isles – not least because English football supporters often carried the Union Jack.

But a phrase such as 'the North-East Atlantic Archipelago' is not only ugly, it worryingly effaces the past. In contrast, names such as 'Great Britain' and 'British Isles' embrace history, attempting to make sense of two thousand years of enmity and amity; they are not just handy geographical descriptions, but testaments to relationships and shared histories, struggles, and conflicts. The history of Great Britain is therefore a grand narrative – an attempt to weave many narratives into one national epic – and the very words 'Great Britain' are a shorthand way of describing this vast story. And retrospectively, looking back from the first decade of the twenty-first century, this history appears to make sense: the fact that Great Britain has mutated and survived – even evolved – imposes a pattern of apparent inevitability and manifest destiny on the chaos of historical process that has brought us to this point. It is in the nature of countries to do so. They present themselves as if they are permanent and eternal, as essential entities rather than political formations. But as the historian John Cannon has remarked in describing the formation and history of England, 'There was no pre-destined goal, no manifest destiny, save perhaps towards a kingdom of the British Isles, which was never quite achieved.'[3]

In the case of Great Britain, this essence is one of unity – unity and disunity are the defining themes of Britain's epic history. The dream of union has been long and for many it has been a nightmare, but it is the one dream from which Britain can never awake: to do so would be to end the 'British Isles' as a meaningful concept. Now, after two millennia in which the kingdoms dreamt of union and then strove to extend that vision of unity worldwide, the past century has seen the Union in decline: the dismantling of the British Empire, the independence of the Republic of Ireland, and more recently in 1999, the limited devolution of Scotland and Wales in the founding of the Scottish Parliament and the Welsh National Assembly. Was the Union, which arguably only lasted from 1746 to 1922, an historical anomaly? Certainly the pattern is now changing and among the ramifications of this gradual breakdown is an ensuing crisis of British identity, and, simultaneously, of English identity, which has long relied on England's primacy within Great Britain to provide its foundations.

The idea of union is, then, at the heart of this book: the union of England with Wales, Scotland, and Ireland to form a United Kingdom. The ebb and flow of the dream of union washes around the British shores like the seas that surround it, confirming to its inhabitants the islands' independence from mainland European geography and history, and the Union Jack, made by laying together the crosses of the realm's national patron saints, is its symbol: the history of the Union and its extension across the globe forms the back-story to the biography of the flag. Some may find all this, in Raphael Samuel's words, to be 'drum-and-trumpet history'.[4] That is unavoidable, as the flag has spent much of its life in the company of drums and trumpets.

Like the United Kingdom, then, the Union Jack is the result of two thousand years of unionist ambitions. Like the United Kingdom again, the Union Jack is an invention, assembled from different parts that have been subtly altered in order to retain their identity as part of a larger whole. The flag is a carefully balanced compromise, a perpetual reminder and emblem of unification. Consequently, as the relationship between the four nations within the British Union shifts, the very concept of Britain itself is being rethought. Where does this leave the flag? On 12 April 2006, it was four hundred years since a flag of the Union had first been raised. Is it finally time to lower the old standard for good, or will the Union Jack stream across new skies, riding on the winds of change as the sign that leads Great Britain ever onward through the twenty-first century?

GLOSSARY

Achievement	the complete armorial bearings, consisting of shield (or coat) of arms, crest, supporters, badges, motto, insignia, and so forth
Argent	(heraldic metal) silver or white
Azure	(heraldic tincture) blue
Blazon	originally a verbal account of a knight's arms, delivered at a tournament by a herald; now means the written description of a coat of arms
Canton	the upper, left-hand quarter of a shield or flag; the most prestigious position
Counter-change	reversing two colours
Dexter	the right-hand side of shield or flag, from the position of the bearer (i.e. the left side as viewed)
Dip	the depth of a flag
Ensign	the adaptation of a national flag for use at sea, flown at the stern of a vessel
Field	the background colour of a design
Fimbriation	narrow white border to distinguish between two colours laid together
Fly	the furthest edge of a flag from the staff
Gules	(heraldic tincture) red
Halyard	rope used for raising or lowering flag up a staff

Hoist	the closest edge of a flag to the staff
Impalement	a form of marshalling: two coats of arms presented side-by-side
Length	the measurement of a flag from hoist to fly
Marshalling	combining coats of arms, for example through marriage
Or	(heraldic metal) gold or yellow
Purpure	(heraldic tincture) purple
Quartering	a form of marshalling: dividing shield or flag into four and alternating different sets of coats of arms
Rampant	an animal represented as standing on its hind-legs, with fore-legs raised
Sable	(heraldic tincture) black
Saltire	a diagonal cross
Sinister	the left-hand side of shield or flag, from the position of the bearer (i.e. the right side as viewed)
Truck	a runner for a halyard
Vert	(heraldic tincture) green
Vexillology	the study of flags

I HERE BE DRAGONS

Edwin, King of Northumberland, had alwayes one Ensign carried before him called in English a Tuffe… King Oswald had a Bannerol of Gold and Purple… Cuthred, King of Wessex, bare in his Banner a golden Dragon at the battel of Bureford… and the Danes in their Standard a Raven.

William Camden, *Remains* (1674), 228

FLAGS ARE AMONG the most ancient of deliberate human signs. Since Biblical times, they have served to identify persons and families of rank, as well as provinces, regions, and peoples. They began as rallying points — emblems or images around which allies could gather on the battlefield or at times of crisis — and so were from the beginning essentially signs of union and identity as well as being statements of distinction and exception. Flags have, as we shall see, always been valued as important objects in themselves, and even been reputed to possess supernatural powers. They have, in different ways, also symbolized the union of Great Britain. Before the Union Jack flag, the idea of a British union was not only expressed in medieval heraldry, but also in the millennium before that in the banners of the Dark Ages. So it is worth tracing the vagaries of the heraldic and the pre-heraldic imagination, as these attempts to represent both visually and symbolically a union of Great Britain are effectively prototypes of the Union Jack. The perspective offered here is therefore necessarily long: Britons have been striking flags and raising standards for some two thousand years; before then, they found other ways of declaring their allegiances and loyalties.

The first references to the earliest inhabitants of the British Isles suggest that, initially at least, the ancient Britons were not known for their flags, banners, or standards. Instead, they bore a more personal, literal form of insignia. The ancient Britons wore their identifying emblems on the body itself, and this communal fashion characterized them across the ancient world. Indeed, these people appear to have named themselves after their body art. 'Britons' literally means 'people of the designs', and is derived from the Celtic '*Priteni*'.* In 320 BC, the ancient explorer Pytheas first circumnavigated the 'Pritannic Isles'; the Greeks adapted the word to '*Pretanoi*', and later the Romans to the Latin '*Britanni*'. Some of these Britons painted themselves: 'Picts' literally means 'the painted people' and, in *The Gallic Wars*, Caesar remarks that 'All the Britains, indeed, dye themselves with woad, which occasions a bluish colour, and thereby have a more terrible appearance in fight.'[1] Tattooing also seems to have been widespread and customary. William of Malmesbury noted that the ancient Britons pricked patterns into their skin, and the pioneering sixteenth-century antiquary William Camden argued that the Picts and Britons were 'painted peoples' who

---

* Modern Welsh for Britain is 'Prydain'.

stained and coloured their bodies and moreover were characterized by 'their cutting, pinking, and pouncing of their flesh'.[2] He even proposed the ancient Britons as the originators of heraldry:

> some give the first honour of the invention of the Armouries
> [insignia] in this part of the World to the ancient Picts and Britains,
> who going naked to the wars, adorned their bodies with figures and
> blazons of divers colours, which they conjecture to have been several
> for particular Families, as they fought divided by kindreds.[3]

These figures were characteristically, if fancifully, depicted in John Speed's *The History of Great Britaine under the Conquests of the Romans, Saxons, Danes and Norwegians* (1611), naked but decorated with head-to-toe depictions of the sun and moon, stars and flowers.[4]

The Brits are currently the most tattooed people in Europe, so perhaps little has changed. But despite this – and the ancient origins of British body art – tattooing is still often frowned upon, particularly as an expression of national identity. As such, it retains some of its earliest stigma – the word is ancient Greek for 'mark' – and ancient British tattoos were called '*Britonum stigmata*'.[5] Like branding, tattooing was a literal stigma: a mark of disgrace or ownership, as well as being associated with barbarians such as the Scythians and Britons. For these reasons, the Greeks and Romans identified criminals and slaves by tattooing them, which was a supremely legible way of both proclaiming a crime and indicating the successful execution and enforcement of the law. It also meant that the *lack* of such marks on the body was itself a form of marking, as it was effectively a way of recognizing civilized and law-abiding citizens. But stigmatizing of this sort generated dissident confederacies, and tattoos became ways in which individuals could declare shared transgressions and identify themselves as members of outlawed subcultures. Tattoos were, for example, popular among the early Christians as ways of bearing witness to their prosecution under the Romans. Tattoos not only permanently recorded a statement of faith and mortified the flesh, they could also be interpreted as an imitation of the stigmata of crucifixion, and it is not impossible that St Paul was tattooed with the five wounds of Christ ('I bear in my body the marks of the Lord Jesus').[6] Christian tattooing remained popular throughout the Middle Ages, and pilgrims were still receiving tattoos to record their visits to shrines in Bethlehem and Jerusalem well into the seventeenth century; at the same time, comparable forms of body marking such as branding and ear-paring were firmly established as sentences in English criminal law.

So when the Romans arrived with their invasion force on the shores of Britain in AD 43, they were faced with tattooed, woad-painted Britons.[7] The armies of the emperor Claudius, in contrast, bristled with ensigns: most notably the iron eagle carried before the legions that bore the legend *SPQR (Senatus Populusque Romanus*: 'The Senate and the People of Rome'). These imperial insignia were typical organizational devices of the seasoned, well-drilled Roman military that made them an all but irresistible force when on campaign, but it is noticeable that later invaders of the British Isles, as well as migrants, took up the idea and bore similar standards: the Danes carried one of the 'beasts of battle', a raven (sometimes actually a live bird chained to a tall staff or mounted in a cage) and the Jutes traditionally rallied to the sign of the white horse. Standards were also soon adopted by the ancient Britons too, but neither eagle, raven, nor horse captured the British imagination in quite the same way as did one particular Roman ensign: the dragon. It would fly across the country for the next thousand years and was the first emblem of a united England, if not a united Britain. In a very real sense, the Union Jack flag evolved out of the sign of the winged serpent.

The use of dragons as military ensigns originated in the East among the Parthians and the Dacians, from where the practice was adopted by the Roman army. A *draco* designated a cohort of soldiers (300–600 men), ten cohorts making one legion. The flying dragon became the cohort's standard, and its standard-bearer was a *draconarius*; it was one of six different Roman military insignia.* Some twenty dragon standards appear on Trajan's Column in Rome (AD 106) and later on the Arch of Galerius (AD 311). St Isidore of Seville wrote in his encyclopaedic seventh-century treatise *Etymologies, or Origins* that the sign of the dragon was borne to battle in remembrance of Apollo slaying Python, a fearsome serpent.[8]

But they were more than just signs: Roman dragons were elaborate constructions. The Greek historian Flavius Arrianus (Arrian), a crony of the emperor Hadrian, wrote in the mid-second century AD that dracontine standards were originally Scythian and 'made by sewing scraps of dyed cloth together':

---

* The word *draconarius* is late Latin; the standard-bearer is described by Flavius Vegetus in *De Re Militari* (late fourth century).

from head to tail they look like serpents ... And when the horses are spurred on the wind fills them and they swell out so that they look remarkably like beasts and even hiss in the breeze which the sudden movement sends through them.[9]

They must have looked terrifyingly spectacular. The fourth-century historian Ammianus Marcellinus described in his *Histories* the entry of Constantius into Rome in AD 357 surrounded by dragons ['*dracones*']:

he was surrounded by dragons, woven out of purple thread and bound to the golden and jewelled tops of spears, with wide mouths open to the breeze and hence hissing as if roused by anger, and leaving their tails winding in the wind.[10]

In other words, these standards were not flags but war machines that roared in the wind and writhed above the invading army like malevolent guardians – instruments akin to bagpipes or the sirens attached to aerial dive-bombers: they deployed noise as a weapon.

Although the dragon was clearly identified with Rome from the second century AD, it was later used by the Byzantines, Carolingians, Vandals, Langobards, and Saxons, and Viking longships were famously dragon-prowed. It also became a favourite image among the original ancient Britons and the Romano-Britons, a diverse people popularly and sentimentally known since the eighteenth century as the Celts.[11] After the Romans finally withdrew in AD 408, Britain began to be settled by the Teutonic tribes – in particular the Saxons from Holstein, and the Angles from the Angeln region, who named their territory Anglia. The process of Anglo-Saxon settlement and the long Celtic withdrawal to Wales, Cornwall, Ireland, and Brittany ('Little Britain', as opposed to 'Great Britain', the largest of the British Isles) was gradual and generally peaceful. But as the Celts were driven further west, they did eventually unite under the dragon standard for a series of battles. It is possibly from these that the legend of King Arthur originated. Arthur was the focus of an invented, imagined unity in early chronicles and histories: the Matter of Britain was effectively a matter of union.

Arthur became intimately associated with the dragon standard. The military emblem of his father, Uther Pendragon, was allegedly a gold dragon which he used 'to carry about with him in the wars'.[12] Medieval heralds claimed that Uther's arms had been two green dragons, back-to-back and therefore presumably rampant (rearing up on back legs), and his succession had purportedly been predicted by a ball of fire shaped like a dragon.[13] Uther's son Arthur was often likewise depicted in a dragon-crested helmet: dragonish. But such details were all derived from legends circulating in the Middle Ages, centuries later than the Arthurian epoch, and they do not square with the scant historical evidence for King Arthur.

He is first mentioned in the *Historia Brittonum*, attributed to Nennius and written in the eighth or early ninth century. Arthur is fighting at Guinnion Fort:

> Arthur carried the image of the holy Mary, the everlasting virgin, on his shield, and the heathen were put to flight on that day and there was a great slaughter made on them through the power of Our Lord Jesus Christ and the power of the holy Virgin Mary his mother...[14]

The *Annals of Wales* for the year AD 516 also possibly refers to the emblem Arthur carried on his shield: 'The battle of Badon, in which Arthur carried the cross of our Lord Jesus Christ for three days and nights on his shoulders and the Britons were the victors.'[15] In other words, the earliest references to Arthur depict him as a champion of the Virgin Mary and bearer of the cross, rather than as marching beneath the howling dragon. But by the twelfth century, Geoffrey of Monmouth pictured the mythical king crowned with the familiar dragon crest, if carrying an image of the Virgin on his shield.[16] Geoffrey subsequently describes Arthur's battle against Lucius Hiberius, where 'he set up the Golden Dragon which he had as his personal standard'.[17]

The dragon may have been developing as a secular symbol of unity between the British people, yet it was also a symbol of the pagan and the diabolical, and the Christian Church had a growing antipathy towards its domestic and military uses. One of the Beasts of Apocalypse described in the Revelation of St John the Divine was like a dragon, and – significantly – able to summon fire: 'And I beheld another beast coming up out of the earth … and he spake as a dragon … And he doeth great wonders, so that he maketh fire come down from heaven on the earth in the sight of men.'[18]

Popular references to fire-breathing dragons did not appear until about AD 500, possibly associated with the invention of the incendiary weapon Greek fire. But although fire had elemental associations with aerial creatures, it was also, of course, the essence of Hell, and so from the late fourth century Christians were encouraged to reject all that was dragonish.[19] The Christian writer Prudentius explicitly outlawed the dracontine standard. He described in his *Peristephanon* how good

Christians had abandoned Caesar's ensigns for the sign of the cross, and 'in place of the swelling draperies of the serpents which they used to carry, led the way with the glorious wood which subdued the serpent'.[20]

This victory of the wooden cross over the fiery dragon is, as we shall see in the next chapter, repeated in many miracles in which serpents are quelled by saints making the sign of the cross. It is symbolic of the victory of the Church over the Devil, over paganism, over evil, and there are more than forty dragon-slaying saints in the Western Church.[21] But although the actual appearance of dragons was considered to be a dire omen and a sighting over Northumbria in 793 was believed to presage famine, the creature continued to be powerfully associated with a unified Britain.[22] Alongside the growing Arthurian associations, the dragon was the symbol of Cadwallader, the last king of the ancient Britons and (it was later claimed) the ancestor of Henry VII. The golden dragon also became the royal symbol of the West Saxon army; in 752, Cuthred, King of Wessex, marched to victory against the Mercians at Burford under the emblem.[23]

How unified was the country at this time? Sceptics of these early unionist claims should bear in mind that in his *Historia Ecclesiastica Gentis Anglorum* (*The Ecclesiastical History of the English People*, 731), the Venerable Bede had already identified England both as a single nation, and as the nation that dominated Great Britain. Bede described 'Engla-land' – *gens Anglorum* – as a region of five languages and four peoples: the English, the British or *Brittones* (the original inhabitants), the Irish who had settled in Argyll and the Western Isles, known as the *Scotti*, and the Picts. The subsequent *Anglo-Saxon Chronicle* (based on Bede) records the information as follows:

The island of Britain is eight hundred miles long and two hundred miles broad; and here in this island are five languages: English and British and Welsh and Scottish and Pictish and Book-language.* The first inhabitants of this land were Britons, who came from Armorica [Brittany], and settled at first in the southern part of Britain. Then it happened that Picts came from the south, Scythia [north-east Black Sea], with long-ships (not many) and landed at first in northern Ireland, and there asked the Scots if they might live there. But they would not let them, because they said that they could not all live there together. And then the Scots said: 'We can, however, give you good advice. We know another island to the east from here where you can live if you wish, and if anyone resists you, we will help you so that you can conquer it.' Then the Picts went and took possession of the northern part of this land; and the Britons had the southern part...[24]

The English themselves were an amalgamation of, among others, Angles, Saxons, and Jutes, as well as remaining the earlier inhabitants – Britons and Romano-Britons – and they occupied the seven kingdoms, or 'Heptarchy' – Northumbria, Mercia, East Anglia, Kent, Essex, Sussex, and Wessex – not to mention the petty Celtic kingdoms of Scotland, Wales, and Cornwall.† Although these kingdoms were not politically or economically united, there was nevertheless a concept – an aim, even – of the *bretwalda* or overlord of the English kings.[25] Bede's *Historia Ecclesiastica Gentis Anglorum* was in one sense, then, a

* Six languages if British (Cornish) is distinguished from Welsh; Scottish refers to Irish settlers, and 'Book-language' is Latin.

manifesto for union. He inspired subsequent rulers to attempt to unite England beyond the sevenfold diversity of the Heptarchy and to secure allegiance from their immediate British neighbours. In the course of this, Bede proposed that the unity of the Church and Christianity had been and would be instrumental in identifying and unifying the English nation. And coincidentally, in Bede's account of the unifying influence of the Church of Rome comes another early reference to flags on British soil. At St Augustine's audience with King Æthelberht in 597, Augustine carried a *vexillum*: 'bearing as their standard a silver cross and the image of our Lord and Saviour painted on a panel'.[26] A *vexillum* could refer to a portable shrine or reliquary, but the word also meant 'banner' – in particular a square flag hung from a crossbar – hence vexillology, the study of flags. The two meanings are probably connected: it is possible that flags developed in Europe at this time from the supernatural properties attributed to reliquary wrappings. Reliquaries – sacred containers in which holy relics were housed – became divine by their association with the relics they protected, and so Augustine's banner may have been either an actual reliquary covered in cloth or just the cloth cover itself. In the seventh century, for example, the remains of King Oswald had been entombed and a *vexillum* of purple and gold placed over the sarcophagus; this fabric wrapping could clearly have been carried into battle as a standard. The tradition

† The kingdoms of the Heptarchy have also been retrospectively attributed their own insignia: Northumbria – a cross between four lions, Mercia – a saltire, East Anglia – three gold crowns, Essex – three swords, Kent – a white horse, Sussex – six swallows, and of course Wessex – the gold dragon.

is, in a sense, continued by honouring those who have died on active service by draping their coffins in the national flag.

Augustine's standards, the silver cross and the image of Christ, may not have been adopted as the emblem of one England under one Church, but the Church did contribute to the unity of the country over the next 150 years, and it was the Viking chieftain Offa who was to be proclaimed variously *rex Anglorum* (King of the English) and *rex totius Anglorum patriae* (King of all England). In 757, Offa became King of the Mercians and thereafter subjugated the surrounding regions, invading Kent, Essex, and London, and by 774 achieving some sort of supremacy. Although the titles *rex Anglorum* and *rex totius Anglorum patriae* were retrospectively applied and during his lifetime Offa was only ever *rex Merciorum* (King of Mercia), it is nevertheless from about this time – over a century before Alfred the Great was crowned – that a more stable idea of England emerged. Relations with the Britons, Vikings, French, Scots, Welsh, and Irish began to settle, and Offa did succeed, for instance, in imposing a common coinage on his territories. Henceforth, the nation gradually crystallized as laws, borders, currency, religion, and trade became standardized, and as political and military forces were consolidated against common enemies such as, ironically, the Danes.

Offa's ambitions were in part inspired by Bede – whom he had read. The germ of the idea of union began to work across south-east England, and eventually became enshrined in the ideology of the English monarchy and in the body of the English king. The strength of this idea, that the monarch was intimately related to the nation, was firmly established by 1016 when Canute the Great, another Dane, succeeded.[27] This proved no threat to English identity: it was the institution of the monarchy rather than the nationality of the monarch that was necessary in maintaining national identity and unity, and this has since been a powerful feature of the English and later the British throne. The Norman invasion of 1066 did not really threaten the identity of England. Although William the Conqueror remained heavily involved in French affairs, this created an opportunity for later English kings to develop interests in Normandy, Anjou, Aquitaine, and other provinces and principalities in France as extensions of Englishness and the English union. More recently, the accession of a Dutchman in 1689 and a German in 1714 presented no discernible threat to English or British identity either; neither did the rise of the House of Saxe-Coburg-Gotha (although they did prudently change their name to Windsor during the Great War), nor does the fact that the current heir to the throne is half-Greek.[28]

Offa's overlordship was not, however, sustained by his immediate successors. Within thirty years Wessex had become the leading English power and Ecgberht, King of the West Saxons from 802, became overlord of the English kings. Although his tenure was very brief (828–9), it is nevertheless from Ecgberht that the British royal family can trace its descent, for in 886, halfway through his own reign, Ecgberht's grandson Alfred became overlord of the English. This is the point that effectively marks the founding of a continuous English identity: Alfred the Great is popularly considered to have been the first ruler of all England, 'the first Good King', and even in his own time was described in 886 as the ruler of 'all *Angelcyn*' – the Anglo-Saxon name for what Bede had called in Latin *gens Anglorum*.[29] He was the sovereign who cultivated the language, established the navy, and secured the country against the Danes – in the course of which in 878 he had symbolically seized one of the Danish raven standards at Cynwit (Countisbury). The cult of Alfred and the belief in a unified England went hand-in-hand from this point, and by the nineteenth century Alfred was considered to be both a model monarch and the archetypal Englishman, 'England's darling'.

Under the *bretwalda*, the union began to stabilize. By the time Alfred's son Edward the Elder was on the throne, he was receiving personal submissions from all sorts of kings scattered across Britain in acknowledgement of his overlordship. In 918, Edward received such submissions from the Welsh kings of Gwynedd and Dyfed, and according to the *Anglo-Saxon Chronicle* for 924,

> the king of Scots and all the nation of Scots chose him as father and lord; and so also did Rægnald and Eadwulf's sons and all those who live in Northumbria, both English and Danish and Norwegians and others; and also the king of the Strathclyde Britons and all the Strathclyde Britons.[30]

Edward the Elder's son Athelstan also took the title *rex Anglorum*, and moreover in 928 he was the first Wessex king to claim the whole of the country, styling himself on his charters and coins *rex totius Britanniae* (King of all Britain). In this, he was acknowledged by the northern kings, the five kings of Wales, and the last kings of Cornwall. Athelstan was also, interestingly, the first English monarch to have his likeness memorialized in a contemporary painting. The accession of Edgar the Peacemaker in 959 was similarly supported by eight kings,

variously of Wales, Scotland, Cumbria, and Scandinavia, who supposedly rowed him up and down the River Dee. Reminiscent of Athelstan,
the Peacemaker styled himself *Albionis Imperator Augustus*, and his
coronation gave a sense that the whole of Britain could be united – if, as
the chronicler Æthelweard rather tartly commented, it was under the
English overlord: 'Britain is now called England,' he wrote, 'thereby
assuming the name of the victors.'[31]

Throughout this period the English fought under the dracontine
standard, and therefore the dragon itself can be seen as a symbol of
unity, raising a national awareness, particularly among the Saxons. Yet
despite the Celtic enthusiasm for curling decorative dragonish motifs,
there are surprisingly few early references to dragons in Welsh and
Irish iconography: the *Historia Brittonum* notes only a fifth-century
report of a sinister confrontation between a white dragon and a red
dragon – an omen that the Welsh red dragon would overcome the
invading Saxons and expel them from Britain (an omen that has been a
long time coming to pass). There are no reports of dragons in the sixth-
century cycle of Welsh poems *Y Gododdin*, and it appears that the Welsh
dragon ensign actually originated in the twelfth century. Likewise,
dragons are absent from Ireland. The English, however, continued to
raise dragons above their armies. A dragon flew at the Battle of
Assandun in 1016 and perhaps most famously fifty years later, at the
Battle of Hastings in 1066, where King Harold's standards were the
golden dragon of Wessex and the shining figure of a warrior.

1066 – the most memorable date in English history – witnessed a
three-way struggle for the country fought between King Harold of
England, King Harald Hardrada of Norway, and Duke William of

Normandy (William the Bastard). Edward the Confessor had supposedly nominated William his successor, to which Harold Godwinson,
Earl of Wessex, allegedly acquiesced while in Normandy in 1064. But
it was claimed that on his deathbed the Confessor had revoked this succession. Instead, he appointed his wife, Edith, to rule with her brother
– her brother being Harold Godwinson. King Harold II was crowned
in Westminster Abbey on 5 or 6 January 1066, whereupon William
immediately began preparing an invasion force. But there was a third
factor: Harold's brother Tostig, the exiled Earl of Northumberland. He
joined forces with the warrior-king Harald Hardrada (also known as
Harald Sigurdsson) with his own plans to invade. The invasion season
opened in the early autumn. Harald and Tostig took York on 20
September 1066 after the Battle of Gate Fulford, before being slain by
Harold at Stamford Bridge on 25 September. Harold then marched his
victorious army down to Hastings, where they met William's force on
14 October and were famously defeated.

Flags feature prominently in the histories and legends of this epochal
year. Harald Hardrada marched beneath his black banner *Landeydan*,
or 'Land-Waster' – a magical flag that had hitherto guaranteed victory
in each of his many battles.* It was, Harald declared, his most treasured
possession; fittingly, after Stamford Bridge 'Land-Waster' was lost.[32] In
one story, however, it is reputed to have been recovered and preserved
by the MacLeod clan in Dunvegan Castle on the Isle of Skye, with a
promise that the fairies will come to the aid of the MacLeods whenever

* 'Land-Waster' may have been a Danish raven banner, designed to intimidate the
enemy by invoking the carrion of the battlefield.

it is flown – although they will only do so three times. The fairy flag has already been raised twice, at the battles of Glendale (1490) and Trumpan (1580). It is now too delicate to be unfurled a third time, but soldiers of the MacLeod clan did take tiny squares of the fabric when they left to fight in the two world wars of the twentieth century.

William the Bastard had no fairy flag, but he did have God on his side. One of his earliest preparations for invasion had been to send a delegation to the Vatican. Pope Alexander II had replied by blessing the campaign with a Papal banner, giving the Normans the blessing of the Church in their invasion: it means that had Harold won, he would have been excommunicated (an early example of English resistance to Rome, perhaps). As it was, after their victory the Normans presented Harold's standard of the golden warrior to the Pope in thanks, suggesting it was a representation of a soldier-saint rather than a figure from classical myth such as Ajax. Papal banners subsequently became popular talismans on the Crusades.

These flags are depicted on the Bayeux Tapestry, which in its commemoration of the invasion offers a fascinating glimpse of the insignia and regalia of the Saxon and Norman knights. The tapestry shows thirty-seven pennons (or pennants) on Norman lances, twenty-eight of which are triple-tailed, and one Saxon pennon even has four streamers.* From the devices carried on shields, it is apparent that these designs are all 'pre-heraldic', with no laws or conventions to govern them. The most elaborate pennon is that borne by Count Eustace II of Boulogne, which may have been the Papal banner secured by Duke

---

* Also called gonfanons, from the Anglo-Saxon *gudfana*, war-flag.

William, whereas the most elaborate standard is the Saxon dragon (actually a wyvern, as it has only two legs). It is last seen languishing on the ground as Harold falls – since the time of Edmund Ironside, it had been conventional for the English king to position himself between his two standards.

The Battle of Hastings marked the end of the years of the dragon. Although for centuries English armies would continue to bear dragon standards into battle, and real dragons still occasionally made spectacular appearances over the English countryside – for instance, at Christchurch in Hampshire in 1113 – they had very little formal status. It was not until the advent of the Tudors in 1485 that dragons received any royal recognition of their symbolic heritage as the fabulous beasts of British union, but even then their tenancy was brief and marginal and in any case based on the later Welsh emblem; they have since been long neglected. But the *draco* of the Romans, the golden dragon of Wessex, and the wyvern of King Harold II were succeeded by an equally fierce – although non-native – creature. From now on, lions held court. They would be adopted, in various guises, by the English and Scottish kings, and by the princes of Wales.

William's own personal standard at Hastings was a pair of lions – he supposedly carried one lion for Normandy and one for Maine, of which he had become count in 1063, and his successors likewise bore two lions. His son, Henry I, the 'Lion of Justice', kept lions at his Woodstock menagerie (probably the first to be on British soil since those brought by the Romans), and he may also have been drawn to the emblem via his wife, Aelis of Louvain, whose seal bore a lion. Henry presented his son-in-law, Geoffrey of Anjou, with a shield bearing at least four golden lions, and they later appeared on the shield of William Longspee, Geoffrey's grandson. This strongly suggests an heraldic inheritance – a significant innovation.[33] Eleanor of Aquitaine, Henry II's wife, used a seal of three lions, and the Great Seal of Henry II's son and heir Richard I *Coeur de lion* (Lionheart) showed a lion (or possibly two) rampant. This seal was lost while the Lionheart was in captivity, and when he returned in 1195 he adopted into his second Great Seal a standard of three golden lions *passant regardant* (crouching and watching) on a red field or background (he is depicted bearing a shield of these three lions in an illustration to the thirteenth-century *Greater Chronicle* of Matthew Paris).[34] Although the Lionheart still took the dragon standard on Crusade, where it was borne by Peter des Preaux, the three lions became the armorial bearings for succeeding Plantagenet kings, and remain on the royal coat of arms to this day.[35] They also form the basis of the team badge on England's cricket sweaters and football jerseys.

King John is clearly shown on his Great Seal with three lions, as is Edward I.[36] A contemporary illustration depicting the young Edward III on his accession shows him being armed by St George and bearing the three lions on his shield and surcoat (a loose garment worn over armour). Interestingly, heraldic lions are always presented individually and 'rampant', and a lion crouching or in the company of similar beasts is technically described as a 'leopard' – a distinction noted by the chronicler of the siege of Caerlaverock (written 1307–14), who described Edward I thus:

his banner were three leopards courant of fine gold, set on red, fierce, haughty, and cruel; thus placed to signify that, like them, the King is

dreadful, fierce, and proud to his enemies, for his bite is slight to none
who inflame his anger; not but his kindness is soon rekindled towards
such as seek his friendship or submit to his power. Such a Prince was
well suited to be the chieftain of noble personages.[37]

It was not until the seventeenth century that the English leopards were
officially designated lions.

The Prince of Wales also bore lions on his shield, and the kings of
Scotland had used the emblem of a lion for centuries: 'the ruddy lion
ramping in his field of tressured gold' (a rearing red lion against a
yellow background, surrounded by a tressure or ornate frame).[38]
According to Hector Boece (*c.* 1520), the 'reid lioun, rampand in ane
feild of gold' image went back as far as 330 BC and was brought to
Scotland from Ireland in the sixth century by Fergus Mor MacErc, who
settled his people in Dalriada.[39] It is first mentioned, however, at the
Battle of the Standard in 1138, where the Scottish king, David the Saint
of Scotland, bore a lion standard – the first reference to the flag being
raised. Traditionally, however, the red lion was attributed to David's
grandson, William I, which subsequently earned him the sobriquet 'the
Lion', and it survives on the Great Seal of his son, Alexander II. In this
early rendering, the lion lacks its tressure and lilies, which were added
later from Scotland's association with France.[40] St Aelred, however,
claimed that in the twelfth century the royal standard of Scotland
depicted – of all things – a dragon.[41]

With the lions were to come other national badges, many of which
reflected the native flora of the Isles, as opposed to the fantastic fauna.
For England, there was the broom plant of the royal Plantagenet

dynasty (Henry II–Richard II), supposedly taken from Geoffrey of Anjou's habit of wearing in his helmet a sprig of yellow broom (in French, *Plante genet*); for Scotland there was the crowned thistle; for Ireland, the shamrock or trefoil; and for Wales, the leek and occasionally the mistletoe. Edward I also adopted a gold rose, and his brother Edmund Crouchback, second son of Henry III and first Earl of Lancaster, took a red rose, as did his descendants – roses having been traditionally brought back from the Crusades by the Lionheart. Edmund's tomb was painted with red roses, and the symbolism possibly gained momentum from his mother Eleanor of Provence, who was likewise characterized by roses.[42] In contrast, Edmund of Langley, Duke of York, adopted the white rose, and the emblems of the two houses would eventually of course christen their struggle for the throne the Wars of the Roses.[43] As Richard of York declares in Shakespeare's *Henry VI (Part 3)*:

> I cannot rest
> Until the white rose that I wear be dy'd
> Even in the lukewarm blood of Henry's heart.
> (I, ii, 32–4)

Eventually, in recognition of the marriage of the Lancastrian Henry Tudor to Elizabeth of York, the Tudors (Henry VII–Elizabeth I) took a variegated red and white rose as their badge, together with a crown. These roses also survive today on England football shirts, as well as on English rugby shirts, and the all-British rugby team is appropriately enough known as the Lions.

Such emblems were not confined to nations or to royal dynasties – they were adopted by all major families and by many individuals.

Richard II, for example, favoured a number of personal devices in addition to the lions of England and the broom of the Plantagenets: a sun shining, a sun in cloud, a recumbent and chained white hart, and even a tree stump – all of which become woven into the imagery of Shakespeare's play *Richard II*.[44] This sign language developed its own conventions and traditions, and, by attempting to impose some sort of order and unity on the world, gradually generated its own logic. The symbolism is strangely folkloric – a sort of visual nonsense poetry mixing incongruous elements. Richard's tree stump, for example, signified Woodstock, a family name; the Lucy family, in contrast, had badges of pike – finless fish which were also known as 'luces' – and so their badge punned on their name too. Simultaneously, powerful Christian symbols such as crosses were incorporated into designs, and patterns like the *fleurs-de-lys* (lilies, the flowers of the Virgin Mary) remain recognizable even today. There is a restless playfulness in this jumble of signs: of blue lions and white harts, foxtails and tree stumps, the crescent moon and seven stars, the shining sun, three leopards creeping by and staring if as one, bugles, seashells, and crowned eagles. Furthermore, they became oddly combined or entangled together when families and dynasties were united in marriage: they could be combined and reworked, as the royal leopards multiplied from two to three, or the Tudor rose grew petals of both red and white, while more complicated patterns could be 'quartered' (divided into four, alternating designs between each quarter) or 'impaled' (the designs placed next to each other). The resulting strange conjunctions conjured up become almost dreamlike, revealing the symbolic world of the Middle Ages to be teeming with an arcane and fantastical hybridity – and it is out of this dazzling ferment that the Union Jack would ultimately emerge. Some account of this sign language and the laws of heraldry is therefore needed to establish the conventions that govern the national flag, while avoiding the blizzard of technical terms that describe Henry de Percy's coat of arms, for instance, as '*azure, a fess of five fusils or*'.

Heraldry is a medieval phenomenon that began in dynastic badges. These could be witty or wry, punning or allusive – perhaps recounting like a rebus or visual puzzle a family anecdote or episode – but they also had to be instantly recognizable and unique. Such early insignia – especially those of martial religious institutions – developed rapidly during the Crusades because it was impossible to identify knights and their men-at-arms beneath helmets and armour. The Knights of St John of Jerusalem (a.k.a. the Hospitallers), for example, uniformly wore silver, eight-pointed crosses on black fields, and later a red surcoat bearing a white cross; the Knights Teutonic could be recognized by their black crosses on white; the Knights of St Lazarus wore green crosses; and the Templars a red, eight-pointed cross on white. The Templars also carried the bloody cross as a banner, but particularly favoured the standard *Beauseant*: a black stripe above a white field (*per fess sable and argent*), sometimes combined with the red cross. '*Beauseant*' ('Be glorious') was also the battle-cry of the Templars.*

---

* Battle-cries often inspired mottoes, such as '*Esperance*' ('Hope') for the house of Percy and '*Crom a boo*' ('I will burn') for the FitzGeralds. The battle-cry of the English kings, '*Dieu et mon droit*' ('God and my right'), was supposedly first used at the Battle of Crécy (1346), and refers to the right to the French throne.

As indicated by the subtly varied badges of crusading fraternities such as the Hospitallers, Teutonics, Lazarites, and Templars, various different designs of Christian crosses developed: at the height of the Middle Ages, there were almost three hundred variations.[45] Other devices were entirely personal: Camden, for example, recounts that at the Siege of Jerusalem, Geoffrey of Bouillon managed to shoot three birds with a single arrow – a feat was subsequently recorded on his coat of arms.[46] Such signs, patterns, and colours were expressed as an enigmatic language: at once a code confined to insiders and yet also a very public statement of a family's position in society and place in history. It was the mark – or rather the seal – of their authenticity.

From these badges developed literally the first 'shields of arms' or 'coats of arms'. The principal heraldic media were shields, surcoats, and standards. Coats of arms often became too complicated to be reproduced in full, so shields carried the primary design: what would be pictured as, literally, a shield in the full coat of arms. Surcoats bore only prominent designs or distinctive badges and colours, and this became the uniform of servants and retainers. These were 'liveried' servants, who received food, clothing, and lodging directly from their lord. Colours were kept simple, even for royalty: Plantagenets – red and white, Lancaster – white and blue, York – blue and murrey (mulberry), Tudor – white and green, Stuart – gold and scarlet (as now); and Hanover (perhaps appropriately, as will become apparent) – red, white, and blue. Evidently you were what you wore in the Middle Ages, and sumptuary laws dictated the materials and cut of what one was permitted to wear, based on social status – ermine, for example, was reserved for earls, and the dimensions of fancy footwear were strictly regulated.

In such a context, livery became crucial in identifying a lord, his kin-folk, and their servants, and it is from such survivals of medieval culture that the Union Jack developed.

With such a proliferation of colours and emblems inevitably came rules to regulate, describe, and catalogue these insignia: these were the laws of heraldry, enforced by heralds or officers-at-arms. Heralds may have originally been minstrels, versed in genealogy and aristocratic culture, but by the thirteenth century they had become eminent officials, overseeing the regalia and entertainments of the noble houses of Europe. The earliest 'roll of arms' described is that of Henry III, and the earliest document that describes heraldry is a Norman French poem, 'The Roll of Caerlaverock', probably written during the reign of Edward II by Walter of Exeter, between 1307 and 1314.[47] Heraldry was evidently firmly established in the thirteenth century, and all knights were by then armigerous (being entitled to a coat of arms), although it was not until March 1483 that Richard III founded the Herald's College, also known as the College of Arms.

The conventions of heraldry developed because of the need to 'blazon' or describe a coat of arms, usually at tournaments. The blazon considers the shield from the perspective of the bearer, so that left (*sinister*) and right (*dexter*) are reversed. Colours are made up of five 'tinctures', such as red (*gules*) and blue (*azure*), and two 'metals' of silver (*argent*) and gold (*or*: essentially white and yellow, respectively). Tinctures may not be laid on tinctures, nor metals on metals. Geometric patterns and shapes, such as the cross or the *fess* (a horizontal bar bisecting the shield), are known as 'ordinaries', and more complex motifs, such as lions and lilies, are 'charges'. The full 'achievement' or 'armorial bearings' also included supplementary devices, such as supporters (various symbolic beasts that held up the shield of arms), crests (a helmet, often topped with a crown or figurehead), and badges, mottoes, and other insignia; this was a way of incorporating other significant emblems.[48]

Medieval heralds also attempted to codify and stabilize the uses and dimensions of standards, pennons, pennoncels, and banners as part of the heraldic communication system, ensuring that these could be reliably interpreted at tournaments or on the battlefield. First, of course, was the personal flag of an armigerous individual: a knight's standard. Standards were long, tapering flags consisting of the cross of the patron saint (St George for England and the Anglo-Normans in Wales and Ireland, St Andrew for Scotland, discussed presently), followed by bands of livery colours containing badges or crests, often separated by mottoes – in the case of the house of Percy, these badges were the blue lion, a silver crescent, golden manacles, a key, an open crown, a falchion (curved broadsword), and a bugle. Pennons (pennants) were designed to be carried on lances and bore the cross of the national saint and the knight's badge positioned so as to be represented correctly when the lance was horizontal; pennoncels were smaller streamers of livery colours such as those on helmets; helmet crests were known as 'tuffes' or 'tufts'.[49]

Heraldic information recorded on standards and pennons was often abbreviated or expressed in an alternative form, but was of comparable symbolic significance to a knight's coat of arms and could brook no dishonour. The Battle of Otterbourne (1388) was allegedly occasioned by the Earl of Douglas seizing such a standard – Harry Hotspur's pennon – and provocatively standing it before his tent.[50] Although doubt has been cast on the 'romantic colour' of this episode, the emphasis placed on knights' pennons in Froissart's account and elsewhere would seem to make it plausible.[51] Robert Rutherford of Chatto fought at the same battle, and was afterwards known as 'Robin of the Tod's Tail', as shortly before battle commenced he had killed a fox and tied the animal's brush to his lance to act as his standard that day, using the 'Tod's Tail' to lead his troops. Foxtails were also characteristic Lancastrian ensigns, and were favoured by the three Henrys of Lancaster (IV, V, and VI).[52]

If the Battle of Otterbourne indicates the extraordinary importance attached to dynastic standards, other insignia such as banners (square or rectangular battle-flags) were even more jealously guarded. They were crucial for battlefield tactics, allowing companies to be positioned and rallied: Froissart describes how, at the Battle of Poitiers (1356), the French army ordered 'that each lord should unfurl his banner and advance, in the name of God and St Denis, in battle order'.[53] The size and shape of banners were an indication of rank and degree, ranging from about a three-foot-square banner for a baron to six-foot for an emperor – which could again provide crucial tactical information.[54] Many barons were in fact 'bannerets', cavalry officers in charge of thirty to forty men-at-arms, named after the rectangular battle-standards they were permitted to bear, as opposed to mere knights, who carried only the triangular pennon.* Knights could be promoted to knights banneret for acts of valour and derring-do, and the ceremony of investiture originally required the monarch to tear the long triangular or forked pennon of the knight into the rectangular shape of a banner.

---

* In the feudal hierarchy, bannerets were higher than knights but lower than earls.

Like the dubbing of knights, this promotion could clearly take place on the battlefield itself.[55]

Banners are the origin of regimental colours. By the sixteenth century, these military standards had begun recording the illustrious feats of the men who served under them, instilling a sense of history and identity, and of pride and loyalty among the troops of a particular company; they were useful too as a subtle means of enforcing discipline during peacetime. These colours became symbolic genealogies of increasing complexity, representing the condensed history of a fighting unit. And like armorial standards, they also became prized war booty themselves: two Scottish banners seized by Sir William Molyneux at the Battle of Flodden (1513) appear on his memorial brass.[56] As an illustration of their disgrace, it was suggested that companies who had lost their colours should fly a black flag until they had won another from their foes.

The Union Jack – a flag that, like regimental colours, it is possible to 'disgrace' – clearly emerges from medieval vexillology, but it does so centuries on. Before then, there were heraldic expressions of British identities and British union occurring in royal coats of arms. The familiar quartered style of the English and later British royal crest emerged in 1340, when Edward III claimed the French crown for the English kings. The three leopards were quartered with the French *fleurs-de-lys*, creating a union of kingdoms in heraldry if not in reality. Interestingly, when the French redesigned their *fleurs* in 1376, the *fleurs* on the English standard soon mirrored this alteration.* There were many

---

* *France Ancient* depicted rows of *fleurs* in a 'wallpaper' effect, whereas *France Modern* carried just three *fleurs-de-lys*. Henry IV adopted the *France Modern*

other innovations: for example, Edward IV sometimes quartered his coat of arms with those of St Edward the Confessor, while Richard II 'impaled' his arms with the Confessor's by placing the two coats of arms side-by-side.[57] With the succession of James VI of Scotland to the English throne in 1603, the royal coat of arms began to acquire the features it retains to this day. James VI and I added the ruddy lion of Scotland to the royal armorial bearings, and he also maintained that the three English 'leopards' should henceforth be regarded as 'lions'.

The French *fleurs-de-lys* actually remained on the English royal banner until 1801, when 'King of France' was finally dropped from the British monarch's titles and the *fleurs* were removed to make space for the harp of Ireland – a device that allegedly dates from 719 BC, when it was brought to the country by the Irish king David. It was Henry VIII who decreed that the harp be regarded as the Irish national emblem when he decided to take the title of 'King of Ireland' for himself. He also added a harp on a blue field to the royal banner, and minted Irish coins bearing the instrument. The harp's wooden body was plain at this stage; it would subsequently be decorated with animals and the figure of a woman. Today, the harp is usually represented with a carved body depicting Tea Tephi, an early Irish queen, whose wings denote her guardianship of the island.

Elements such as lions and the harp are familiar today, as the royal arms have not changed substantially since the time of Queen Victoria; the two quadrants, each of three lions, now symbolize both England

design. The Black Prince adopted a similar badge of ostrich feathers (he also mentioned in his will badges of 'swans, ladies' heads, and mermaids of the sea').

and Wales, as well as the six colonies; in addition, there is the ruddy lion of Scotland and the Irish harp. But as if this carnival of strange couplings were not enough, there's more: in addition to the three lions, England also had a single lion as an independent national emblem, while Scotland was likewise identified by the unicorn as well as the red lion, and these are added to the royal coat of arms as a crest and 'supporters'. These supporters, first ordered by Henry VI, are particularly curious – another fantastical element: the animals stand on their hindlegs on either side of what appears to be a gigantic shield, skittishly tossing their manes and waving their tails. Occasionally, they also bear flags as well, cupped in paws or hooves, or have significant little idiosyncrasies: for instance, the unicorn is depicted with a loose chain to indicate freedom, and a crown around the neck to indicate a crowned democracy or a constitutional monarchy. Commenting obliquely on their role as joint supporters of the royal shield of arms, Lewis Carroll for one saw the absurdity of embodying Anglo-Scottish tension in the two creatures:

> The Lion and the Unicorn were fighting for the crown:
> The Lion beat the Unicorn all around the town.
> Some gave them white bread and some gave them brown;
> Some gave them plum-cake and drummed them out of town.[58]

A list of the various English and British supporters that have come and gone similarly reads like a whimsical circus inventory. Supporters have been part of the royal arms since Edward III supposedly adopted a lion and a falcon. Henry VI had two antelopes, and sometimes paired a lion with, variously, an antelope, panther, or tiger. Edward IV's bearings were supported by two lions, or a lion with a black bull or a hart. Later monarchs used various combinations of the lion with a chained hart (Edward V), lions and white boars (Richard III), lions, white greyhounds, and red dragons (Henry VII), lions, dragons, bulls, greyhounds, antelopes, stags, and cocks (Henry VIII), lions, dragons, and greyhounds (Mary and Elizabeth), and a lion and an oryx or ante-lope (James VI and I). James later introduced the unicorn, and, expanding the creaturely theme, gave the Irish harp a body carved in the likeness of an animal. Since James, the lion and the chained and half-crowned unicorn have remained as supporters, but James also introduced banners for them to hold. Originally these were the curved cross of St Egbert (borne by the lion) and the arms of Edward the Confessor (unicorn); these were later changed to the crosses of St George and St Andrew, respectively. Meanwhile, a particular royal Scottish banner was 'marshalled' (or designed) to be used in Scotland, in which the order and therefore the precedence of the English and Scottish elements were reversed.

The appearance of the crosses of St George and St Andrew in the royal coat of arms is a reminder of just how closely the story of the Union Jack is tied to the history and practice of heraldry, and the heraldic iconography and combination of these two saints' crosses is discussed in the following chapters. But although the Union Jack is undoubtedly indebted to heraldry, it has also superseded it. The flag may not be completely stable and unambiguous, but because it is a national flag there is far less instability and ambiguity associated with it than those coats of arms created by the extravagant individualism of heraldry.

Even at its apogee in the High Middle Ages, heraldry and its associated media could cause profound problems on the battlefield. The medieval historian Jean Froissart, for instance, records that before the Battle of Poitiers (1356), a parley between Sir John Chandos (companion of the Black Prince of England) and Sir John of Clermont (France) ended in a fit of pique when the two discovered that they were both wearing the same insignia of a blue Madonna haloed by rays of light.[59] Negotiations broke down, much to the subsequent detriment of the French. They were catastrophically defeated in the ensuing battle, and their king was captured by the Black Prince and cripplingly ransomed, causing instability across Europe. Heraldic confusions were also common. During the Battle of Barnet in 1471, the Earl of Oxford fought under the emblem of a silver star, but this so resembled Edward IV's white Yorkist rose against the sun that the Earl of Warwick mistakenly attacked his own allies. In the words of the contemporary chronicler John Warkworth,

> divers times the earl of Warwick's party had the victory and supposed that they had won the field. But it happened that the earl of Oxford's men had upon them their lord's livery, both before and behind, which was a star with streams, which was much like King Edward's livery, the sun with streams; and the mist was so thick that a man might not properly judge one thing from another; so the earl of Warwick's men shot and fought against the earl of Oxford's men, supposing them to be King Edward's men; and soon the earl of Oxford and his men cried, 'Treason! Treason!', and fled away from the field with 8,000 men.[60]

The most telling and resonant example of the course of history being shaped by heraldry, however, comes after Poitiers and before the Wars of the Roses. In terms of insignia, the Battle of Shrewsbury (1403) could be seen as the turning point between medieval and modern warfare, between chivalry and politics, even between aristocratic heraldry and national insignia, yet intriguingly suggests how certain elements of the heraldic imagination are tenacious enough to survive in popular culture today. Significantly, Shrewsbury is also the tale of a failed union of Britain; moreover, the story begins with a dragon:

> And now after these shall come out of the North a Dragon and a
> Wolf, the which shall be the help of the Lion, and bring the realm
> great rest with peace and glory, with the most joy and triumph that
> the like was never seen this many years before … These three shall
> rise against the Moldewarpe [mole], which is accursed of God …
> Also, they shall thrust him forth from the realm, and the Moldewarpe
> shall flee and take ship to save himself, for he shall have no more
> power over this realm; and after that he shall be glad to give the third
> part of his realm to have the fourth in peace, but he shall not get it,
> for the will of God is that no man shall have mercy but he that is
> merciful.[61]

So – dragon, wolf, and lion contrive to send mole away in a boat, and having done so, will thank God. Nursery rhyme? A religious allegory? Christianity has a whole symbolic language made up of comparable images: pelicans and doves, apple trees and keys, even snakes and ladders. Do these creatures represent Satan (a serpent in the Garden of

Eden, a dragon in the Book of Revelation), St Francis of Assisi (he is often depicted with 'Brother Wolf', whom he converted), and St Jerome (who considerately removed a thorn from a lion's paw)? Or perhaps the dragon indicates St Margaret or St Martha, both of whom vanquished similar beasts. What of the short-sighted mole, though? Moles barely feature in Christian symbolism, although along with many other creatures that 'creep upon the earth' the Bible does declare them to be 'unclean'.[62] Gathering three saints together to deal with a velvety animal – comparable in the order of things to a tortoise or a snail – does seem, however, a mite excessive, and to make sense of this peculiar narrative we must look instead, of course, to heraldry, and to the state of Britain at the end of the fourteenth century. It will reveal how the heraldic imagination functioned and was debated.

In 1399, the usurper Henry Bolingbroke seized the crown from his cousin Richard II to become Henry IV – which immediately threw the land into turmoil: not only was there a stubborn loyalty to Richard, but there were also stronger claimants to his throne than Bolingbroke. The whole kingdom was tottering – there were rumours of insurgency at home, persistent border raids from the Scots, and threatened uprisings in Wales – and so in 1400 Henry declared his intention to march north and invade Scotland. Mobilizing against the Scot was a traditional act of union, and this ferocious theatre of battle had a bloody history of vindictive attrition. The Northumbrian house of Percy in particular bore an ancient enmity towards the Douglas clan, one which had in 1388 exploded in the wilful carnage of the Battle of Otterbourne. But in 1398 the Percys had signed a truce with Scotland and attempted to make peace with their traditional enemies, although the border skirmishing continued. Eventually it was the wildly chivalric son of the Earl of Northumberland, Harry 'Hotspur' Percy – so named for his speed across the field of battle – who roundly defeated the Scots at Nesbitt Moor in May 1402, and then massacred them later that same year at Homildon Hill. Homildon Hill has been called 'perhaps the most complete victory of the longbow in English history' – the Scottish army of more than a thousand was utterly annihilated; there were reportedly just five English casualties and no English lord or knight got near to engaging the enemy in combat.[63] Hotspur also captured the Earl of Douglas to boot. But despite the English successes north of the border, at the same time in Wales Owen Glendower was taking advantage of Henry's precarious position to raise his own rebellion.* On 16 September, Glendower declared himself Prince of Wales, and Henry dispatched the ubiquitous Hotspur to quell the insurgent.

Allegiances during these times were fluid. Many Welsh troops joined Hotspur during his campaign, while for his part Glendower was, like many of his countrymen, a veteran of the English army: after studying law at Westminster he had in 1385 fought with King Richard against the Scots. Moreover, Glendower's rising was the catalyst for an Anglo-Welsh rebellion. His attention was focused on the English nobleman who commanded the Welsh Marches: Edmund Mortimer, fourth Earl of March. Glendower captured Mortimer but declined to ransom him; instead, Mortimer was married to Glendower's daughter, Catherine. To Henry, this had all the appearance of a rebel alliance cementing before his eyes, as Mortimer's nephew, also called Edmund, was a direct

* The original spelling of Owen Glendower's name was Owain Glyndŵr.

descendant of Edward III and considered by many to be the rightful heir to the throne.

Henry had no answer to this western coalition. It was not simply a matter of sending in Hotspur to strike the renegades – Hotspur had married Edmund's sister Elizabeth and so was tied not only to the Mortimers but now of course to the Glendowers as well. Furthermore, Hotspur also favoured the sovereign legitimacy of young Edmund over Henry, and was in any case for his own part refusing to hand over the captive Douglas to Henry.

It was perhaps inevitable, then, that Hotspur should raise his own rebellion in 1403, supporting both Edmund Mortimer, whose estates were by now being confiscated, and his erstwhile foe Owen Glendower. All three were united – part of a magnificent new dynasty through which the fragmenting country would be restored to peace and stability. These allies even mooted the idea of what later became formalized as the 'Tripartite Indenture': Britain would be ruled by Hotspur in the north, Mortimer in the south, and Glendower in Wales, each pledging mutual support. It would be a rebel union.

So it is against this background that early English chroniclers such as Edward Hall, Raphael Holinshed, and John Speed tell the tale of the mole being ousted by the combined force of the dragon, the wolf, and the lion. The dragon was the emblem of Glendower, the wolf of Mortimer, and the lion of Percy; the mole, in contrast, was Henry, cursed by God: this was a mix of heraldry and Christian symbolism. The prophecy was already old by the fifteenth century, but it was enthusiastically revived in the cause of the rebellion – enthusiastically by some, at least. Holinshed was dismissive of the 'foolish credit giuen to a vaine prophesie', and in his play on the rebellion, *Henry IV (Part 1)*, William Shakespeare has Hotspur impatiently dismissing the character Glendower's elaborate prophecies and the extravagant accounts of the wondrous portents that accompanied his birth:

> sometimes he angers me
> With telling me of the moldwarp and the ant,
> Of the dreamer Merlin and his prophecies,
> And of a dragon and a finless fish,
> A clip-wing'd griffin and a moulten raven,
> A couching lion and a ramping cat,
> And such a deal of skimble-skamble stuff
> As puts me from my faith...
> (III, i, 142–9)[64]

Hotspur's lively exaggeration parodies the tone of Glendower's sonorous mysticism, but this passage is also about the language and imagery of heraldry. A dragon, a fish, a griffin, and a couching (lying down, or *couchant*) lion – 'such a deal of skimble-skamble stuff' – are all familiar charges on coats of arms. For Hotspur, these signs are primarily battlefield devices: dynastic insignia identifying friends and foes. It is essential that the symbols are practical, stable, and unambiguous. Glendower's way of reading them, however, as part of a supernatural system of correspondences, threatens to put Hotspur 'from his faith' – his faith in the lance and longsword. Hence with typical penetration, Shakespeare determines that contests of signification, representation, and identity run through the whole of this play, culminating at last on the battlefield, where the question of recognition critically determines the final confrontation of the rebels with Henry IV. It is perhaps appropriate that the main reason Hotspur is remembered today is by association with such heraldic emblems.

To battle, then. With the old prophecy ringing in their ears, Hotspur's rebel army marched through Yorkshire with their new ally, the Earl of Douglas. They followed the blue lion banner (the blue lion had been adopted by the Percys from the standard of Louvain), which was quartered with the arms of Hotspur's stepmother, Maud de Lucy: that is, the shield was divided into four quarters, two of the blue lion, two of the Lucy 'luces', or finless fish.* But these were not the sole standards borne. Since Henry's coronation there had in fact been several risings in the name of Old King Richard, and the rebels were fêted by supporters of the old regime, often identified by Richard's emblem of the white hart. Hotspur's archers, for instance, were the elite Cheshire bowmen who had been the personal guard of King Richard, and they still bore the white hart on their surcoats. And by adopting Richard's old standard, the rebels encouraged rumours to spread that the old king was not only still alive, but was actually leading the army – such was the power of symbols to raise the dead.

Hotspur met Henry at Shrewsbury, and his tactics for the fight were dictated by the insignia of the king. He launched his attack at Henry's banner, expecting to find the king beneath it. The standard-bearer was slain and the standard actually taken – but Henry had quietly withdrawn. Where was he? They fought three hard hours before the king, identified by his regal armour and house of Plantagenet livery,

---

* *A field or, a lion rampant azure; azure, five fusils in a fess argent.*

broke ranks with a cry of 'saint George victorie' to lead a charge.[65] The Douglas struck him down with his axe. Or at least he appeared to. In an uncanny repetition, the Douglas then found himself killing the king a second time, a third time, and a fourth time – King Henrys were apparently sprouting up everywhere:

> Another king! They grow like Hydra's heads:
> I am the Douglas, fatal to all those
> That wear those colours on them.
>
> (V, iv, 24–6)[66]

All were impostors arrayed in the king's armour, and although this information may be later anti-Henry propaganda, it seems that there were doubles actually slain on the field in the king's own personal colours: Adam of Usk mentions two noble knights, 'each made conspicuous as though a second king', to frustrate the common tactic of bands of knights targeting the opposing leader.[67]

Hotspur's style was quite different from Henry's – to rally his troops he fought with his visor up, crying the Percy motto, '*Esperance!*' As a tactic, it was also considerably less successful than the king's: he was killed by a chance arrow that struck him full in the face. This too may be later anti-Henry propaganda – perhaps Hotspur had simply removed his helmet through exhaustion, or perhaps he simply fell to an anonymous sword thrust. But the result was the same: the rebels fled. Young Edmund would not succeed to the throne, and a different prophecy, one predicting the defeat of Percy, was instead fulfilled: 'The cast-off beast shall carry away the two horns of the moon.'[68] The horns refers to another heraldic badge of the Percys, the crescent moon.

The Battle of Shrewsbury was the end of the Percy Rebellion and the beginning of the slow descent into the chaos of the Wars of the Roses half a century later; it also signalled the passing of the age of chivalry.[69] The new king had triumphed by low cunning, by duplicity, by breaking the laws of engagement: it was clearly unchivalrous to use such tricks and decoys that made a mockery of heraldry and medieval traditions. It would be rather like the captain of a soccer team today wearing the colours of the opposing side – which is of course where Hotspur's name lives on. In a sport obsessed with a contemporary form of heraldry (if not with chivalry) in the form of strips, badges, and mottoes, the London football club Tottenham Hotspur named itself in 1882 after the local Hotspur Cricket Club. They themselves had taken their name from Shakespeare's rash hero and man of honour. When in 1899 Spurs moved to a professional ground, they christened it after the local public house. Was it simply a coincidence that the pub bore the same image as one of the standards under which the Percy Rebellion marched – or did it stir a faint memory, suggest a noble pedigree? Whatever the case, for over a century now Tottenham Hotspur have played their home matches at White Hart Lane.

The Percy Rebellion reveals the degree to which the practicalities of medieval politics and warfare were heraldic, and to what extent the world was seen in terms of signs and correspondences – whether pragmatically or mystically. Among all the abundance of heraldic sign-making and media, the rebellion also reminds us that the dragon, that first sign of union, continued to prowl around the fringes of British iconography as the national emblem of Wales, occasionally rearing to greater prominence in coats of arms as a supporter, or carried into battle as it was, for example, at Lewes (1216), Crécy (1346), and Bosworth (1485).[70] This persistent presence was in part because of the sustained – indeed, growing – popularity of King Arthur Pendragon, a national folk hero who mixed legendary and religious motifs. It was also, however, the result of the growing popularity of another hero – a soldier and a saint. Significantly, the early images of the Once and Future King began to overlap with this martial saint, who was also profoundly associated with dragons, and whose standard constitutes the primary component in the Union Flag. It is to him we now turn. In a scene from Thomas Malory's *Morte D'Arthur* (1470), Arthur is greeted by a particularly telling vision of religious iconography:

> And when he [Arthur] saw day break he went to the chapel to pray, expecting to find the hermit's coffin uncovered. It was not; it was covered by the finest tombstone ever seen, with a bright red cross upon it; and the chapel seemed to be filled with incense.[71]

The red cross of St George: the dragon-king and the dragon-slayer would thenceforth be warriors-in-arms.

11 WHERE IS ST GEORGE?

Bar Harry England, that sweeps through our land
With pennons painted in the blood of Harfleur.
French King, *Henry V* (1599), III, v, 48–9

THE BLOODY CROSS is one of the oldest Christian symbols and stands as a vivid depiction of the crucifixion. St Michael sometimes carries a white shield emblazoned with the red cross, and medieval illustrations of Revelation often depicted Christ armed with a sword and a red-cross shield. Saints such as Ursula and her eleven thousand virgins, and Ansanus, the patron saint of Sienna, carried the standard, and it was also linked to early English Christians such as Constantine the Great, Emperor of Rome (324–37), and Joseph of Arimathea, who in 72 was supposedly given,

A shield of silver white
A cross endlong and overthwart full perfect.[1]

Its most powerful association, however, is with another English Christian: the patron saint of England, St George – warrior, dragon-slayer, and protector of fair maidens.

St George is popularly imagined as a knight in shining armour, a paladin from the gilt pages of medieval romance. Piety, miracle-working, and martyrdom have little place in his legend – he seems less a paragon of Christianity than a daring knight errant, pricking on the plain, questing to win his spurs, battling with gruesome foes to save damsels in distress from the clutches of evil. And he is consistently identified by his pure white shield emblazoned with a crimson cross. It is this emblem that for centuries was the flag of all England, and which today forms the central component of the Union Jack.

Yet St George's appeal was not simply to the English, and the red cross has been raised across Europe and the Middle East. For over fifteen hundred years he was celebrated and venerated in shrines, chapels, and churches from Doncaster to Antioch, and his martyrology and legend were, with countless local variants, told and retold from Libya to Scandinavia. St George has been the guardian variously of Aragon, Armenia, Braganza, Beirut, Byzantium, Canada, Cappadocia, Catalonia, Constantinople, Ethiopia, Ferrara, Genoa, Georgia, Germany, the Greek army, Hanover, Hungary, Istanbul, Lithuania, Malta, Moscow, Portugal, Schleswig, Slovenia, and Venice, as well as England, and he was adopted by rulers such as Charles the Bold (Duke of Burgundy, 1467–71) and Maximilian I (King of Germany, 1486– 1519, and Holy Roman Emperor, 1493–1519).

Why did the cult of St George gain such popularity, and how did it become so strongly identified with England? And where did his distinctive red-cross regalia originate? Clearly such a figure of chivalry incarnate captivated the medieval imagination, and a fighting saint would inevitably be associated with the almost invincible English army.

But St George is a much more complicated figure than the knight-in-shining-armour image suggests. He has mysterious affinities with folklore and lost legends – as well as with other cultures and traditions – and is representative as much of Falstaff's 'Merrie England' as he is of Henry V's clinical annihilation of the French at the Battle of Agincourt (1415):

> Where is St George, where is he, O,
>
> He is out in his longboat all on the salt sea, O,
>
> And in every land, O, the land that ere we go,
>
> And for to fetch the summer home,
>
> The summer and the May, O,
>
> >   For summer is acome and winter is ago.
>
> Unite! Unite![2]

In the story of the Union Jack, St George's banner of the bloody cross is more than just a simple Christian symbol. It is rather a standard that proclaims the unity of England, a unity that is embodied in all the contradictions of the land, the life, and the history of the country.

The St George of the first thousand years or so of his cult was certainly no knightly champion battling fiery serpents. Indeed, the whole dragon episode is, it transpires, a comparatively late addition, not appearing until about the ninth century – at least six hundred years after his canonization – and only gaining widespread popularity from the twelfth.*

---

* St George slaying the dragon appears on the arms of Moscow in the ninth and tenth centuries, and in carvings in Prague.

Until then, St George was a Christian martyr – and not just a martyr who died once for his faith: he was a *megalomartyr*, a martyr among martyrs. The earliest accounts of St George's martyrdom dwell on the many and various tortures he endured, during which he regularly dies only to be resurrected for further protracted suffering. In these versions, St George is a Christian officer in the Roman army who refuses to honour the Roman gods. He throws down Roman idols and miraculously heals the sick, who promptly convert to Christianity. He is brought before the emperor Dacian and complains about the persecution of Christians, is tried, and tortured. Thousands of witnesses to his suffering also convert before his ultimate demise.

The range of tortures to which St George is subjected suggests that his suffering was representative of all the martyrdoms of all the other martyrs: he was capacious, emblematic of total suffering through his repeatedly racked body. Indeed, no specific torture is associated with St George; there is consistency only in the variety of tortures endured between his trial scene and final execution. Writers and artists portray a ghastly litany: St George has nails knocked into his head, is flayed with rakes or whips or morning-stars, broken on a wheel or a rack or a contraption involving millstones, variously sawn up and dismembered, boiled or roasted in a cauldron or shod with red-hot iron shoes, and ultimately – having been restored to life two or three times to challenge further the ingenuity of his torturers – he is beheaded. St George is also often crucified on a variety of differently shaped crosses. During his ordeals, the martyr George is frequently pitted against the sorcerer Athanasius, who attempts to poison him, but who is converted by the spectacle of martyrdom and is himself eventually executed. The emperor Dacian, who orders the tortures, remains, however, unmoved.

The extravagant martyrdoms of St George provided a favourite subject for medieval artists in church paintings and carvings and on stained glass, the deliciously gruesome images being ostensibly to demonstrate the fortitude of the true believer. They also retained a hint of pagan notions of sacrifice, in which the willingness of St George to undergo repeated tortures suggests the renewal of fertility through ritualized slaughter. The repeated cycle of death and renewal is characteristic of the celebration of folk and pagan figures such as the Fisher King, whose lands die with him, but which are seasonally revived with the coming of the spring. Those mysterious practices that are the English mummers' plays may also be a faint survival of such rituals. St George is a common and often central character in these strange performances, but the only shared mumming motif is of a character's death and subsequent resurrection – and consequently the only character common to all the different versions of the English mummers' play is not, as one might think, St George but the figure of the Doctor.

His association with the rhythms of the pagan year is also evident in George's name. William Caxton's *Golden Legend* (1483, written originally by Jacobus de Voragine, 1265), which widely popularized St George's hagiography, gave the etymology of his name thus:

The name George is derived from *geos*, meaning earth, and *orge*, meaning to work; hence one who works the earth, namely, his own flesh... Or George is derived from *gerar*, holy, and *gyon*, sand, therefore, holy sand; for he was like sand, heavy with the weight of his virtues, small by humility, and dry of the lusts of the flesh. Or again, the name comes from *gerar*, holy, and *gyon*, struggle; so a holy fighter, because he fought against the dragon and the executioner. Or George comes from *gero*, pilgrim, *gir*, cut off, and *ys*, counselor, for he was a pilgrim in his contempt for the world, cut off by gaining the crown of martyrdom, and a counselor in his preaching of the Kingdom.[3]

The name George does indeed derive from the Greek 'a tiller of the soil', and in his Christianized form George is sometimes considered to be the patron saint of farming. In this capacity he is linked to the Green Man, and in Eastern Europe, St George is sometimes known as 'Green George'. But the kinship with non-Christian fertility figures does not end there. A mosque to the Islamic prophet Al-Khidr is adjacent to St George's chapel in Lydda – supposedly the founding chapel of his cult – and locally the two are considered to be almost synonymous. Al-Khidr is the 'Green Man' or 'Evergreen' in Islamic and pre-Islamic lore; he discovered the Fountain of Youth and could be resurrected after death, and an ambulance service in Turkey actually ran under the title of the 'Khidr Service'.[4] St George is – like the healer Al-Khidr, like the Doctor in mummers' plays – also reputed to have powers of intercession for sufferers from such conditions as leprosy, syphilis, herpes, plague, snake venom, and also mental illness.

All this seems to be at some distance from slaying dragons. The episode was perhaps introduced into the life of the saint to capitalize on the idea that George was a soldier (he is usually represented as wearing armour) and to provide an explanation for his mass conversion of a whole city, and hybrid versions of the St George martyrdom narrative combine the grisly relish of human torture with dragon-slaying. Such accounts commence with the dragon terrorizing the city of Silene in Libya. It is only prevented from laying waste to the area by the citizens placating it with a tribute of sheep, and then, as the sheep diminish, with children, drawn by lots. Eventually the king's daughter draws the fatal lot and is chained up outside the city, awaiting the dragon – for whom she is sometimes dressed as a bride. The monster's breath is so terrible that none has dared to approach it, but St George arrives, subdues the dragon, and binds it with the princess's girdle or garter, before dispatching it. George then converts the king's household and subsequently the entire city, before the emperor intervenes, whereupon he is tried and tortured. In some cycles St George is resurrected to kill the dragon, and there is an earlier legend in which he was resurrected in order to assassinate the Roman emperor Julian the Apostate.

As already indicated, in addition to its strong Roman, Saxon, and British associations, the dragon was also a Christian symbol of irredeemable evil, and when St Michael fights the Devil in the Revelation of St John, Satan has assumed just such a shape for the confrontation. Although the episode of St George and the dragon probably originated in the East, it was popularized by the *Golden Legend*, in which George's adversary is explicitly described as 'the Devil'. In early versions of the story, the saint could dispel the loathsome creature merely by making the sign of the cross, but the encounter soon developed into a full-blown combat and an identifiable motif in the George narrative. The confrontation culminated with a cross of blood being incised on the dragon's head – emblematic of the victories of the sign of the cross over the Devil, of the holy wood over evil.

In Greek iconography St George overcomes the dragon of the Apocalypse in the presence of the Church, which is represented by a crowned virgin. Hence the bridal princess St George rescues is symbolic of the whole faith, and also of the Virgin Mary. Indeed, St George is often described as 'Our Lady's Knight', and was strongly associated with the Cult of the Virgin, which contributed to his role as a model of chivalry and courtly love. The connection between the saint and the Virgin is explicit in compound dedications in English churches, and they are also combined in designs such as that of the Great Seal of Edward III. Although in later secular adaptations George marries Fair Sabra (the princess) and fathers the next exemplar of medieval superheroes, Guy of Warwick, in Christian hagiography George's invulnerability to the dragon and his devotion to the Virgin Mary were symbolic of his spiritual purity and chastity. This also made George a somewhat androgynous figure, and the extreme suffering he endures bears similarities to that of virgin female martyrs such as Agatha, Barbara, Catherine, Lucy, and Margaret, who also undergo extended patterns of torture. Moreover, Sts Margaret and Martha both vanquished dragons with the cross, and St Ursula even carries a standard of a white banner with a red cross. To determine whether the bloody cross is characteristic of all martyred virginal dragon-slayers, we must consider in more detail the spread of the cult of St George.

George's origins were probably in Palestine during the reign of the Roman emperor Diocletian (AD 284–305), although he may have been a citizen of the Turkish city of Nicomedia on the Bosphorus and there is a Nubian tradition that situates George in the Nile Valley.* Lydda, now Lod, in Palestine was possibly the site of his martyrdom, traditionally on 23 April 303. By 530 there was a shrine at Lydda supposedly consecrated by his remains, but the cult was already well established by then and the earliest churches to St George had appeared in Shaqqâ, and Ezra (south-west Syria) within a few years of his death, *c.* 346. The church still holds what are allegedly St George's remains. The earliest identifiable image of St George appears on a sixth-century icon of the Virgin Mary, where he is represented as a warrior: the champion of Mary. His iconography also took over that of Mars, the Roman god of war. Some depictions of Mars, such as a bas-relief depicting the god mounted and aiming a lance at a foot-soldier, can be seen as St George prototypes. Before the advent of the dragon motif, the saint was often depicted as an armoured rider engaging enemy infantry, which obviously increased his appeal to mounted knights.[5]

The cult of St George was established in Europe by the sixth century, particularly in France. Clovis, King of the Franks, had dedicated a monastery near Cambrai to the saint; his wife, Clotilda, dedicated a nunnery near Paris to him; and their son Chilebert 'translated' or conveyed a relic of St George to a monastery dedicated to St Vincent he had built near Paris. His relics were also venerated by St Gregory of Tours (539–94). In the mid-sixth century, a church in Heidesheim (close to Mainz in the Rhineland) was dedicated to St George, and others followed suit. By 751, Zacharius (the last Greek Pope) had discovered in

---

* Edmund Gibbon erroneously identified him with the archbishop George of Cappadocia (iii, 131); this was later refuted by Samuel Pegge.

Rome the relic of St George's head, which he presented to San Giorgio in Velabro. There were at least five 'heads' of St George, probably various cranial remains encased in head-shaped reliquaries; one of these was eventually translated to St George's Chapel in Windsor.[6]

Traditionally, the cult reached Britain in the sixth century, although in all likelihood it did not arrive until much later, possibly through the influence of Arculf, a Frankish bishop, who landed on Iona in 683.[7] From his earliest incarnations in the Isles, St George was celebrated as a fighter, and in a forerunner of the legends of Arthur and the Knights of the Round Table, Antonius, a mythical Count of Britain, chose the saint as the patron of an elite cavalry brigade. In 679, Adamnan (Abbot of Iona) recorded a miracle of St George later noted by the Venerable Bede in his *Ecclesiastical History* – which was, as we have seen, an early piece of English propaganda – and George also appears in Bede's martyrology, the Old English martyrology, and the Irish martyrology of Oengus the Culdee; furthermore, Ælfric Grammaticus wrote a metrical homily on St George for his *Lives of the Saints* (*c.* 1000). Several religious houses and churches were dedicated to St George before the Norman Conquest of 1066, but at this time he was in no way considered a specifically English national saint.

The adoption of St George as the patron saint of England was a post-Conquest phenomenon and ultimately a consequence of the Crusades. It was in the tenth century (*c.* 930s) that Odo of Cluny had developed the concept of a 'just' war fought by 'soldiers of Christ' (*miles Christi*), which became the theological justification for the Crusades.[8] St George naturally appealed to soldiers, especially to military leaders – aristocratic warriors who fought from horseback – hence, with St Michael the Captain of Hosts and St Maurice of the Theban Legion, he became a patron of the Crusades, the first of which was launched in 1095.[9] By the beginning of the eleventh century German knights were blessed in the names of three saints – Maurice, Sebastian, and George – and, come the end of the century, this trio were providing the same service for the entire English army. St George – soldier, horseman, lately dragon-slayer, and *megalomartyr* – was clearly particularly suited to such a role and he soon became literally manifested as *miles Christianus*.

The first recorded vision of St George was to Norman knights fighting Sicilian Muslims at Cerami in 1063. He was manifested again, in the company of St Demetrius, at Antioch in 1098, and thereafter frequently at Jerusalem, where he was identified by his 'white armour marked with the red cross'.[10] The Lewes Group of wall-paintings (Sussex) is the earliest visual cycle in England of the St George martyrdom (*c.* 1080–1120); it includes the vision of St George over Antioch.[11] The visions of St George aiding the Crusaders in their battles may also be related to the wandering Elijah, who provides help when it is needed, and to Al-Khidr, again, who was a patron of travellers.[12]

St George's livery was instantly recognizable. He usually appeared in armour emblazoned with the cross, and an early carving (*c.* 1100) at Fordington in Dorset depicts him brandishing a lance bearing a pennant with his characteristic insignia. The red cross became firmly associated with St George simply because the Crusaders marched under the sign of the cross and the patronage of the warrior saints. 'Putting on the cross' was proverbial for taking pilgrimages and crusading, and the chronicler Jean Froissart, for example, describes how 'over three hundred thousand people put on the Cross, and embarked on this crusade'.[13] Possibly Crusaders popularized the red cross after seeing it in Middle Eastern shrines, but it was already a generic Christian symbol, and a thirteenth-century illustration of Christ leading the Crusaders clearly shows the standards and shields of the bloody cross. But in any case, the colour of the cross of St George was not confined to red until the advent of heraldry. During the Third Crusade (1190–92), for example, Norman knights wore the red cross, while the English knights bore the white.[14]

There were many stories of soldier-saints appearing to 'fight the good fight' on the side of Crusaders, among them George, the two Theodores (one a recruit, the other a general), Demetrius ('The Great Martyr', d. *c.* 305) and Mercurius (d. *c.* 250) – all soldiers who had been persecuted by the emperors Dacian and Diocletian in the fourth century – as well as the black warrior St Maurice (leader of the Theban Legion, executed at the end of the third century). The supreme commander of this divine squadron was the Archangel Michael. The Theodores were popular in Italy, Demetrius and Maurice in the Balkans and around the Mediterranean respectively. St George was particularly favoured by the north European Crusaders, for whom Lydda became a place of pilgrimage. Between 1150 and 1170 the first Crusader cathedral was built there; it was razed by Saladin twenty-one years later.

The Crusaders' enthusiasm for St George added significant momentum to the pan-Christian cult that had been spreading for centuries, but also began to confine his patronage to England. This identification of St George with England started to be cemented during the reign of Richard I *Coeur de Lion*. He adopted St George as his personal patron for the Third Crusade – although he also took a dragon standard with him for good measure – and was subsequently rewarded by a vision of the saint at Acre. The Lionheart possibly rebuilt the tomb at Lydda and was later married in St George's Chapel at Limassol. It is important to note, however, that St George was not the only saint venerated by the Lionheart – or indeed by the English in general at this time.* The bloody cross was carried by Crusaders alongside the blue standards of St Edmund (three golden crowns) and the cross of St Alban (a yellow saltire or diagonal cross; both on blue). St Edmund was a Saxon king of East Anglia, martyred by the Vikings, who was specifically invoked at coronations as a figure of English heroism, independence, and Christian forbearance; his body was re-enshrined in 1198 during the reign of the Lionheart.[15] The Wilton Diptych, dating from the end of the fourteenth century, depicts Edmund as one of the patrons of England presenting Richard II to the Virgin and Child; the other national patron depicted is St Edward the Confessor, traditionally the monarch's protector rather than the patron saint of the country. His arms were traditionally an ornate golden cross (*cross flory*) between four doves or martinets on a blue field.

Edward the Confessor was invoked not only for his reputation for sanctity and purity and his founding of Westminster Abbey, but because he had recognized the Norman succession and at the same time

---

* The Lionheart possibly had less time for Arthur, allegedly giving Tancred of Sicily, a brother Crusader, a sword that he claimed was Excalibur.

been the last of the Old English kings. So despite the Norman invasion and the defeat of Harold II at the Battle of Hastings, the cult of Edward the Confessor flourished after the Conquest. He had been exiled in Normandy for nearly thirty years before he became king in 1042, and as he remained chaste throughout his marriage to the Earl Godwin's daughter, Edith, and would die without issue, he had in 1051 allegedly nominated William the Bastard, Duke of Normandy as his heir. The Confessor was therefore a reminder of how England had been united pre-Conquest, and how the succession of a Norman monarch somehow ensured the continuity of this union. Both Edmund and Edward the Confessor remained popular national saints during the Middle Ages and, although not *miles Christi*, they too were called upon by soldiers: for instance, at the Siege of Calais (1351), where English troops invoked both saints, George and Edward. The third-century St Alban was another favourite because he was considered to be the first saint martyred in England (the '*proto-martyr*'). He was possibly a Roman citizen who was tried for sheltering a Christian priest and subsequently sentenced to decapitation; one of his executioners converted, while the other's eyes literally popped out of his head, a frequent occurrence at martyrdoms.

But despite the popularity of Edmund, Edward, and Alban, it was St Gregory the Great (540–604) who was at this time venerated as a general national saint for the English. His sympathy towards the Anglo-Saxons was proverbial – it was Gregory, then a prefect of Rome, who famously noticed three fair, golden-haired boys in the Roman slave market and asked after their nationality.

'They are Angles or Angli.'

'They are well named, for they have angelic faces and it becomes such to be companions with the angels in heaven.'*

Gregory instantly set off to preach in Britain, but was rapidly recalled by the then Pope, Pelagius II, due to a public outcry – Gregory was too popular at home to be allowed to vanish into Britain. As Pope Gregory I (590–604), however, he enthusiastically masterminded the conversion of the Anglo-Saxons, sending a beflagged St Augustine and a task force of forty missionaries to England in 597 and further envoys in 601. He was later celebrated in 747 as the 'apostle and patron of the English' who would present the English people to God on the Day of Judgment. Many churches were dedicated to Gregory, although he was slightly eclipsed by later national interest in the active missionary work of St Augustine of Canterbury (d. *c.* 604), St Aidan (d. 651) of Iona and Lindisfarne, and St Cuthbert (*c.* 634–87), north England's most popular saint, to whom 135 English churches were dedicated. Cuthbert's relics were translated to Durham in 999, and the cathedral also had the saint's famous standard: the burial shroud in which his uncorrupted body had been wound. This shroud was reputedly Cuthbert's own corporal (the cloth on which he had placed the consecrated communion host) and so was a similar relic to the *vexillum* of St Augustine.[16] It was carried into battle before the Conquest by King Edgar, and afterwards at such encounters as the Battle of the Standard (1138), Neville's Cross

---

* This was only the start of St Greg's punning – he continued by enquiring after the name of their king. 'Aella,' he was informed. 'Then must Alleluia be sung in Aella's land.' (For an alternative version, see Camden's *Remains*.)

(1346), and Flodden (1513), before being publicly burnt during the Reformation by the Dean of Durham's wife.

There was, then, evidently a strong sense of English identity within the Church of Rome, focused on individual national saints and expressed through hagiographies and sermons, feast days, and insignia. But over the next 250 years of Crusades and then the Hundred Years War with France and her allies, George replaced Edmund, Edward, Alban, and Gregory to become the undisputed patron saint of England, and his bloody cross became the nation's standard. By the end of the Middle Ages almost two hundred parish churches were dedicated to him. Interestingly, in these dedications he often succeeded St Gregory, the English apostle.

In the course of this rise to pre-eminence among the English saints, St George became a popular subject in a variety of sacred and secular contexts – such as wall-paintings, books of hours, and popular literature – which further secured his position. His legends and cycles were elaborated and the cult generated its own rituals. The medieval St George was, as we have seen, a multi-faceted hero, 'symbolic of both fertility and charity; a tortured martyr oppressed by a heathen ruler as well as a figure of noble authority; and a symbol of English nationhood in general while also representative of quite discrete parts of English society'.[17] He was by this time additionally claimed as the patron saint of farmers, husbandmen, saddlers, horsemen, knights, soldiers, archers, armourers, and sailors; invoked as a healer; and even considered to be a protection against nightmares. The charm 'For the Night-Mare', which called on 'St Jeorge' and the Virgin to ward off hauntings, could be copied out and tied to a horse's mane.[18]

Unsurprisingly, the English cult of St George was developed to include such incidents as the saint visiting England as a tribune from Beirut. He arrives on the western shores via a circuitous route south of the Irish Sea (since called St George's Channel) and forms a special relationship with his supposed contemporary, Queen Helena (*fl. c.* 248–328/9). Helena was a traditional British heroine, reputed to be the mother of the first Christian emperor, Constantine the Great, the discoverer of the True Cross, and a model of piety for Anglo-Saxon queens. During his trip, George also visits the tomb of Joseph of Arimathea at Glastonbury,* and of course slays a dragon – although precisely where is disputed.[19] Caxton produced the first sustained elaboration of George's travels to England in the *Golden Legend* (1483), his most popular work; in 1515 Alexander Barclay translated Spagnioli's *Georgius*, which added further spurious detail; and from 1576 to 1577, Richard Johnson published his popular and influential *Seven Champions of Christendom*, in which George by now hails from Coventry and is father to Guy of Warwick. Johnson's *Seven Champions*, derived from romances such as *Bevis of Hampton*, includes such details as George's body being marked with birthmarks of a dragon, a bloody cross, and a garter, as well as his marriage and three sons. There is of course no martyrdom in these later secular versions. By the eighteenth century, George's lineage had developed so that he was descended from the Trojan hero Aeneas, and was now buried at Windsor. English visual cycles, meanwhile, were charac-

---

* In plates accompanying the *Prose Lancelot*, a French romance of 1300–20, Lancelot finds the tomb of the son of Joseph of Arimathea, who is depicted as a knight carrying the cross of St George on his shield.

terized by the resurrection of St George by the Virgin Mary in order to slay the dragon – the visual image which eventually grew to dominate the legend. These cycles do, however, stress the Christian heroism of George, who converts the city to Christianity, for which he is then persecuted, and they do not incorporate elements such as the marriage of St George to the princess Sabra.

Although there are claims that 23 April was observed as a national feast day as early as 1222, it was not until 1399 that St George's Day was officially recognized 'as a holiday, even as other nations deserve the feast of their patrons'.[20] Thomas of Chobham (*fl.* 1190–1236) recorded St George's Day as merely a local celebration, and instead invoked St Gregory as the English patron:

> *Bidde we þanne þene holie man: apostle of Engelonde þat he bi-fore ihesu crist: ore neode ounder-stonde.*

> [Then let us pray to our holy man, the apostle of England, to represent our needs before Jesus Christ.][21]

But local St George pageants can be traced back to Durham as early as the ninth century, and activities really began to flourish in the thirteenth century; and although most of the evidence about these tableaux or 'ridings' dates from the sixteenth century, they are first recorded in 1408. It is possible that mummers' plays are a folk remnant of such early rituals, and if so they demonstrate the significant development of the martial aspects of the legend. A mandate in 1244 may refer to such a ritual; in it Henry III orders:

a dragon to be made in fashion of a standard, of red silk sparkling all over with gold, the tongue of which should be made to resemble burning fire, and appear to be continually moving, and the eyes of sapphires or other suitable stones, and to place it in the Church of St Peter, Westminster, against [in full view of] the King's coming.[22]

In mummers' traditions, however, the dragon is usually alluded to but seldom appears – instead, St George's foes are human – whereas in written sources, St George fighting human foes is a relatively late development, although it does appear in some early carvings. Mummers' plays also include non-canonical detail such as the marriage of St George to the King of Egypt's daughter. The productions were often patriotic and sometimes inclusively British – with St George in the company of Sts Patrick, David, and Andrew – but sometimes for England alone.

Edward I hung the banner of St George alongside those of Sts Edmund and Edward the Confessor at the Siege of Caerlaverock in 1300.[23] Edward was the first Plantagenet to regard himself as English rather than French and could also perhaps be considered the first monarch who seriously attempted to unify Great Britain: the Gaelic *Annals of Connacht*, for instance, describe him as 'king of England, Wales and Scotland, duke of Gascony and lord of Ireland'.[24] But although he attempted to unite the kingdoms as much through diplomacy and invitation as through force and suppression, Edward's unionism was an explicit combination of internal colonialism with Anglicization, and he should perhaps be more properly regarded as the progenitor of the 'first English empire'.[25]

This imperialism was reflected in Edward's cultural ambitions too. In addition to his devotions to St George and to the royal protectors, Edward was also a keen Arthurophile: his court was based on Camelot, and Pierre de Lantoft claimed that 'Of chivalry, after King Arthur, was King Edward the flower of Christendom.'[26] Consequently, during his reign the English began to appropriate the Matter of Britain for their myths of national destiny and for a non-classical legendary history, often Arthurian in content. Geoffrey of Monmouth's *Historia Regum Britanniae*, for example, which ended by lamenting how the 'odious race' of Angles and Saxons had driven the indigenous Britons into Wales and Britanny, where they await the fulfilment of Merlin's prophecies, nevertheless became a source book for English Arthurianism and English history. Monmouth's account inspired, for example, the *Brut*, a thirteenth-century poem by Layamon that traced the history of England from Brutus to Cadwallader, and also Robert of Gloucester's chronicle of England (*c.* 1260–1300), which includes a paean inspired by Bede:

> England is a well good land; in the stead best
> Set in the one end of the world, and reigneth west.
> The sea goeth him all about, he stint as an yle:
> Of foes it need the less doubt, but it be through gile:
> Of folk of the self-land, as me hath I sey while.
> From south to north it is long, eight hundred mile,
> And two hundred mile broad from east to wend
> Amid the land as it might be, and not as in the one end.
> Plenty men may in England of all good see,

But folk it agult [wrong], other years the worse and
  worse be.
For England is full enough of fruit and of treene,
  Of woods and of parks, that joy it is to seene.[27]

England had engulfed the 'island of Britain', and, as will become apparent, Edward did succeed in ruling England, Scotland, and Wales for a decade.

If Edward I's adoption of the banner of St George can be seen as a declaration that England was an independent nation – independent of the Normans – and the dominant power in Great Britain, it remained for his grandson Edward III to definitively champion St George as the national saint and in so doing give the country a clear identity and a firm destiny. Edward was represented on his accession as being armed by St George, who is identified by the bloody cross, while the young monarch bears his royal badge of the three lions on his shield and surcoat. Edward's throne had a depiction of George and the dragon adorning the back, he possessed a relic of St George's blood, and had his family painted with St George depicted as their patron. Froissart records that during Edward III's victory over the Flemish at the island of Cadsand (1337), 'the English decided to approach in the name of God and St George'.[28] At the start of what was to become the Hundred Years War, the king had definitively adopted the most warlike of the English saints.

'For St George and Merrie England' had become a battle-cry in the thirteenth century, but following the fall of Acre and the end of crusading in 1291 the shout had only been heard in England's British and European campaigns. The cry was raised, for instance, at the Battle of Evesham (1265) by English troops loyal to Henry III in opposition to

Simon de Montfort's rebels. At this encounter, soldiers loyal to the king wore red crosses; de Montfort's barons marched under a white cross. Against the French at the Battle of Sluys (1340), Edward III's navy of some 140 ships called on 'God and St George' and his vessels flew the bloody cross, and shortly thereafter he ordered replacement eighty-six pennoncels for his ships, and eight hundred for his troops.[29] The Normans 'were delighted to see that King Edward's standard was flown, for they were eager to fight with him'.[30] In response, the English crushed the French and their fleet.

Edward III has been criticized for pursuing glory on the battlefield at the expense of England, despite promoting such institutions as the House of Commons within the English Parliament. But his military expeditions were driven by a long-term strategy for stability and unity. His campaigns in France were in direct response to the collapse of the French succession in 1337 and his own claim to the throne through his mother, Isabella, as well as to the French sympathy for Scotland. Edward III was the grandson of Philip IV of France and through his mother a nephew of the last Capetian, Charles IV. He had first staked his claim to the French throne on Charles's death in 1328, but as this was through the female line, the crown had gone to Philip VI. But Philip VI's hostility to England encouraged Edward to revive his claim in 1337. In 1340, Edward declared himself to be 'King of England and France' and quartered the royal arms of three gold leopards against red with the golden French *fleurs-de-lys* against blue. In prosecuting this claim, he was strengthened by support from the Netherlands, Flanders and Germany.

Edward's ensuing victories at Sluys (1340), Crécy (1346), and Poitiers (1356) were clear demonstrations that God fought with the English. It is important to emphasize the astonishing success of the English war machine during this period, for it appeared to be driving forward a powerful national destiny. Froissart, for instance, commented that, 'The English ... will never love or honour [their king] unless he is victorious and a lover of arms and war against his neighbours', and in 1373, a commentator noted that, 'the English are so filled with their own greatness and have won so many big victories that they have come to believe that they cannot lose. In battle, they are the most confident nation in the world.'[31]

The remarkable and almost unbroken run of stunning English victories at home and on the Continent seemed to confirm that the English were God's Chosen People – and led to some absurd exchanges: when Edward assumed the title of King of France in 1340, he invited his French rival, Charles IV, to enter a cage full of lions if he thought *he* was divinely appointed; Charles, a man who feared that he was actually made of glass, declined.

Edward's interest in the French crown also shows that English national destiny was intimately tied to a concept of union: uniting the crowns of England and France would also unite Britain, and all would be united under the name of St George and the sign of the bloody cross. In such a scenario, George's fight with the dragon seemed to embody two myths. On the one hand, the dragon could signify the old Britons, the Celts, who traditionally favoured such symbols. In other words, Edward I's invasion of Wales had been a straightforward reworking of the George-and-the-dragon motif, in which the Englishman St George was clearly destined to defeat the Welsh dragon. There is, moreover, a clear reference to the cross of St George in Edward I's 1277 campaign against the Welsh, where it was used to identify infantrymen and archers by means of pennoncels (pennons on helmets or lances) and bracers (arm-bands) – 340 pennoncels were ordered from Admetus, the tailor to the king.[32] On the Continent, however, the man-against-monster model became a David-and-Goliath myth that pitched the English against the rest of Europe in general and against France in particular. The flexibility of this aspect of the legend meant that other details – principally George's gory martyrdom – were increasingly played down.

Within a few years, then, St George was generally considered the patron saint of England. Against the French at Calais (1349), the king again brandished his sword in the name of king and country: 'Ha Sant Edward, Ha Sant George'.[33] It also seems that for his various campaigns, Edward III

appoynted his souldiers to wear white Coats or Jackets, with a red Crosse before and behind over their Armoure, that it was not onely a comely, but a stately sight to behold the English Battles, like the rising Sunne, to glitter farre off in that pure hew; when the souldiers of other Nations in their baser weedes would not be discerned.[34]

Wardrobe Accounts show ships being decked out with St George crosses and royal arms from 1350, and on 13 August 1351 the Patent Rolls recorded the attributes of 'the blessed George, the most invincible athlete of Christ, whose name and protection the English race invoke as that of their patron, in war especially'.[35] When, in contrast, in 1396 the French Comte d'Eu called on St George under the banner of the Virgin Mary, his allies considered it to be a 'very foolish speech'.[36]

The French had St Denis instead, and since 1119 had fought beneath his *oriflamme* – a standard of divine origin consisting of three tongues of scarlet silk flown from a golden staff; Saracens were allegedly struck blind or even killed outright if they glimpsed it. Froissart described the flag at the Battle of Rosbeque (or Roosebeke, 27 November 1382):

> The oriflamme is a precious banner, and was sent first from Heaven as a great mystery, the which was ever a great comfort to them that saw it. And the same day it showed some of its virtue, for all the morning there was a great thick mist, that one could scant see another, but as soon as it was displayed and lifted up on high, the mist broke away, and the sky was as clear as any time in the year before… this greatly did comfort them.[37]

When this flaming banner was flown at Crécy and Poitiers, it signalled that no prisoners were to be taken. Such a declaration to fight to the death was rare – vanquished noblemen were usually captured rather than slain, and ransomed for fantastic sums, which of course encouraged chivalry and maintained bloodlines. But at both Crécy and Poitiers, the bloodthirsty French tactic of *guerre mortelle* backfired so badly that the flower of their nobility was almost completely destroyed. Consequently, at Poitiers some quarter was given – indeed, the triumphant English were outnumbered two to one by the prisoners they had captured and ransomed, among them the French king, John II.

The emphatic sequence of victories over France also gave support to an early movement identifying the English with various Biblical ancestors. In the succeeding centuries, this was to develop into the theory that the English, the British, and ultimately the countries of the Commonwealth were the tribes of Israel and therefore literally God's Chosen People. As it was, Adam Houghton, Bishop of St David's, would subsequently declare at the opening of Parliament in 1377: 'I truly believe that God would never have honoured this land in the same way as He did Israel through great victories over His enemies, if it were not that He had chosen it as His heritage.'[38]

In the winter of 1347–8, Edward sealed his successes on the battlefield by formalizing the military ethos of his court. He created one of the most enduring institutions to unite the military glory of the nation with Christian chivalry: the Order of the Garter, founded under the patronage of the Holy Trinity, the Virgin Mary, Edward the Confessor, and St George. The order was formed as a brotherhood of chivalric knights and uniquely among such orders survives to this day. St George had long appealed to orders of chivalry across Europe, the first being the apocryphal and angelic Knights of St George, supposedly founded in 312 by the Roman emperor Constantine the Great. More recently, a religious order, the Order of St George of Alfama, had been founded in 1201 by King Pere II of Aragon (members of which bore the bloody cross), and a tournament form of the Order of the Round Table developed in the 1240s, headed by Ulrich von Lichtenstein, who invited any knight who broke three lances with him to join his order.[39] The first lay order based on Arthurian chivalry and dedicated to St George was founded around 1325 by Charles I of Hungary (the Fraternal Society of Knighthood of St George), and other orders were formed from 1307 in response to the suppression of the Knights Templar, including the Order of the Band (or Sash), founded by Alfonso XI, King of Castile and Leon.[40] The idea of the knight had developed from the middle of the eleventh century, and by the beginning of the thirteenth century had been formalized as a concept, both a title and a code of values.*

   In 1344, Edward had first mooted a new Order of the Round Table of no fewer than three hundred knights, who would be seated at a table two hundred feet in circumference at Windsor Castle. Edward promised that any knights from France, Scotland, and elsewhere who attended the St George's Day feast at Windsor would be peacefully received.[41] The French heir, John of Normandy, managed to put a similarly ambitious idea into practice by inaugurating the Order of the Star in 1352 – but in the same year its knights were massacred at the Battle of Mauron. Yet even before then, Edward had radically revised his ideas, and in 1348 the Garter knights were formed at Windsor, accompanied by the inevitable Arthurian ceremony. Just twenty-six companions were admitted, nearly all of whom had fought at Crécy, and many of whom were minor knights; they may even have already worn the insignia there.† This shared battle honour, together with the blue and gold colours of the garter, suggest that the order was a reference to Edward's claim to the French throne, or alluding to the Knights of the Band. More colourful and salacious explanations were, however, proposed by romance writers of the time, who suggested, for example,

---

* These values were summed up in the idea of chivalry: military values of skill at arms, valour, and loyalty; aristocratic courtliness; and religious devotion as a soldier of Christ.

† Membership is today confined to the monarch, the Prince of Wales, and twenty-four knights; very few commoners are so honoured.

that the king was sporting a garter he had acquired from a damsel named Honeysuckle. But the garter is more likely to be a reference to the legend of St George and the princess's girdle or garter that bound the subdued dragon. The elite badge, which bore the cross of St George at the centre of a star, was designed to be worn as insignia outside the armour, just above the knee, thereby identifying champions of the field.[42] The Garter legend *'Honi soit qui mal y pense'* ('Cursed be he who thinks dishonourably') was added to the royal coat of arms by Edward, and the Crécy motto *'Dieu et mon droit'* ('God and my right' – the right to the French throne) was also quoted.

St George soon usurped his divine compatriots – the Trinity, the Virgin, and the Confessor – as the embodiment of the order's ideals, and perhaps symbolically, St George's Chapel at Windsor, the inner sanctum of the order, was a royal chapel originally dedicated to St Edward.[43] St George was powerfully identified with the order. The Bedford Book of Hours (1423) actually shows St George as a Garter knight. This volume was prepared for the Duke of Bedford – Henry V's brother John – who led the English army to victory at Verneuil. Bedford was described at the time in his regent's robes: a blue surcoat (the colour of the heavens and hence of truth), emblazoned with a red cross of St George, itself imposed on a white cross, which is a rather suggestive prototype for the later Union Flag. A fifteenth-century image of Edward III as the patron of the Garter Order shows him with the cross of St George prominent on his robe, but still wearing his surcoat of quartered English leopards and French *fleurs-de-lys*. This regal distinction between king and country is significant: on a coin minted during his reign – a gold noble – Edward is shown captaining a man-of-war;

on his shield he bears his own coat of arms, not the bloody cross, which was reserved for England and St George.

St George continued to bring aid to the English armies in France and elsewhere – the Black Prince and King Don Pedro of Portugal both wore the bloody cross against the French and Spanish at the Battle of Nájera in 1367 – but other orders continued to take him as their patron. The Enterprise of the Knights of St George, for example, was formed in the 1370s to protect Catalonia under the sign of the red cross, and the 1325 Fraternal Society of Knighthood of St George itself continued until about 1395.* An associated order, the Society of the Dragon, was formed in Hungary in 1408 by Sigismund von Luxemburg-Brandenburg, taking the device of the dragon in the spirit of crushing 'the followers of the ancient Dragon, and … the pagan knights'. This, too, invoked the iconography of the bloody cross:

> the sign or effigy of the Dragon incurved into the form of a circle, its tail winding around its neck, divided through the middle of its back along its length from the top of its head right to the tip of its tail, with blood [forming] a red cross flowing out into the interior of the cleft in a white crack, untouched by blood, just as and in the same way that those who fight under the banner of the glorious martyr St George are accustomed to bear a red cross on a white field … [44]

* Other groups include the Company of the Grail-Templars of St George (Austria, c. 1337–c. 1380), the Order of St George with the Pelican (Electoral Palatinate, 1444–9), and the Knightly Order of St George (proclaimed by Pope Paul II in 1469).

The Draconists were, however, a political rather than a chivalric order. One of their members, Vlad II, Prince of Wallachia, received into the order in 1431, became known as 'the Dragon' ('*Dracul*'); his son, also Vlad, was known as 'the Dragon's son', or '*Draculea*' – the historical Count Dracula.

The red cross of St George was by now indisputably the standard of England. In 1374, Edward ordered thirty-one more standards of St George for his navy, and in 1375, twenty-six 'jacks' and St George streamers.[45] On 17 June 1385, his grandson Richard II sent an army to repel the Scots. Ninety-two banners of St George flew above the English army and Richard's men were again ordered to wear the cross of St George emblazoned on their surcoats:

> that every man of what estate condicion or nation thei be of, so
> that he be one of our partie, bere a signe of the armes of Saint
> George, large, both before and behynde, upon parell that yff he be
> slayne or wounded to deth, he that hath so doon to hym shall not
> be putte to deth for defaulte of the crosse he lacketh. And that non
> enemy do bere the same token or crosse of Saint George upon
> payne of dethe.[46]

This became known as 'the George *jacque*'; the Scots, in contrast, bore the cross of St Andrew.[47] When the Earl of Northumberland attempted to raise a rebellion in 1408, culminating in the Battle of Bramham Moor (near Tadcaster), the *St Albans Chronicle* recorded that the rebels were engaged by forces loyal to the king, displaying 'the banner of

St George, with the pennon of his [the sheriff's] arms spread out'.[48] It was certainly a loyalist emblem – the Wilton Diptych depicts Richard kneeling before an angel bearing the banner of the bloody cross and an orb of Britain – but despite the regality of many of its associations, it was also the standard of the people. In 1381, the Peasants' Revolt had marched against the king, Richard II, under the same cross of St George.

St George also continued to make propitious appearances on the battlefield. In response to Henry V's invocation at Agincourt (25 October 1415), 'In the name of Almyghti God and Saynt George avaunt banarer! and Saynt George, this day thyn help!', witnesses reported that the saint 'halpe hym to fighte, and was seyne aboven in the eyre, that day they faught'.[49] Henry had ordered the population to pray to St George during his campaigns in France, and he obligingly manifested himself again on Henry's triumphant return to London. Following the battle, Archbishop Chichele raised St George's Day to a principal feast day, a 'greater double' festival, celebrated in a comparable fashion to Christmas Day. Moreover, Henry insisted that his troops (and only his troops) be identified by the cross of St George. His ordinances of war made at Mantes in July 1419 stipulated

> that every man of what estate, condicion or nacion that he be, of oure partie, bere a band of Seint George suffisant large, upon the perile, if he be wounded or dede in the fawte thereof, he that hym wounded or sleeth shall bere no peyn for hym: and that none enemy bere the said signe of Seint George, but if he be prisoner & in the warde of his maister, upon peyn of deth therefore.[50]

Among Henry's effects at his death was a pennon of St George valued at 6s 8d – equivalent to four weeks' wages for a labourer.[51] Shortly afterwards, the heart of St George was translated to the chapel at Windsor, a gift of the Hungarian king, Sigismund, who brought it to Windsor in 1416 on his induction to the Order of the Garter, and the event was celebrated with a feast of cakes and pies depicting scenes from the legend of the George. Finally, 'A Carol of St George' patriotically celebrated the victory at Agincourt by linking the Virgin and the dragon to the battle against the French, before promising

> In his virtu he wol us lede
>
> Againis the Fend, the ful wight,
>
> And with his banner us oversprede,
>
> If we him love with all oure might.[52]

At the same time, St George was also being woven into legendary English history. The chronicler John Hardyng (1378–*c.* 1465) claimed that after his conversion the second-century English king Lucius 'bare of sylver a crosse of gowles [gules] in fourme of seynt Georges armes', as did King Arthur's knight Sir Galahad.[53]

The nation identified powerfully with St George at all levels. English popular culture was saturated with the saint: there were already taverns named after him by the beginning of the fifteenth century, celebrating

> Saint George that swinged the dragon, and e'er since
>
> Sits on's horseback at mine hostess' door.
>
> (*King John*, II, i, 288–9)

And this rise in St Georgery went with a burgeoning sense of English national identity. London brewers, drawing up their ordinances in English, remarked that 'our mother tongue, to wit, the English tongue, hath in modern days begun to be honourably enlarged and adorned ... and our most excellent lord, King Henry V, hath procured the common idiom ... to be commended by the exercise of writing.'[54] Despite the Plantagenet claim on the French crown, Henry V actively discouraged the use of French language, fashions, and culture. It was a popular policy. This sense of national pride extended, for instance, to the English delegation attending the Church Council at Constance in 1414–17. They patriotically argued that 'England is a real nation':

> whether a nation be understood as a people marked off from others by blood relationship and habit of unity, or by peculiarities of language (the most sure and positive sign and essence of a nation in divine and human law) ... or whether a nation be understood, as it should be, as a territory equal to that of the French nation, England is a real nation ...'[55]

Henry VI maintained his father's devotion to St George, and the saint appeared at the infant monarch's coronation in 1422. At this manifestation he had St Denis at his side, thereby supporting the Plantagenet's claim to France, and the pairing again confirms that St George was now considered to be the patron saint of England. Indeed, William Caxton later described the saint as 'patrone of this royame of Englonde and the crye of men of warre' in his *Golden Legend* (1483).[56] George was, however, still invoked by other nations and regions. The Hundred Years War encouraged the spread of St George to Normandy, which was occupied by the English in the early fifteenth century. There,

George is often depicted simply in armour and the red cross is absent because of its associations with the English enemy rather than the regional saint; Henry V had even ordered that subjugated Normans should wear the red cross as a sign of submission. Elsewhere, St George was invoked by opposing armies of Swedes and Danes at the Battle of Brunkenberg in 1473.

Each side in the Wars of the Roses attempted to legitimate their respective claims with Georgist imagery. In 1462 the Yorkist Edward IV attended a George and the dragon pageant at Bristol and in 1475 began rebuilding the chapel at Windsor, incidentally incorporating the white rose of York into the design; he was also a keen Arthurian and the first to assume the royal crest. Likewise, the Tudors sought to add lustre to their dynasty with St George. The bloody cross was flown by the Tudors – rather ironically, it transpired, as it was flown beside the Welsh dragon. Henry VII won the Battle of Bosworth Field (1485) under the banner of St George, marched into London beneath the flag, and presented it to Westminster Abbey. For his subsequent coronation, the new king commissioned a sumptuous George cross that consumed six yards of crimson velvet. His family were depicted in an altarpiece with St George, and the saint appears twice on Henry's own tomb. And Henry, too, was an Arthurian: his eldest son was born at Winchester – which then as now is home to an Arthurian Round Table – and was christened Arthur.

Prince Arthur did not, however, live to succeed his father, and it was his brother who was crowned in 1509 as Henry VIII. Henry had several suits of armour decorated with Georgist motifs, and issued the George noble, a gold coin showing the saint. He also invoked the idea of a united Arthurian empire in justifying his break with the church of Rome as he instigated the English Reformation from 1534 onwards: England could exist as an 'empire, entire unto itself'.[57] But Henry VIII did not dissolve simply the monasteries: one of the consequences of the Reformation was the dissolution of the ritual year. St George's Day had become a major event in the calendar: it had been flourishing as an annual mandatory festival for over a century, and one could even be fined for not attending. Such activities greatly contributed towards the growth of the cult.[58] The day was celebrated with costumed civic and guild pageants or ridings featuring mounted knights and effigies of dragons. A procession would precede mass, and the day would culminate in a feast. It is worth noting that the St George's Day ridings were not carnivals that turned the social order upside down for a day; instead, they embodied and supported the existing hierarchy, and it is possible therefore that the more mysterious and anarchic mummers' traditions developed into a sort of 'anti-riding'.

There was a famously spectacular St George riding at Norwich in the early sixteenth century, featuring George in white armour and red cross, a dragon – known as 'the Snap' or 'Old Snap' – and St Margaret. An eighteenth-century Snap survives in the city museum and local morris men made a new Snap in the 1980s for the Lord Mayor's parade. Other towns such as Bristol, Chester, Coventry, King's Lynn, Leicester, Newcastle upon Tyne, Reading, Stratford-upon-Avon, and York also had lavish pageants, but despite the adoption of the cross of St George for its own arms, there are no records of celebrations in the City of London (the public arms of London are the cross of St George with the sword of St Paul, the city's patron).[59]

The flora adorning the body of
'A Young Daughter of the Picts'
represents her intimate union with the
land (Jacques le Moyne de Morgues,
*c.*1585).

A fantastically quartered heraldic tattoo
borne by a nineteenth-century British
soldier (1899). The motto 'Caen Cressie
Calais' is that of the campaigns of Sir
John Radcliffe.

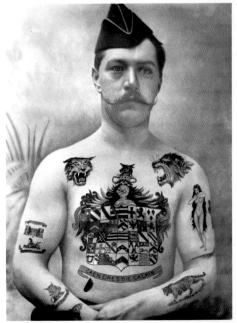

The Papal banner that served as one of the Norman standards in 1066.
(Bayeux Tapestry, c.1070s).

The dragon standard of the Saxons, descended from the Roman draco.
Note the fallen dragon beneath the slain warrior (Bayeux Tapestry, c.1070s).

The tomb plaque of Geoffrey Plantagenet, count of Anjou, showing on his shield the charge of golden lions presented by his father-in-law, Henry I (from the Cathedral of St. Julien, Le Mans, *c*.1151–55).

Richard I, recognizable by the three lions he supposedly adopted for his shield and Great Seal (illustrated copy of Matthew Paris's *Chronica Majora*, thirteenth century).

St George arming Edward III with the shield of the royal lions. Note the reversed leopards on Edward's surcoat (Milemete Treatise, 1326–7).

Christ leading a Crusade; the Lamb of God is also frequently depicted bearing a flag of the bloody cross (illuminated manuscript, thirteenth century).

The Wilton Diptych: Richard II is presented to the Virgin and Child by Sts Edmund, Edward, and John the Baptist. The angels, like Richard, wear white hart badges and also collars of broom – the *plante genet* of the Plantagenets (*c*.1395).

After the Reformation, the crown was obliged to continue to observe St George's Day in some fashion in honouring the Knights of the Garter, which prompted Henry VIII to declare that while George should not be worshipped as a saint, he could still be celebrated as a person. But despite reforming its rites in line with Protestant sensibilities in 1550, the Garter ceremonies still had more than a smack of Catholic and pagan superstition about them.

Henry's son, the precocious boy king Edward VI, objected: 'My Lords, I pray you what saint is S. George that we heere so honour him?'

The Marquess of Winchester responded, 'St George mounted his charger, out with his sword and ran the dragon through with his speare.'

The lad replied, giggling, 'I pray you, my lord, and what did he with his sword the while?'

'That I cannot tell your Majestie.'[60]

The ceremony was abandoned in 1552, but revived again two years later when the Catholic queen Mary I came to the throne and briefly returned the country to pre-Reformation ritual. Mary and her husband, the future Philip II of Spain, paid special attention to St George. Philip led the Garter knights on the saint's day in 1555, and images of George were re-erected nationwide.[61] But this pageantry soon began to fall away – not least because Britain entered a period of depressed temperatures that drastically affected the weather and forced outdoor celebrations to move to warmer dates. Queen Elizabeth I abolished St George's Day festivities again in 1567, and any Georgery henceforth took place on May Day.

Despite all this, by the end of the sixteenth century, the national trinity of St George, the bloody cross, and England was firmly established. The cross of St George was also the favoured ensign for both military and merchant vessels (the royal arms were only hoisted by the Admiral of the Fleet), and among the flags provided for the mariner cousins Sir Francis Drake and Sir John Hawkins in 1594 were thirty of the cross of St George, at 16s 8d each.[62] As one of St George's biographers has put it, during the reign of Henry VIII the saint's emblem 'came to be recognised as a true flag of England, and many sixteenth-century paintings of the English army feature this banner, sometimes as the sole standard flown'.[63]

The cross is explicitly described, for example, at the outset of Edmund Spenser's Elizabethan poem *The Faerie Queene*. The first book of this national epic (published in 1590) is titled 'The Legende of the Knight of the Red Crosse, or Of Holinesse' and it quaintly recounts in a lilting archaic language the temptations of Redcrosse, a knight identified as 'Saint *George* of mery England, the signe of victoree' (I, x, 61). As his name suggests, Redcrosse bears the emblem of a red cross, signifying Christ's blood and the crucifixion as well as the cross of St George:

> But on his breast a bloudie Crosse he bore,
>> The deare remembrance of his dying Lord,
>> For whose sweete sake that glorious badge he wore,
>> And dead as liuing euer him ador'd:
>> Vpon his shield the like was also scor'd,
>> For soueraine hope, which in his helpe he had.
>> (I, i, 2; also I, ii, 11)

Redcrosse is a descendant of ancient Saxon kings, and is also, like Arthur, explicitly a figure of national unity:

High reard their royall throne in *Britane* land,

And vanquist them, vnable to withstand.

(I, x, 65)

The Faerie Queene is an epic of English antiquity. It marries the idea of a single Britain to legendary figures such as Arthur and Redcrosse, in a landscape inspired by medieval romance and populated by heraldic charges – effectively a pagan Protestant unionism. This imagined England was a sleek political hybrid, and it was symbolized by the cross of St George.

Spenser was writing at a time when England felt very little affinity with Europe – indeed, when it was comprehensively cut off from mainstream European culture and identity. The country turned its attention to its own stability, its relations with its immediate British neighbours, and its interests in the world beyond Europe. In the wake of the English Reformation, England made its way primarily through Protestantism, imperialism, and a renewed sense of national destiny, variously established by works such as John Foxe's *Book of Martyrs* (1563), *The Faerie Queene*, and William Camden's *Britannia* (1586) and *Annales* (1616). Camden, for instance, recorded that before the Conquest, Brithwold the monk, concerned at the royal succession of English sovereigns, 'had a strange vision, and heard a voyce, which forbade him to be inquisitive of such matters, resounding in his ears, "The kingdome of England is God's own kingdome, and for it God himself will provide."'[64]

One of the consequences of this English separation from Europe was the settlement of the centuries-long feud with Scotland. Within a few short years, this momentous change would fundamentally alter the political nature of Britain by uniting the two crowns – and, in doing so, would create the first Union Flag. But to arrive at the accession of King James I of Great Britain in 1603, it is necessary first to turn to the histories of Wales and Scotland, to consider their relations with England and their place both in the union of Britain and in the fabric of the Union Jack.

III THE OLD ENEMIES

It has beyne seyne in thir tymys bywent,
Our ald ennemys cummyn of Saxonys blud,
That neuyr yeit to Scotland wald do gud.

Blind Harry, *The Wallace* (1470s), I, 5–7

ALBA IS GAELIC for Britain, and from it we have the word 'Albion'. Oddly – or then again, typically – Albion has become a mystical name for England rather than Britain, perhaps most resonantly in the visionary work of the poet and artist William Blake, although both Bede and Camden stress that it describes the whole of Britain.* Even the etymology of the word has been denied its Gaelic roots, with suggestions that

---

* For example, *Visions of the Daughters of Albion* (1793) and *Jerusalem* (1804–20) (see also Ackroyd). Avalon, possibly named after the apples of Somerset and Devon, might be more appropriate. Bede's *Ecclesiastical History of the English People* begins 'Britain, once called Albion...'; the first sentence of Camden's *Britannia* is '*Britain, called also, Albion...*'. Blake was known as 'English' Blake.

it derives from the Latin *albus*, which means white and therefore allegedly refers to the chalk cliffs of Dover. Of course, this slippage once again demonstrates how the lion's part, England, imagines itself in relation to the whole of the British Isles. But this is an ancient complaint, and there are more intriguing implications in the word.

Traditionally, the first king of Scotland was Kenneth I MacAlpin (d. 859). In the 840s, Kenneth united the kingdoms of the Picts and the Gaels with Albany (the region from Humber to Caithness) under the name of Alba, and its inhabitants called themselves Albanaig – the name Scotia (or Scotland) did not appear until about the tenth century. Alba was a union of kingdoms under one crown, and the concept of Alba actually laid claim to the entire realm of Britain. In other words, the union of Alba was both Scotland and Britain, and in the word 'Albion' one can discern the unionist aspirations of the ancient Scots, whose ambition was to unite the land from the north. Moreover, Kenneth's united kingdom of Albion was traditionally identified by a single flag, taken from the middle of the ninth century as the national standard: the cross of St Andrew.

St Andrew's silver *crux decussata* or saltire (a diagonal cross) on a field of blue is therefore as much a flag of attempted union as the bloody cross of St George. Its origins are, however, more distinct, and its history too is clearer, for there was not an Andrean cult to the same degree as there was the Georgist. But the St Andrew silver saltire does have a long and illustrious career before – and indeed after – its incorporation within the two Union Flags. Its story begins on the Sea of Galilee, during the life of Jesus Christ.

St Andrew (d. *c.* AD 60), *pie, sanctorum mitissime* ('most gentle of the saints'), was originally a fisherman. He had been a disciple of John the Baptist, and with his brother Simon (latterly Peter) was the first of Jesus's apostles to be called; he was actively present, for example, at miracles such as the feeding of the five thousand. Indeed, in the east and the Orthodox Church he is 'Andrew the First-called', giving him at least equal status with Peter, and therefore with Rome, while in Scotland the primacy of St Andrew was cited when asserting Scottish independence from England, and specifically from York, itself the see of Peter. After the crucifixion, Andrew became a missionary. Traditionally, each apostle was given a part of the world to evangelize and Andrew was allotted the north, as far as Russia. In the event, he probably preached in Greece, although he is also linked with Scythia and Epirus, and was supposedly crucified in Patras, Achaia, after two days' sermonizing. He is a patron of Patras but also of Russia too, where he bears a saltire in colours reversed from the familiar Scottish design, that is, a blue cross on a white field. In Russia it is claimed that *'Andreeski'* converted Georgia and the Ukraine. There is a rich apocryphal tradition associated with St Andrew related to this tradition – *The Acts of Andrew and Matthias* [Matthew] *among the Anthropophagi* – which gruesomely describes his series of missionary journeys, most notably to Ethiopia, where he rescues Matthew from hungry cannibals. A version of this appears in the Old English poems *Andreas* and *Fates of the Apostles*, both written in the ninth century.

Later traditions attributed to Andrew the founding of the Church of Constantinople. The arrival of Andrean relics in Constantinople in about 357 has certainly been seen as a founding moment for the Church there, although the documentation for the translation of his relics to the city is likely to be a medieval forgery. Nevertheless, Constantinople basked in the reflected glory of St Andrew, the equal of St Peter: Constantinople was a 'new Rome', and Andrew's cult accordingly spread to Italy and Gaul. In Rome, the 'apostle of England', Pope Gregory the Great, founded a monastery to St Andrew, and it was from here that Augustine went in 597 to convert the English. Andrew proved popular in England, where there were eventually about six hundred churches dedicated to him. By the sixth century, St Andrew's Day (30 November) had become a universal feast.

From England, the cult spread to Scotland. In the early eighth century (*c.* 740) a church was dedicated to St Andrew at Kinrymont, supposedly founded by St Rule (also known as Regulus). St Rule, a native of Patras, dreamt that an angel commanded him to take the relics of St Andrew into the north-west; arriving at Fife, he built the church at Kinrymont to house the remains, and Kinrymont was later renamed St Andrews. In this enterprise, St Rule was aided by one Angus (Oengus or Hungus), a king of the Picts, who occupied the Highlands and who gave St Rule land and protection. It is not clear which King Angus was instrumental in the foundation of St Andrews – he may have been a king who had already adopted St Andrew as a patron, or who did so shortly after the consecration of the church, or it may have been a later Angus who championed the saint. Nevertheless, the symbol of the silver saltire traditionally originates from a vision witnessed by this Pictish king.

The kingdom of the Scots arose from the remains of the kingdom of Fortriu (the Gaelic name for a Pictish region recorded in fourth-century

Latin as Verturiones) and the Caledonii (a confederation of Highland tribes who had fiercely resisted the Roman invasion). The inhabitants of the region were usually referred to as Picts. They survived from the seventh to the tenth centuries, enduring almost constant attacks from the Vikings. It was during the course of these raids that King Angus adopted St Andrew as the patron saint of his people in the eighth or ninth century. Angus dreamt that the saint appeared to him on the eve of battle, and the next day a silver saltire shone in the bright blue sky: 'ane schinand croce was sene in the lift, strauncht above the army of the Pichtis, not onlik to the samin croce that the appostil deit on. This croce vanist nevir out of the lift quhil the victory succedit to Pichtis.'[1] The Picts cried 'Sanct Andro our patron be our guide', and the enemy was routed. Angus then went barefoot to the kirk of St Andrew to offer his thanks for the saint's deliverance of him and his country, and thereafter the Picts adopted the diagonal white cross as their national banner. In 843 it was taken by Kenneth MacAlpin as the flag of all Scotland.

The tradition that St Andrew was crucified on an X-shaped cross is a puzzle. He was originally depicted iconographically as a fisherman either carrying or crucified upon the instrument of his martyrdom: a tree, a Latin cross, or occasionally a Y-shaped cross. But from the tenth century, the conventional cross was gradually superseded by the saltire, and it is not known where this tradition comes from. There is no specific source for the adoption of the saltire, and there are no early references to St Andrew being crucified on a diagonal cross.[2] It is tempting to speculate that King Angus did indeed see a silver saltire in the sky, and that in the Pictish mind this formed a connection with St Andrew that had not previously been endorsed by images of the saint – in other words, that the saltire tradition emerged in the Middle Ages through its association with the Scots and was gradually incorporated into the religious iconography of St Andrew. Alternatively, the adoption of the diagonal cross may simply have been the result of a mistaken reading of an overly stylized crucifix. The adoption of the saltire does seems to have been a British innovation, however, appearing as early as the eleventh century on a font in Langtoft, Yorkshire, and on the twelfth-century seal of St Andrews Priory and the Bishop of St Andrews's seal in 1279. By the fourteenth century, its symbolism was firmly established. In his *De Cruce* of 1593, Justus Lipsius describes the *crux decussata* as the cross 'on which a sufficiently old tradition tells us St Andrew died', and the saltire is often referred to as 'the St Andrew's cross'.

The colour of the field was not important until much later, and might have been influenced by the royal French use of blue. Despite the vision beheld by King Angus in the bright blue morning sky, the azure field on which the silver saltire lies was only fixed in the sixteenth century in Lindsay's *Armorial* (1541) and previous to this the silver saltire appeared as the St Andrew's cross on other fields, such as black. The background of the cross of St Andrew has in any case become progressively darker from the almost sky-blue heraldic azure of the sixteenth century to the indigo of the nineteenth. And despite the field being finally fixed as azure in the mid-sixteenth century, in less than a lifetime the silver saltire would in any case be braided together with the bloody cross of St George.

The translation of the relics of St Andrew being in some way accompanied by a vision of the diagonal cross and by a Pictish victory blended together in the iconography of the emerging cult. The miracles on the battlefield justified the presence of the holy relics of St Andrew in Scotland and simultaneously authenticated them as genuine, and they also gave impetus to Scottish unity by the authority of a divinely sanctioned emblem. Interestingly, King Angus is also attributed with another of Scotland's national emblems – the thistle. An impending Viking raid was thwarted during his reign by one of the Danish invaders treading on a thistle and crying out, thereby alerting the Scots.* Both of these symbols of Scottish national unity – the silver saltire and the thistle – were tied to the landscape in some way, then, and both were strongly associated with repelling invaders: for the next five hundred years, Scottish identity would be built on keeping its lands free from outside interference.

Obtaining the relics of the first apostle also proved to be a significant religious coup, and the city of St Andrews became a major Christian centre in the north. By the tenth century, the Bishop of St Andrews was effectively the head of the Scottish Church and the city had become a place of pilgrimage, although Constantinople remained the principal shrine to the saint.† But although St Andrews was the seat of Scotland's primary bishop, prior to the Reformation only two dozen churches

---

* The thistle legend is attributed to Achaius, a semi-mythical king of the Scots in part derived from Angus. In fact, the thistle probably wasn't used before the reign of James III.

† After the fall of Constantinople in 1204, the Crusaders took the remaining relics of St Andrew to the Italian city of Amalfi, and in 1461 his head was presented to the Pope; it has since gone back to Patras. Any relics that were housed in St Andrews did not survive the Reformation.

were dedicated to the saint in the country; meanwhile, St John the Evangelist had twenty and St Peter almost twice that. This was in part because there were already other patrons of Scotland. In 848 or 849, following persistent Viking raids, Kenneth had translated the relics of St Columba to a church in Dunkeld. St Columba (*c.* 521–97) was a peaceable missionary Irish saint and bard who had founded monasteries at Derry (546), Durrow (*c.* 556), and possibly Kells, before arriving on Iona and establishing the monastery there. He converted Brude, the King of the Picts, evangelized in the Western Isles, and has the reputation of being the 'apostle of Scotland'. Columba's crozier was called 'Battle-Victory' and carried to war in Scotland and Ireland by, for example, William the Lion – the twelfth-century king traditionally named for first raising the ruddy lion standard of Scotland – as was the Monymusk reliquary containing Columba's relics.[3]

Another popular legendary saint was St Mungo (or Kentigern, d. 612), supposedly the illegitimate grandson of a British prince, who preached in Strathclyde and Cumbria. It is to St Mungo that Glasgow owes its city arms, which depict four of his folkloric miracles:

> Here's the bird that never flew,
> Here's the tree that never grew;
> Here's the bell that never rang,
> Here's the fish that never swam.
> (Trad.)

The bird he brought back to life, with the tree he kindled a fire, with the bell he mourned the dead, and in the belly of the fish was found the wedding ring of a queen, so saving her from execution. There are fishy tales associated with other Scottish protectors too. St Ronan (a.k.a. Romayn, Ruan, and Rumon) was a seventh-century Scottish hermit who rode on a whale to the island of North Rona, in order to escape the evil tongues of women.

Nevertheless, it was St Andrew who gradually became identified as the country's patron. This was in a large part due to attempts to express a national and institutional identity and cohesive culture in the face of emergent Anglo-Georgism. Like Flanders and Normandy, Scotland had risen out of the desolation left by the Vikings, the tribes uniting against their common enemy under a common leader. By the early tenth century, the descendants of Kenneth MacAlpin had established a Gaelic royal line in east Scotland and a single dynasty was identified with the united kingdoms of Alba. The emergence of Alba was in particular aided by the long reign – some forty or more years – of Constantine II, who succeeded his cousin Donald (the first recorded 'King of Scotland') in 900. Further Viking assaults were resisted by military consolidation and marriage alliances, which also expressed the unionist ambition to overrun the rest of Britain. Most notably, an alliance of Scots, Danes, and Irish Britons marched against the English king Athelstan and his brother Edmund in 937.

Despite this union, the alliance was crushingly defeated at Brunanburh, and the *Anglo-Saxon Chronicle* celebrated the English victory in carrion rhymes, possibly alluding to Celtic symbols (the raven, for example, was not only the standard of the Danes, but was also linked to Arthur) and the 'beasts of battle':

> king and aetheling, exultant in war,
> sought kith, the land of Wessex.

> They left behind to divide the corpses,
>
> to enjoy the carrion, the dusky-coated,
>
> horny-beaked black raven,
>
> and the grey-coated eagle, white-rumped,
>
> greedy war-hawk, and the wolf,
>
> grey beast in the forest.[4]

Thereafter, tenth-century Britain developed into two power blocs: what would become England, with its stronghold in Wessex, and Scotland, the focus of a larger Gaelic and Nordic identity. Their enmity slumbered for the next three and half centuries.

With the Conquest and its aftermath, the Anglo-Norman supremacy in the south had more than enough to occupy itself with without looking for trouble in the north – not least by quelling Wales. It was a hundred years before the complexities of the royal succession had been disentangled and English internal affairs stabilized, by which time Henry II (1154–89) ruled England and most of France, including the territories of Normandy, Brittany, Anjou, and Aquitaine: a realm that stretched to the Pyrenees. Hence, it was French and European foreign policy, and also, inevitably, the Crusades, that occupied the kings of England. Scotland was too poor, too inhospitable, and too comparatively remote to draw much attention.

There was nevertheless a certain amount of inevitable political manoeuvring. William Rufus succeeded in placing Edgar, an Anglo-Norman descendant of Edward the Confessor, on the Scottish throne in 1097, and Henry I married one of his eight illegitimate daughters to Alexander I of Scotland (he had about a score of illegitimate children, but only one legitimate heir: Matilda). There was also intermittent conflict, notably at the Battle of the Standard (Northallerton, 1138), where King David, known as 'the Saint of Scotland', cried 'Albany' and raised the ruddy lion for the first time in response to a combination of English holy banners – St Cuthbert of Durham, St John of Beverley, St Peter of York, and St Wilfrid of Ripon – flown from the mast of a ship and topped by a silver pyx (a vessel in which the consecrated host was stored); indeed, a wagon was required to move the massive ensign, which doubled as a rallying point and a refuge.[5] Despite being defeated at the Standard, the Saint of Scotland subsequently seized Northumbria in 1149 during the civil wars sparked by Stephen of Blois's acquisition of the English crown. He held the region until 1157, when Henry II negotiated for the restoration to England of Cumberland, Westmorland, and Northumbria, and an uneasy peace was restored. But in any case, the Scottish kings seemed more concerned with strengthening their position by uniting under the crown of Scotland northern regions such as the Western Isles, then governed by Norway, and by marrying into European royalty, than they were with the Anglo-Normans south of the border.

Things were generally quiet until the Treaty of Paris in 1259, in which Henry III negotiated an Anglo-French peace and surrendered most of the Plantagenet lands on the Continent. For the next few decades, the attention of English monarchs became necessarily confined to Britain. In Scotland, events began to move when Alexander III died after falling from his horse. His infant granddaughter Margaret, known as 'The Maid of Norway' after her father, Eric II of Norway, was recognized as the heir to the throne and guardians appointed until she achieved her majority. Among other things, this required the creation of an appropriate royal seal (1286). As the infant monarch could not be represented herself, she was replaced on the seal of the Guardians of the Realm of Scotland by an image of St Andrew being martyred on the *crux decussata* – the diagonal cross or saltire. It was a significant development: the symbol now stood for more than the young princess and her guardians, more even than the institutional apparatuses of state and Church – it represented the Scottish people: as the motto declared, '*Andreas Scotis Dux esto Compatriotis*' ('Andrew be leader of your Scottish compatriots').[6]

The two peoples and two crosses might have been united within a few years of the premature succession, as Edward I of England proposed his own son as a suitor to little Margaret. The arrangement was accepted, and a peaceful union looked possible until Margaret died in 1290, aged only six. Undeterred, Edward then began to interfere in Scottish affairs, and his heavy-handed meddling was to provoke three hundred years of bitter strife.

The Scottish campaign was driven by Edward's endeavour to incorporate Scotland into his own united kingdom. Following the death of Margaret, Edward was invited to arbitrate the succession because of fears of civil war. He threw himself into this 'Great Cause', mooting a union of the kingdoms before proposing John Balliol for the Scottish throne, ahead of the Bruce candidate, Robert the Noble. King John was crowned on St Andrew's Day 1292 and adopted the lion and tressure as the Arms of Dominion of Scotland; in return, Edward took for himself the title of 'lord superior' of Scotland.[7] But in 1295 the Scots began to distance themselves from England by negotiating with France and Rome, to which Edward responded in 1296 by insisting that King John and the Scottish nobility should pay feudal servitude to the English crown. This propelled the Scots into a far closer relationship with France – what became known as the Auld Alliaunce: in various incarnations this alliance was to last for the next 450 years. And it provoked the first engagements of the Anglo-Scottish wars.

Edward attacked and deposed King John and now treated Scotland as a conquered enemy, which inspired Sir William Wallace to lead a united army of Scotland in the revolt of 1297, which was put down in 1298. Fighting continued intermittently. In 1300, for instance, Edward besieged Caerlaverock Castle, the campaign that inspired the Anglo-Norman poem 'The Roll of Caerlaverock'. At least two-thirds of this heraldic epic is a meticulous – almost a ritualistic – rehearsal of the knights and their respective coats of arms. Even the conclusion of the siege is a piece of vexillological symbolism: 'when they saw that they could not hold out any longer or endure more, the companions begged for peace, and put out a pennon, but he that displayed it was shot with an arrow, by some archer, through the hand into the face'. When the garrison finally surrendered, 'the King caused them to bring up his banner, and that of St Edmund, St George, and St Edward'.*

Wallace was executed in 1305 and his dismembered body scattered to the four corners of Scotland, but the coronation of Robert the Bruce as Robert I a year later provided a new focus for Scottish patriotism and unity.[8] The Bruce's reign instigated a persistent and corrosive conflict, culminating in a legendary victory over the English at Bannockburn in 1314. Interestingly, for his divine patron King Robert favoured St

* St Edmund's banner displayed three golden crowns on a blue field; St Edward the Confessor's was a red banner with the triangular device of the Holy Trinity.

Columba, whose relics were carried on to the battlefield. But following the engagement, history was rewritten. The dedication of St Andrew's Cathedral in 1318 offered particular thanks to St Andrew for the victory at Bannockburn. The saint was a powerful propaganda weapon. For example, the Declaration of Arbroath (1320) and various Papal bulls suggested that St Andrew had visited Scotland as part of his northern mission and had converted the Scots while the English were still pagan, suggesting that it was the north Britons rather than the southerners who were actually God's Chosen People.[9]

The Scots maintained a campaign of border raids until, in 1328, their independence was reluctantly recognized by the newly installed Edward III at the Treaty of Northampton. This agreement withdrew the English crown's claim to overlordship of the Scottish lands – after which the raids continued anyway, and so Edward subsequently renewed his title and campaigned north of the border when not fighting elsewhere. Inevitably, England and Scotland became implacable enemies, and from the late 1370s there was almost continuous warring between the two, fuelled by increasingly entrenched mutual distrust, scorn, and hatred, and by English fears of the hardening Scottish alliance with France. Edward III's policy in Scotland was hamstrung by fears of encouraging Franco-Scottish relations, to the extent that the concurrent and equally devastating English campaigns in France were in part a response to the Auld Alliaunce and rumours that French fleets would sail to the aid of Scotland (for example, in 1335 and 1337). Such support was indeed tangible: in 1385, the French sent their allies 1,200 sets of armour, thereby reducing the Scots' vulnerability to the Welsh and English longbows.

For these protracted campaigns, the Scots were, like the English, identified by the livery and coats of arms of their noble houses, by the cross of their national patron saint, or by standards emblazoned with both designs. Froissart gives some of the heraldic devices of the Scottish lords in 1327, suggesting that the troops fought in household companies, but the cross of St Andrew was regularly worn to counter the cross of St George, especially after 1385, and Andrew was instinctively invoked by Scottish warriors. The ballad of 'The Battle of Otterburn', for example, describes the Scots crying 'Sent Androwe' while the English call on 'Sent George the bryght, owr ladyes knyght', and the *Walsingham Chronicle* records that when plague broke out during one set of hostilities, the Scots prayed, 'Gode and Saint Mungo, Saint Romayn and Saint Andrew shield us this day from Goddis grace, and the foul death that the Englishmen dien upon.'[10]

But as St George had replaced Alban, Edmund, Edward, and Gregory, so St Andrew gradually superseded the other Scottish saints. The cross of St Andrew was declared the national emblem by the Scottish Parliament on 1 July 1385, to be worn by Scottish and French soldiers on the front and back of their *'jacques'* (surcoats) when fighting the English:

Item que tout homme francois et escort ai un signe devant et derrer cest assamoir une croiz blanche Saint Andrieu et se son jacque soit blanc ou sa cote blanc il portera la diete croize blanche en une piece de drap ronde ou quarree.

[Item: every man French and Scots shall have a sign before and behind, namely a white St Andrew's Cross, and if his jack is white or his coat white he shall bear the said white cross in a piece of black cloth round or square.][11]

The year 1385 was, of course, also when Richard II ordered the English army to don the cross of St George – possibly in response to this Scottish initiative. The saltire was also taken up by Burgundy shortly afterwards, and indeed St Andrew became a patron of the knightly Order of the Golden Fleece, founded in Burgundy in 1430/31 (and still active); a saltire of ragged staves is included in the regalia of the order.[12] Like St George, St Andrew also appeared on coins and other instruments of national unity: the English noble of Edward III had St George's cross and *fleurs-de-lys* on one side, and the king in armour on the other; the gold noble of David II of Scotland was the same design, replacing the cross of St George with that of St Andrew.[13] Like George too, Andrew's adventures were described and elaborated upon in the *Golden Legend*, and he also appears in the Scottish *Legends of the Saints* (c. 1400), although surprisingly there is no mention made there of St Andrew's patronage of Scotland, or even of the translation of his relics.[14] By 1510, St Andrew had been declared *Scotorum sanctissimus patronus*, and was honoured by a weekly prayer.[15]

The silver saltire tied the Scottish nation together, and united them against the detested English. The English would occasionally take an army over the border to hammer the saltire-clad Scots – for example at Neville's Cross (1346, where King David II was taken), Homildon Hill (1402), and Flodden (1513).* These defeats both devastated the Scots

---

* The Scottish receipts for their flags at Flodden survive, including four shillings

and inspired a profound loathing of the old enemy.[16] When Aeneas Sylvius Piccolimini (later Pope Pius II) visited Scotland during the reign of James I, he recorded that 'Nothing pleases the Scots more than abuse of the English.'[17] Scottish ballads described the English as having tails so that they could be dragged to the gallows and Highlanders allegedly enjoyed playing football with the decapitated heads of Englishmen. For his part, Edward I had literally set the seal on the relationship when in 1296 he presented the Great Seal of Scotland to his new governor, declaring that he was glad to be getting out of the shit: '*Bon basoigne qy de merde se deliver.*'

But it would be wrong to suggest that the English had it all their own way. Following defeat at Otterbourne in 1388, and despite victories such as Homildon Hill, they were on the defensive against Scotland for much of the fifteenth century: the Scots, for example, took Roxburgh Castle and Berwick in 1460–61. The war was effectively being fought on two fronts by the English, because they frequently encountered Scottish soldiers in their continental campaigns. Scotland persistently delivered aid to France during the Hundred Years War. In 1428 the poet Alain Chartier described the Auld Alliaunce as 'inscribed not upon sheepskin parchment but engraved upon the flesh of men; written not in ink but in blood', and in 1429 it was a combined force of Scots and French defending Orléans that saw Jean d'Arc leading a relief force towards the besieged town, of which the nineteenth-century poet and historian Andrew Lang later commented: 'Alone of all the people with whom she was concerned, the Scots never deserted, sold, betrayed or condemned

'to ane woman ... for making them in haste'.

La Pucelle.'[18] The oppressed peoples of Europe were finding an identity defining themselves as allies against the English, and in 1442 a Scot declared that, 'The tyranny and cruelty of the English are notorious throughout the world, as manifestly appears in their usurpations against the French, Scots, Welsh, Irish and neighbouring lands.'[19] It was only from 1462 that a series of truces with Scotland eventually led to a 'perpetual peace' treaty in 1502 – the first since Edward III's in 1328. Although there continued to be great mistrust and as late as 1490 the English Parliament passed a restrictive statute 'Against Scotsmen', a new phase in Anglo-Scottish relations was beginning.[20]

In 1486, Henry VII formed the 'Union Rose': he married his red rose of Lancaster to the white by taking Elizabeth of York as his wife, and he combined their respective badges in his livery. He later endeavoured to marry the rose with the thistle by giving his daughter Margaret to James IV, but it would be a century before any seeds of unity began to sprout.[21] His son Henry VIII tried to ease the ongoing quarrel by marrying the English Prince Edward to the Scottish Queen Mary, but negotiations broke down and there was further conflict and confusion. Moreover, at the ensuing Battle of Ancrum Moor (1545) some seven hundred Scottish sympathizers fighting for the English against their own countrymen decided to change sides by removing their St George *jacques*. The 'rough wooing' of Scotland continued after Henry's death in 1547, and even Scottish chroniclers such as John Major (or Mair, 1467–1550), by attempting to develop notions of British as opposed to English and Scottish history, implicitly condoned a united British kingdom.[22] These ambitions seemed doomed, however, with renewed hostilities culminating in the Battle of Pinkie (1547) and the departure of Mary to France.

Mary married the Dauphin, Francis, in 1558, and he was offered the Scottish crown. Meanwhile, Elizabeth came to the throne in England, following the death of her sister Mary Tudor, a succession seen as illegitimate by Catholics, who believed that the English crown should go to Mary Stuart, Queen of Scots. Yet Elizabeth's claim was supported by Scottish Protestants, who feared for their independence under French Catholic rule, and who were uniting under the powerful influence of John Knox. With the sudden death of Mary Queen of Scots's French husband, Francis II, in 1560, the threat of Franco-Scottish union swiftly dissolved, because all the while Elizabeth remained a Virgin Queen without a direct heir, the two kingdoms were moving inexorably towards a union of crowns in a common heir: James VI of Scotland.

The English had, of course, also been involved in both Ireland and Wales. Indeed, after the bloody cross and the white saltire, the Irish cross of St Patrick is the third component in the Union Jack. It is, like the cross of St Andrew, a diagonal: a red saltire on a white or silver field. Historians have claimed that this cross has nothing specifically to do with St Patrick and even that it did not exist prior to its 'incorporation' into the Union Flag. Indeed the link with St Patrick is at best tenuous, at worst a convenient fiction, and certainly has no hagiographical authority: strictly speaking, only crucified martyrs are entitled to crosses, yet Patrick died peacefully.*

Yet the flag was used intermittently for centuries before Ireland's union with Great Britain. The design seems to have been adopted from

---

* He is supposedly buried at Saul on Strangford Lough.

the badge of the FitzGeralds or Geraldines, the royal house of Ireland since 1169, and was taken specifically from the arms of the earls of Desmond, who were descended from the twelfth-century Maurice FitzGerald de Windsor, the Anglo-Norman 'Invader of Ireland'. The cross of St Patrick was on occasion flown as the flag of a united Ireland, but since its incorporation in the Union Jack it has seldom been independently flown in Ireland and was unlikely to be adopted by the Republic after 1922. Nevertheless, the prehistory of the flag of St Patrick can be traced, before its formal adoption at the end of the eighteenth century.

St Patrick (*c.* 389–*c.* 461), the 'apostle of Ireland', is in any case a useful point at which to begin an outline of Irish history within the union because he gives a keen insight into early Irish culture and society. Patrick (or Patricius) was a Romano-Briton born between the rivers Severn and Clyde: the son of a deacon, Calpornius, and grandson of a priest, Potitus – although in his early years he 'knew not the true God', neglected his studies, and generally ran wild. Shortly before his sixteenth birthday, he and many of his family were captured and enslaved by Irish pirates; Patrick then got to know the true God a little better. Employed as a herdsman, he spent this time praying and was eventually rewarded with an angelic visitation in a dream, informing him that he would be delivered back to his own country in freedom: 'Lo, your ship is ready.'

After six years Patrick escaped his captors, wandered in exile, and was drawn to board a particular craft which, following a succession of lengthy and legendary adventures, indeed returned him home, aged twenty-two or three. Angelic voices continued to haunt his dreams, however, calling him in 'the voice of the Irish', and specifically calling him to return to the place of his captivity (probably Killalo, Co. Mayo): 'We ask you, holy boy, to come and walk among us once more.' Patrick thenceforth turned his attention to the Church, possibly studying in France and being ordained by St Germanus, yet he found little support for his maverick missionary project to Britain – not least because Pope Celestine had already sent Palladius, the first bishop in Ireland, to attend to an existing congregation there. Details are, however, confusing and it is impossible to disentangle completely our Patrick from Palladius, the mysterious 'Elder Patrick', and St Patrick of Nevers, whose relics at Glastonbury were later claimed to be those of the 'apostle of Ireland'.

Whatever the truth, Patrick soon got back to Ireland – probably by selling his family estates – and commenced his mission, which was of course directed against the Celtic orders of Druids and cults such as sun-worship, from which he converted 'so many thousands'. He found favour with King Laoghaire and established his see at Armagh, performed various miracles and feats of mass conversion, and, as is well known, expelled snakes (and dragons) from the island – indeed, he is usually depicted as trampling on serpents. He also famously used a shamrock or trefoil clover leaf to explain the Trinity, thereby giving Ireland another national emblem and another iconographic motif by which he is known. Moreover, Patrick is reputed to have first distilled the liquor potheen.

Such tales are, however, the stuff of later lives and folklore – the earliest popular association of St Patrick with the shamrock, for example, comes as late as 1674, when Dublin ha'pennies carried St Patrick as a bishop bearing the leaf. Shortly afterwards, on St Patrick's Day 1681, an English visitor noted that 'ye Irish of all stations and condicions were crosses in their hatts, some of pins, some of green ribbon, and the vulgar superstitiously wear shamroges'.[23] Early traditions, however, had begun to emerge in the late seventh century; until then, St Brigit (or Bride) was Ireland's most popular saint: she was a patron of dairymaids, poets, scholars, blacksmiths, and healers, and her miracles included turning her bathwater into beer. But Church politics dictated that Armagh championed their founding bishop, St Patrick, and in doing so they conflated Patrick with many aspects of earlier Irish saints – including Brigit herself. Patrick was also incorporated into the great Celtic myth cycles of the period: for example, 'The Phantom Chariot of Cú Chulainn' (later retold by W. B. Yeats) described how in his attempts to convert King Lóegaire, St Patrick resurrected Cú Chulainn from Hell; he is later obliged to flee from Lóegaire in the form of a deer. St Patrick was also to be found adventuring with heroes such as Oisín and Caílte. Most notably, during one Lent St Patrick pitted himself against no less a personage than God Himself. In the course of this confrontation, Patrick had to contend with swarms of dark birds sent to plague him, which he dealt with by hurling his bell about. Having endured a forty-day trial, however, Patrick secured the release from Hell of many Irishmen, and also received the divine promise 'that the English should not dwell in Ireland, by consent or force, so long as I abide in heaven'. The site of this contest, Croagh Patrick, remains a place of pilgrimage. By this time, St Patrick was already revered as the national saint: indeed, as early as the mid-seventh century the *Liber angeli* of Armagh (*c.* 650) was making the claim that St Patrick was the 'apostolic teacher and chief leader for all the tribes of the Irish', and that 'he himself will judge all the Irish' on Doomsday.

Patrick also wrote, and his surviving work constitutes the earliest Christian literature in Britain, part of a literate culture that ran alongside the old traditions of oral story-telling and myth-making. The saint's writings on Ireland indicate that it was an educated, cultured, and literate society, and, when taken together with later evidence, suggest that a complex social hierarchy existed between the 'sacred' (kings, clerics, and poets) and the secular, as well as between the free and the bonded. Kings in Ireland were, though, almost literally ten-a-penny: Gerald of Wales noted at one point there were over ten dozen kings in the country. In fact, there were many levels of kingship, and it was a position that was not inherited but won, often on the battlefield. Hence the Irish kings were nearly all, to a man, heroes tested in battle, and as warriors they were identified by their own military colours.

Evidence of these ensigns or *shannachies* comes from early chronicles and epic poems. At the Battle of Mag Rath (Magh Rath, or Moira), every division had a captain identified by a standard so that alliances were visible to the protagonists and the progress of combat could be followed. In the chronicle of the battle, *Cath Maige Ratha*, the *shannachie* of the hero Suibne (Sweeney) is described unfurled in the breeze:

> The standard of Suibne, a yellow banner,
>
> the renowned king of Dal Araidhe,
>
> yellow satin over that wild man of hosts,
>
> the white fingered stripling himself in the middle of them.[24]

In one of the epic poems on the same battle, Congal Claen, King of Uladh (Ulidia), appears bearing a more sophisticated device with an illustrious pedigree:

> A yellow lion upon green satin,
>
> The standard of the Craebh-Ruadh,
>
> As borne by noble Concobar,
>
> Is now by Congal borne aloft.[25]

A later chronicler, Geoffrey Keating (*c.* 1570–1650), attributed this practice of flying ensigns to the Chosen People:

> It was, indeed, long before this time, that the Gaels (that is, the descendants of Gaedal), had adopted the custom of bearing distinctive devices upon their standards, after the example of the Children of Israel, who had already practised this usage in Egypt, and when the children of Israel were marching through the Red Sea, with Moses for their captain-in-chief.[26]

The passage in the Old Testament is in Numbers: 'And the children of Israel shall pitch their tents, every man by his own camp, and every man by his own standard, throughout their hosts.'[27]

Likewise, the Viking account of the battle (*Njal's Saga*) places considerable emphasis on insignia, describing the banners flown before each army, the death of one of the Viking standard-bearers, and the near-rout of the invading force as it mutinies over the superstitions attached to its standard:

Then earl Sigurd called on Thorstein, the son of Hall of the Side, to
bear the banner, but then Amundi the white said, 'Don't bear the
banner! for all they who bear it get their death.' 'Hrafn the red!'
called out earl Sigurd, 'Bear thou the banner.' 'Bear thine own devil
thyself,' answered Hrafn. Then the earl said "Tis fittest that the
beggar should bear the bag'; and with that he took the banner from
the staff and put it under his cloak.[28]

Soon afterwards they are all slain. This may be a reference to a Norse
belief in the relationship between spinning and magic. In this saga, the
Valkyrie spin the fate of battle literally out of human guts, knitting
together the grisly fabric of war that will determine who will die. In the
Orkneyinga Saga, a witch weaves a battle-standard for her son; the
banner guarantees victory to the army that fights beneath it, but the
soldier who bears the standard will die.

The ravages of the Norsemen against Ireland inspired the same
response as in Scotland under Kenneth MacAlpin: the disparate Irish
tribes combined their strength in order to resist the common enemy.
Brian Boru (*c.* 941–1014) campaigned across the country to become High
King of Ireland in the earliest attempt to unite the island in opposition
to the Viking raids. Contemporaries were aware how Brian was binding
together the different strands of tribal identity into a single, parti-
coloured coalition – into a rainbow union – as seen in the account of
Celtic heraldry in *The War of the Gaedhil* [Irish] *with the Gaill* [Vikings]:

Brian looked out behind him and beheld the battle phalanx, compact,
huge, disciplined, moving in silence, mutely, bravely, haughtily,

unitedly, with one mind, traversing the plain towards them; and three
score and ten banners over them, of red, and of yellow, and of green,
and of all kinds of colours; together with the everlasting, variegated,
lucky, fortunate banner, that had gained the victory in every battle
and in every conflict, and in every combat; by which seven battles had
been gained before that time, namely, the gold-spangled banner of
Fergal Ua Ruairc, chief king of the territory of Brefni and
Conmaicni...[29]

Although Brian was eventually killed by a Viking force at the Battle of
Clontarf (1014), his initiative proved to be the first time that a united
Ireland had fought and fallen together. His union would remain a legendary memory until three centuries later, when the Scottish raids
inspired a similar stand.

The Viking threat to Ireland was replaced by that posed by the
Norman Conquest of England, but the Anglo-Normans ignored the
country for a century, much as they ignored Scotland. By 1155,
however, Henry II was entertaining invasion. He sent in a force
between 1169 and 1170, and in 1171–2 campaigned there himself,
having received a Papal licence to invade Ireland in order to speed the
reform of the Irish Church (admittedly this permission was granted by
Pope Adrian IV, the only English pontiff in Vatican history). Things
began well and in 1171 the overall leader of the Anglo-Norman force,
'Strongbow' (Richard de Clare, Earl of Pembroke), proceeded to marry
the daughter of the King of Leinster. Henry himself visited, imposed
English law, and an Anglo-Irish community was established – but the
union almost immediately went into a perpetual decline. Subsequent

attempts by the Anglo-Normans to take the island were piecemeal and their hold on power was only ever precarious, despite a military campaign led by King John in 1210. In the meantime, the Anglo-Norman knight John de Courcy had discovered the remains of Sts Patrick, Brigit, and Columba in Co. Down in 1185. De Courcy was keen to promote St Patrick as an Anglo-Irish patron. The relics were translated to Down Cathedral (the graves remain in Downpatrick to this day), St Patrick coins were struck, and a new life of the saint commissioned – the first to record, for instance, his expulsion of the snakes. All this only helped to bind an independent Irish identity.

As for the occupying force, the invaders merely succeeded in creating the Pale, partitioning counties Louth, Meath, Kildare, and the south-west regions. Beyond that – 'beyond the Pale' – remained a lawless hinterland, united now against the English rather than against the Vikings. Indeed, no English king dared to visit Ireland for almost two centuries (1210–1394). During this time, the rebel Scottish monarch Robert I the Bruce had his brother Edward declared High King of Ireland in 1316, an action which, according to one contemporary commentator, set the whole country in 'one trembling wave of commotion'. There was an ensuing revival of Gaelic culture and the Bruce visited to rally further the Celtic Fringe against the English. The country was exploited by the Anglo-Normans as much as they dared, until Richard II's expeditions at the end of the fourteenth century (1394–5 and 1399).

English rule was briefly revitalized, although again this could not be sustained and in 1460 the Irish Parliament declared itself independent. English influence shrank once more back to the Pale, which had a markedly different identity from the rest of the country. In 1498, the

Irish Parliament determined that troops from the Pale should confine themselves to 'English' weapons, such as crossbows and swords, and not use 'Irish' ones, such as spears and darts. They were also forbidden to use Irish war-cries: instead, they were to restrict their calls to St George or the king of England – hence Anglo-Irish knights of the period are depicted bearing the cross of St George on their shields.* The aristocratic families descended from the Norman nobility that had settled in the twelfth century, such as the FitzGeralds of Kildare, always regarded themselves as English, but they were sometimes described as being more Irish than the Irish and were held in high esteem on the island for their antipathy to being ruled from the mainland.

Until 1541, Ireland had been designated a 'lordship'; in that year, it became a kingdom of the English crown. The change came about following the rebellion of Thomas FitzGerald, tenth Earl of Kildare, in 1534. Kildare's uprising was crushed by Henry VIII, who to avenge the killing of the Archbishop of Dublin then mercilessly executed all the male heirs of the Kildare dynasty. Henry asserted his power by having the Irish Reformation Parliament of 1536 appoint him supreme head of the Church, and in 1541 declare him King of Ireland – the first King of all Ireland since Edward the Bruce. Henry in turn appointed a lord deputy to govern the country, retained the Irish Parliament, and began the resettlement or 'planting' of Ireland by Protestants.[30] Predictably there followed a succession of Irish rebellions, which by the 1590s also involved the Scots, who were led by James VI.

---

* Another English patron, St Gregory, had been revered in Ireland for centuries and indeed been given an ancient Irish royal genealogy.

It was from the Kildares, Irish rebellions, and also perhaps piracy that the red saltire of St Patrick emerged. By the fifteenth century, the arms of the house of Kildare were *'argent, a saltire gules'* (a silver field with a red diagonal cross), and Gerald FitzGerald VIII, the Great Earl of Kildare and an early advocate of Irish self-determination, was fined for flying this standard from his castle in 1467. A century later, this diagonal cross appears on map of *Hirlandia* by John Goghe (1567), where it forms the arms of Kildare and is also pictured flying from the mast of a ship. This may possibly be an Irish pirate ship, which would therefore connect the flag with St Patrick in a somewhat wry fashion.[31] The saltire next appears in a more exalted position in the arms of Trinity College, Dublin (1591), and ten years later a contemporary picture-map of the Battle of Kinsale (1601) shows the Irish troops rallying under flags bearing the cross of St Patrick.[32]

This confrontation took place during the Nine Years War (1594–1603), when the rebel Irish earls Tyrone and Tyrconnell invited Philip III of Spain to rule Ireland. An Irish army, led by the two Hughs O'Neill and O'Donnell, and their Spanish allies were confined by the English for two months at Kinsale, before finally succumbing. By the time of the battle, it seems that the device had been adopted by Irishmen outside Kildare, despite its similarity to the cross of St George, and it is just possible that their choice of standard was influenced by the Spanish Cross of Burgundy, a 'saltire raguly' or ragged cross with arms like a tree that has had its branches lopped off. This was also of course connected with St Andrew, and therefore antagonistic to the bloody cross of St George. By 1612, however, the seal of Trinity College Dublin depicted the St Patrick saltire flying from a castle battlement alongside the cross of St George, and from there it was adopted into the arms of both Cork and Enniskillen.* It also incidentally became the flag of Jersey – possibly through a misreading of an entry in a Dutch flag book of 1700. The book describes the Irish flag thus, '*Yrland heeft een witte Vlag, met een rood Andries Kruys*', illustrating the red saltire with the caption 'Ierse', for 'Irish', which may conceivably have been miscon-strued as 'Jersey'. Nevertheless, in the seventeenth century the cross of St Patrick was evidently recognized as the flag of a united Ireland, and it is therefore the oldest such standard – centuries older than the Tricolour, and even older than the harp flag, although the harp was already the national emblem of Ireland.[33]

The Scots have the silver saltire of St Andrew, the Irish have St Patrick's cross – what of the Welsh? The 1895 *Encyclopaedia Britannica* entry for 'Wales' runs: 'For Wales – see England.'[34] Unfortunately, this is essentially true in both the history of the Union and the biography of the Union Jack – Wales has no independent representation on the Union Flag because Wales is not a kingdom: it is a principality.[35] And despite the historian Nennius's eighth- or ninth-century record of the Welsh red dragon overcoming the white wyrm of the Saxons, the rise of Welsh national symbols comes much later. The English army raised the sign of the dragon, for example, at the battles of Lewes (1216), Crécy

* The red saltire on white is also the state flag of Alabama (1895), and forms the basis for that of Florida (1900). One of the Confederate flags in the American Civil War was based on the saltire of St Andrew, because the Confederates claimed Scottish Covenanters among their ancestors.

(1346), and Agincourt (1415), but the Welsh dragon, '*Y Ddraig Goch*', probably began to arise as a national badge or emblem only in the twelfth century, and it was not formally recognized for another three hundred years; its history has been contested again in recent times.

England's annexation of Wales was only completed after 350 years of resistance. The campaign began shortly after the Norman invasion and was completed in 1536 and 1542–3, with retrospective legislation confirming the Act of Union, which was passed alongside Henry VIII's dissolution of the monasteries. The pill of incorporation was, however, sweetened by the ascendancy of the house of Tudor – a Welsh dynasty that had succeeded to the throne of England with the triumph of Henry VII over Richard III, the last English king, at the Battle of Bosworth Field in 1485 – a victory gained moreover under the eyes of Henry's dragonish standard, subsequently lodged in Westminster Abbey. (This standard also carried the cross of St George in the first compartment, neatly representing the union of the two countries.) The Welsh house of Tudor remained on the throne until the succession of the Scottish house of Stuart in the seventeenth century.

The Welsh themselves – the original Britons – were, like their fellow inhabitants of the British Isles, also keen on uniting the land. From ancient *Triads of Britain* (translated by the nineteenth-century Welsh antiquarian William Probert) we learn that:

1. There were three names given to the Isle of Britain from the first: before it was inhabited it was called the Sea-girt Green Space; after it was inhabited, it was called the honey Island; and after the people were formed into a commonwealth, by Prydain the son of Aedd

the Great, it was denominated the Isle of Britain. And no one has any right to it but the tribe of the Cambrians, for they first took possession; and before that there were no persons living in it, but it was full of bears, wolves, crocodiles, and bisons.[36]

They migrated west, however, during the *adventus Saxonum* (the coming of the Saxons), and from about the fourth century gathered in the three communities of Wales, Cornwall, and Brittany. At about the same time, the Cuneddas, leaders of the Votadini tribe of southern Scotland, migrated to north Wales, possibly on the recommendation of Vortigern, who was king of the Britons immediately after the Roman withdrawal in 410. The Cuneddas secured north Wales from Irish incursions, although Vortigern was less successful when he invited two Saxons, Hengist and Horsa, to help defend southern England; they promptly revolted and established their own principality in Kent in the 450s.[37] In general, however, the exchange of lands was more like a gradual assimilation than an invasion – although admittedly the very name of the country, 'Wales', derives from the Anglo-Saxon *wealh*, meaning foreign.[38]

The country had a distinct geographical identity, and in the later eighth century was separated from England by the great earthwork of Offa's Dyke, much as Ireland was cut off by the natural defence of the sea. Moreover, like Ireland and its dozens of petty kings, Wales was made up of tiny kingdoms: it was not a single country but a region of the three primary kingdoms of Gwynedd, Powys, and Deheubarth, alongside many small locales. This situation had evolved out of Welsh inheritance laws, which were governed by partibility rather than primogeniture, as well as by the mountainous geography of the country, which made travel and communication – and, indeed, ruling – difficult. Again, as with Ireland, the English king might claim lordship over the territory, but it was a title in name only. As early as the eighth century Bede noted that the Welsh 'have a natural hatred for the English', and much like St Patrick in Ireland, St David became a vehicle for expressions of independence from England.[39]

St David (or Dewi, as opposed to Dafydd, d. 589/601) is an increasingly marginal figure. He originally settled in Mynyw (Menevia, now St Davids) in the south-west corner of Wales, founding an order of extreme austerity there and winning himself the name 'The Waterman' for his ascetic habit of standing in cold water. There are references to David from the eighth century, and his feast day was fixed as 1 March by the ninth century, but his cult only really dates from the eleventh, when St Davids was asserting its independence from Canterbury. A tenth-century poem, *Armes Prydein vawr* (*The Great Prophecy of Britain*), suggests David's primacy among the Welsh saints. The poet argues that English overlords have abused the Welsh sainthood and that rising against the English in the name of St David would be blessed with success.

The Conquest of England in 1066 left Wales open to Norman invasion, but this too was to be a gradual absorption. Despite Anglo-Norman incursions directly after the Conquest in 1067–75, the English earls could only assume command over the lowland south: the mountainous regions were impossible to control and, in the aftermath of the Conquest, there followed two centuries of low-level warfare. Wales was therefore divided into *pura Wallia*, ruled by the Welsh princes, and *marchia Wallie*, the Marches, ruled by Anglo-Norman barons. These barons gradually built up what amounted to micro-empires against the remaining Welsh kingships, but it was a gruellingly slow and cripplingly expensive enterprise. In Glamorgan alone, the Anglo-Normans built twenty-six castles in the thirty years between 1117 and 1147. Theirs was a slow seizure. The Welsh, confident in the belief that King Arthur would shortly return, bided their time and abided by the words of Gerald of Wales: 'The English are striving for power, the Welsh for freedom; the English are fighting for material gain, the Welsh to avoid a disaster; the English soldiers are hired mercenaries, the Welsh are defending their homeland.'[40]

By then, Rhigyfarch ap Sulien had written the first surviving life of St David, possibly in response to the first full-scale Anglo-Norman invasion of 1093. Again, there is an intimate relation to the lives of St Patrick and a similar assertion of independent identity. David's birth was forecast to both King Sant of Ceredigion and St Patrick, coming to pass thirty years later when Sant (or *Sanctus*, literally, a saint: 'Sant by name and merits') went out and raped a woman Non (or Nonna or Nonnita, literally, a nun). David was subsequently born to Non during a thunderstorm, raised piously, and took the monastic life. He founded twelve orders, including those at Glastonbury and Bath, before setting up his own at Mynyw, where he died at the ripe old age of 147 after a life spent performing modest miracles, such as divining wells. Although David's cult never established itself among the Welsh in the same way as St Patrick's did among the Irish, it not only survived the Anglo-Norman conquest but many of the invaders became adherents. In, for instance, the *Song of Dermot and the Earl*, a Norman-French *geste* describing the later Irish campaigns, the invading knights repeatedly rally to 'Sein Davi!'[41] Whether they wore leeks in their hats too is not recorded, the leek being David's legendary contribution to Welsh iconography: he advised his countrymen to wear leeks in their headgear in order to distinguish themselves in battle from the Saxons. Other Welsh saints were also fiercely patriotic: the sixth-century St Beuno, the most significant saint in north Wales, planted an acorn in his father's grave that grew into an oak able to kill any Englishman who passed beneath it; Welshmen were not harmed by the tree.

Despite the Anglo-Norman fortification of south Wales, attempts to annex the whole country failed. Henry II tried three times to take Wales: first by diplomacy and then, in 1157 and 1165, by invasions, the second of which was led by Strongbow, who later led the Irish expedition. But the Welsh kings Owen of Gwynedd and Rhys of Deheubarth resisted both Henry's political force and his military might, the latter by mounting a campaign of guerrilla warfare in the treacherously mountainous regions of mid- and northern Wales. Gwynedd, ancient seat of the Cuneddas, became the focus for anti-English insurgency, and in 1244 the first Prince of Wales was proclaimed: Dafydd ap Llywelyn. His claim to princedom was based on his father's title as King of Gwynedd. But it transpires that Welsh independence from Norman England was evidently not a shared – or even necessarily a recognizable – national cause. English armies had long employed Welsh mercenaries: even Strongbow's invasion force of the country recruited many Welshmen.

Henry III endeavoured to intervene diplomatically rather than militarily by supporting Dafydd, Prince of Gwynedd, against the claims to

principality made by his half-brother Gruffudd, whom Dafydd impris-
oned along with his son Owen. This helped to secure Wales as a satellite
of England, until another of Gruffudd's sons, Llywelyn ap Gruffudd,
claimed Gwynedd as his and hounded Henry III out of Wales. So
began a sustained Welsh resistance to the Anglo-Normans. Llywelyn
set himself up as 'Prince of Wales and Lord of Snowdon' in 1262, and
by 1267 at the Treaty of Montgomery had forced Henry to recognize his
hereditary right to the title. The rebel states seemed secure against the
English. But this security was an illusion, and the Treaty of Paris in
1259, which had freed England from many of its continental interests,
was to have much the same implications for Wales as for Scotland.

The coronation of Edward I in 1274 was accompanied by earth-
quakes, thunder, and lightning, as well as a comet and a fiery dragon
scudding across the sky. The king of Scotland was there to pay his allegiance, but not Llywelyn ap Gruffudd, and soon Edward began
preparing an interventionist force with which he intended to divide
Llywelyn's land between his brothers and set them up as puppet rulers.
When he invaded in 1277, large numbers of Welshmen again fought
with the English against Llywelyn, who had also faced various con-
spiracies and assassination plots devised by his own family. However,
gaining confidence from his successful campaign, Edward set his sights
on total domination. By 1282 the Welsh had rebelled and the English
responded by invading in force. They fortified themselves within their
extensive castles and imposed English law. For this campaign,
Edward's troops were provided with armbands of the cross of St
George: 'a primitive form of uniform and a sign of the quasi-religious
nature the war had taken in Edward's eyes'.[42] Llywelyn ap Gruffudd

was slain, possibly ambushed by conspirators, and his head was cut off and sent to London. There it was crowned with ivy, a macabre mocking of the Welsh prophecy that a Briton would be crowned king of England. Sporadic rebellions followed in 1287 and 1294–5, but without a leader such as Prince Llywelyn, the rebels faltered and the country was taken.

The king proceeded to secure his position both physically and ideologically. In an era when a mason earned less than two shillings a week, between 1277 and 1301 the king spent over £75,000 building castles in Wales; Rhuddlan Castle alone (1277–82) cost almost £10,000. And Edward laid claim not only to Wales but also to Arthurian legitimacy, deriving his descent from that slumbering unionist king. He exhumed what were claimed to be the bodies of Arthur and Guinevere at Glastonbury and had them reinterred in marble tombs – simultaneously celebrating and dispelling the legend – and in the process of this enterprise he also acquired Arthur's crown. Inevitably, Edward's union was compared to that of Arthur, in the words of Pierre de Langtoft:

> Ah, God! How often Merlin said truth
>
> In his prophecies, if you read them!
>
> Now are the two waters united in one,
>
> Which have been separated by great mountains;
>
> And one realm made of two different kingdoms
>
> Which used to be governed by two kings.
>
> Now are all the islanders all joined together,
>
> And Albany [Scotland] reunited to the royalties
>
> Of which King Edward is proclaimed lord.
>
> Cornwall and Wales are in his power,

> And Ireland the great at his will.
>
> There is neither king nor prince of all the countries
>
> Except King Edward, who has thus united them;
>
> Arthur never held the fiefs so fully.[43]

In a comparable gesture of consolidation, Glastonbury claimed to have relics of St Patrick and adopted St David as a patron. But the new united kingdom was not solely symbolic, and Edward also delivered a contemporary political statement of union by investing in the office of the Prince of Wales.

There is a legend that Edward promised the Welsh a prince who was born in Wales and who spoke no English – before presenting them with his baby son Edward, born at Caernarfon. But anointing his eldest son the first English Prince of Wales was a gesture of high diplomacy. It was a shrewd act of incorporation, for it recognized Welsh identity without subsuming it into a 'Great England'. In 1301, it was determined that the 'territorial endowment of the heir to the throne' – half of Wales – should 'never be separated from the crown, but should remain entirely to the kings of England for ever', and from the sixteenth century the endowment was regarded as the whole of the country.[44] In acting so, the English gave dynastic attention to Wales and it became traditional to make the heir to the throne of England the Prince of Wales. Since the Norman annexations, south Wales and the Marches had been considered English, but the north – Gwynedd in particular – was a different country, and following the death of Llywelyn had been fomenting further rebellion. The region was strictly subjugated after the revolt at Caernarfon (1294), which destroyed half of the castle, but the more subtle means of control proved to be the more effective. The degree of

integrity afforded to the country by maintaining the title of Prince of
Wales proved sufficient to quell serious risings for more than a century.
Welsh identity was cultivated, and its status as a principality maintained by the English throne through events such as the ceremonies of
investiture held at Caernarfon Castle.

There were also crucial practical benefits to be derived from building a firm union. During the twelfth century, Welsh archers had
developed the most lethal weapon of the age, the longbow – a weapon
that over the next four hundred years was virtually to guarantee
English military supremacy across Europe.[45] Despite frequent brawling
between Welsh and English foot-soldiers, they fought side-by-side
throughout the fourteenth century. At the Battle of Falkirk (1298),
where William Wallace was comprehensively beaten, 10,500 of the
12,500 'English' infantry were born in Wales.[46] There were five thousand Welsh archers and spearmen at Bannockburn (1314), and they also
fought at, for example, Dupplin Moor (1332) and Halidon Hill (1333;
'Thaire was thaire banner born all doune').[47] And it was the same on the
Continent: at the Battle of Crécy (1346), the Cornish and the Welsh
fought alongside the English, which may explain the use of the dragon
standard there and on other French campaigns.[48]

Yet despite the castles, the Arthurianism, the dynastic incorporation,
and the battlefield camaraderie, the union was also fraught with problems. When, in 1294, war again broke out with France, Edward looked
to Wales for troops – and in doing so provoked another revolt. Master
James of St George wrote to Edward I in February 1295, warning the
monarch of the potentially catastrophic instability that the Welsh could
cause by joining the Auld Alliaunce: 'As you know, Welshmen are

Welshmen and you need to understand them properly; if, which God forbid, there is war with France or Scotland, we shall need to watch them all the more closely.'[49]

Minor revolts continued throughout the next hundred years. Despite its reliance on Welsh firepower across the battlefields of Europe, England still considered Wales to be a backward colony, and avaricious English landowners oppressed the populace and refused positions of responsibility to Welsh natives. It was typical colonial mismanagement. Eventually, following the ravages of plague, the popular uprisings grew in intensity and ferocity, and it was in 1400 that Owen Glendower stepped on to the stage of British history. Glendower led disturbances that lasted for the next eight years, and to a degree succeeded in mobilizing the Celtic Fringe. Scotland and Ireland lent support in 1401, as did France in 1403, and Glendower also allied himself with the revolt of the Northumbrian Percys – Hotspur and his ilk – against Henry IV.

The tide turned back in England's favour with the capture in 1406 of James I of Scotland, which calmed the Anglo-Scottish conflict until 1424, and in 1407 with the negotiation of an Anglo-French truce. But by this time Wales was perceived to be a potential danger to the union. It was a region in disarray, and come 1449 it 'daily abundeth and increaseth in misgovernance'.[50] Wales also threatened to provide potential enemies of the English crown with an undefended coastline – a route into England – as well as with rebel sympathizers:

> Beware of Wales, Christ Jesus must us keep,
>
> That it make not our child's child to weep,
>
> Nor us also, if so it go this way

By unwariness; since that many a day

Men have been afraid of there rebellion ...[51]

Wales remained a feared region until the advent of the house of Tudor in 1485, but it never presented a sustained threat to the concept of a united Britain. Once the Tudors were established, Henry VIII further consolidated the relationship between England and Wales. With his divorce creating problems with Rome and the Church, Henry needed stability and uniformity within his own kingdom, and as an expression of monarchical authority he engineered two Acts of Union with Wales, in 1536 and 1542–3, that 'incorporated, united and annexed' Wales to England.[52] The legislation reorganized the region into shires under English law with Parliamentary representation, while a Council of Wales was established to be responsible for defence and the judiciary, and a Court of Great Sessions was established.

After several centuries of gradual unification, this transition was relatively painless, and a continued degree of autonomy was permitted. English became the language of choice, but the Welsh clergy and gentry remained dedicated to the Welsh language, and to Welsh literature and culture, maintaining a strongly historical and linguistic identity – one made possible in part because shortly after the Act of Union the language was canonized in the Welsh Bible and Welsh Book of Common Prayer, a century before similar versions were prepared in Irish Gaelic and two centuries before they appeared in Scots Gaelic. Indeed, an abiding sense of Welshery is clear in that, even in the eighteenth century, the Welsh were still referring to the English as '*saison*', or Saxons.[53] But their incorporation as a principality under the crown of England was total, and Wales has no independent representation on any of the Union Flags. The only monarchs to have included the Welsh dragon in the royal crest were the Tudors, and even then the dragon was only a supporter of the shield of arms. Welsh heraldry itself was late to develop (there are only ten coats of arms recorded before 1300) and also tended to ignore heraldic conventions, mixing colours and metals in proscribed ways. Despite the strong association with the dragon emblem which dates from about the twelfth century, the earliest armorial bearings recorded are those of the sons of Llywelyn the Great (d. 1240), Prince of Gwynedd. Dafydd and Gruffudd carried four alternating red and gold lions, a shield that became associated with the princedom of Wales and was later borne by Owen Glendower, who was distantly related to the house of Gwynedd (*quarterly or and gules, four lions passant counter-changed*). But the princes, though often described as being 'lions' or 'eagles', were most often called 'dragons'. Glendower is depicted in his Great Seal as bearing a wyvern crest (a two-legged dragon) on his helmet and on his horse, and had a dragon and lion supporting his shield. Adam of Usk recorded that Glendower's standard at Caernarfon was a golden dragon on a white field.[54] In other words, despite the popularity of dragon charges, it was not until Henry VII – who claimed descent from the seventh-century semi-mythical Welsh king Cadwallader – that the red dragon became firmly associated with Wales, and since the time of the Tudors the personal flag of the Prince of Wales has been based on the ancient device of the four lions, with the addition of a shield bearing a coronet.

England had unified in response to Viking raids, and thereafter in response to changing relations with Continental powers, especially

France – an object of peculiar odium. Although England's immediate neighbours had also been originally inspired to unite by the need to defend themselves against the Vikings, in the aftermath of the Conquest, Scottish and Irish, and to a lesser extent Welsh, identities were formed in direct response to Anglo-Norman invasion and annexation, and in direct antagonism to England's efforts to unify or subjugate them. So while the English found their national identity and destiny on the medieval battlefields of Europe, the Celtic nations of Britain found theirs in immovable resistance to the English. It would have been an extraordinary stalemate but for the blithe English acceptance of a succession of alien kings: William of Normandy was French and Henry Tudor Welsh; the house of Stuart was Scottish and the Hanoverian dynasty German. Despite the apparently insoluble antagonisms between the four nations of the British Isles, by the beginning of the seventeenth century, Great Britain would be more united than it had ever been before.

IV   1606 AND ALL THAT

Shake hands with Union, O thou mighty State
Now thou art all Great-Britain and no more,
No Scot, no English now, nor no debate;
No borders but the Ocean and the shore.

Samuel Daniel, 'A Panegyrike Congratulatorie to
the Kings most excellent Majestie' (1603), I, 143

IN 1603, thirty-three years after he had been crowned King of Scotland, James VI succeeded Elizabeth to become James I of England and King of Ireland.[1] His coronation was the culmination of the 'rough wooing' of Scotland – the policy of uniting the kingdoms by dynastic marriage and the ensuing succession – rather than by military power and oppression. James was descended from Henry VII on both sides: his mother, Mary Queen of Scots, was the granddaughter of James IV of Scotland, who had married Henry's daughter Margaret Tudor, and Margaret was also the grandmother of James's father by her second marriage. Henry VIII's will had insisted that the crown could only go to English blood, and consequently the descendants of his younger daughter,

Mary, had priority over those of her older sister, Margaret. But James VI was male, Protestant, and politically experienced: English pragmatism won through and James Stuart was crowned.[2]

James's vision was one of unity, for which he had good historical precedents: the ancient unification of 'Alba', the *bretwalda* of the Anglo-Saxon Heptarchy (the overlord of the seven kingdoms of Old England), and the Anglo-Norman assumption of Wales:

> Doe wee not yet remember, that this Kingdome was divided into seven little Kingdomes, besides *Wales*? And is it not now the stronger by their Union? And hath not the Union of *Wales* to *England* added a greater Strength therto? ... I desire a perfect Union of Lawes and Persons, and such a Naturalizing as may make one Body of both Kingdomes under mee your King. That I and my Posteritie (if it so please God) may rule over you to the Worlds End; Such an Union as was of the *Scots* and *Pictes* in *Scotland*, and of the Heptarchie heere in *England*.[3]

More than a union of crowns, James sought a union of the two kingdoms of Great Britain: 'The blessed Union, *or rather* Reuniting, *of* two Kingdoms, anciently but one, under *one Imperial Crowne*'.[4] His language was physical, almost carnal, describing a 'golden Conquest, but cymented with Love': a marriage of two kingdoms.[5]

Some commentators were thrilled by this rhetoric of wedlock. In *The Miracvlovs and Happie Vnion of England and Scotland* (1604), for instance, William Cornwallis described the means to proper union:

Beholde how we are joyned, God, Nature, & Time, have broght vs together, and so miraculously if wee obserue the reuolutions of time, as me thinketh the very words after the consummation of a marrriage, shal not be vnproperly vsed, *Those whom God hath ioyned together, let no man seperate* [*sic*].[6]

He went on to discuss Plato's theory of paired lovers: 'England hath founde her other halfe, she is nowe doubly furnished with the strength of a Kingdome, she hath foure armes, foure legs, two hartes (made one) two powers, and double forces.'[7] Likewise, John Gordon's *Enotikon* [Uniter]*, or a Sermon of the Union of Great Brittainie in Antiquitie of Language, Name, Religion and Kingdome* (delivered 28 October 1604), observed that Britain is the 'holy place wherein this admirable union of God and man is conjoined in the person of a Britain King'.[8] James himself alluded to the marriage ceremony in the words he had inscribed on the joint crown, '*Quae Deus Coniuxit Nemo Separet*' ('What God has joined let no man separate').[9]

King James presented himself as the first British monarch. There was to be free trade within the union and the naturalization of Scots born after his accession; laws, governments, and churches would be brought together under the name of 'Great Britain' – a name that he himself proposed. He established his ideological and genealogical credentials for union by claiming descent from the last Welsh prince, Llywelyn ap Gruffudd, as well as from Henry VII and the Anglicized Tudors, and obviously from the Scottish Stuarts. James came from a legendary line of 109 Scottish kings – an alternative tradition to the English foundation myths – but notwithstanding this, James's union did invoke the legendary history of Brutus. According to Geoffrey of Monmouth, Brutus (or Britto), reputedly the great-grandson of Aeneas, had been guided by the goddess Diana to settle his people on a new island. He had landed at Totnes in Devon more than a thousand years before the Roman invasion and, after vanquishing the giants of the land such as Gog and Magog, had founded Trinovantum – the New Troy – which became London. On his death, Brutus's three sons had divided up the kingdom between themselves: Kamber inherited Wales (Cambria), Albanactus received Scotland (Albany), and Locrinus the land of Loegria (England without Cornwall, which was ruled by Corineus, father of Gwendolen, whom Locrinus had married). This three-way split was to persist for the next 2,500 years. Although from the earliest sorties of Edward I both sides in the Anglo-Scottish wars had invoked the tradition, it was not until the accession of James that Britain was finally reunited and the Brutus legend seemed to have been peacefully fulfilled.

There were other myths of unification as well. James's Scottish supporters remembered the prophecies of the otherworldly thirteenth-century seer Thomas the Rymer, who had predicted that Scotland and England would have one king when the rivers Tweed and Powsail met at Merlin's grave; on the day Elizabeth died, the Tweed flooded into the Powsail at Drumelzier, the legendary resting place of Merlin. The Arthurian allusion was also apt in another way. Arthur had suffered from the arch-scepticism of the influential historian and humanist Polydore Vergil, whose *Anglica Historia* (*History of England*, 1534) savagely attacked Geoffrey of Monmouth's *Historia Regum Britanniae*, dismissing it in its entirety and therefore effectively removing both

Brutus and Arthur from the nation's past. But under Henry VIII, early English historians such as the poet and antiquarian John Leland and John Bale (author of the first English history play, *Kynge Johan*, in 1538) revived the legendary history of Britain and reinvented King Arthur as an archetypal Protestant and unionist hero (they also canonized Joseph of Arimathea as the first English apostle). James's union of the two crowns therefore presented an opportunity to reinstate these popular myths of unification as supporters of the new monarchy, creating a composite British history out of centuries of strife. In the words of the poet and statesman Sir William Alexander,

> The world long'd for thy [James's] birth three hundreth years,
> Since first fore-told wrapt in prophetic rimes...[10]

In assuming power, James had actually invoked one of Merlin's unionist prophecies. The new king had declared that that 'the island shall be called by the name of Brutus, and the name given it by the foreigners abolished', and Francis Bacon recorded him announcing 'that the island was Britany [*sic*], as Brutus and Arthur were, who had the style, and were kings of the whole island'.[11] James proclaimed himself King James I of Great Britain, and to a degree modelled his union upon that of King Arthur. Arthur's stock looked like it was rising again. As a paragon of virtue, a knight of chivalry, and a national and, significantly, a peculiarly *British* Protestant hero, he offered a mythic legitimation of James's reign. William Camden even noted an Arthurian anagram on the monarch's name, *Charles James Steuart*: 'Claims Arthur's seat'.[12]

And yet this Arthurian credo did not exactly soar. The physician, poet, and lyricist Thomas Campion offers an exemplary example of what one might expect to find following the accession of James. In *The Discription of a Maske, presented before the Kinges Maiestie at White-Hall, on Twelfth Night last*, honouring the marriage of Lord Haye (1607), appears 'An Epigram':

> To the most puisant and Gratious IAMES King of great Britaine.
>
> *MErlin*, the great king *Arthur* being slaine,
>
> Fouretold that he should come to life again,
>
> And long time after weild great Brittaines state
>
> More powerfull ten-fold, and more fortunate.
>
> Prophet 'tis true, and well we find the same,
>
> Saue onely that thou didst mistake the name.[13]

Although Campion's 'Epigram' could not have cost the lyricist much effort, it does identify Arthur/James with 'great Brittaines state'. Campion's 'Epigram' is precisely what one would expect to find following the accession; the extraordinary thing, however, is that it appears to be among the very few examples of unionist verse invoking Arthur. Most royalist refrains, such as the lines by Alexander's friend William Drummond of Hawthornden, are far less explicit:

> This is that king, who should make right each wrong,
>
> Of whom the bards and mystic sybils sung;
>
> The man long promis'd, by whose glorious reign
>
> This Isle should yet her ancient name regain.[14]

There are two principal reasons for this immediate failure of Arthurian symbolism. First, Edmund Spenser had already extensively reinvented Arthur for *The Faerie Queene*, and secondly, the union was not in any degree a popular policy – indeed it was only with profound hindsight, in part inspired by imperial successes, that the union came to be seen as positively defining Great Britain.

The Faerie Queene celebrates the Welsh origins of the Tudor dynasty, which it seeks to consolidate with the legends and significance of Arthur. The central figure in the poem is Gloriana, who symbolizes Queen Elizabeth, and it is Gloriana to whom Prince Arthur pays homage; as we have seen, the epic also has a strong Georgist theme running through it in the figure of Redcrosse.[15] But by the time James was crowned, the Arthurian motif was not simply exhausted by the six published books of *The Faerie Queene*; the whole strategy for developing a Tudor myth of sovereignty derived from the legends of Arthur had simply become irrelevant now a Scottish dynasty had succeeded to the throne. In fact, after the initial flush of excitement, it is difficult to find anything save passing references to Arthur in the court writings of the first decade of the seventeenth century: he almost completely vanishes.

Popular references are, however, rather more frequent, and do give voice to a sense of British identity coming to terms with national traditions. The actor-dramatist Samuel Rowley's only surviving play, a chronicle of Henry VIII called *When You See Me, You Know Me* (1605), has a character allude to the ballad 'The Legend of King Arthur' in a veiled reference to Henry's dissolution of the monasteries and his contemporaneous Acts of Union with Wales: 'king Arthur, and his Knights of the round Table . . . were buried in Armour, are alive again, crying Saint George for England, and meane shortly to conquere Rome…'.[16] Here Arthur is very much the Protestant hero. And perhaps the most famous mention of Arthur in this period also derives from the popular stage. In Shakespeare's *Henry V* (1599), we learn that Sir John Falstaff has died: 'he's in Arthur's bosom, if ever man went to Arthur's bosom' (II, iii, 9). Despite the fact that this allusion is actually the Hostess's comical error for 'Abraham's bosom', the mistake is made because Arthur is already associated with Falstaff: in *Henry IV (Part 2)* he enters one scene singing, 'When Arthur first in court', the opening of the ballad of 'Sir Lancelot du Lake' (II, iv, 32).[17] In the same way as the Green Man connotations of St George showed him to be as much a mysterious spirit of the English landscape as a warrior saint and a polit-ical figurehead, so King Arthur and his Knights of the Round Table are made part of the teeming fabric of Merrie Englande, forerunners of 'plump Jack' and his gang, as well as Arthur being the grandfather of British – or unionist – history.[18]

But Falstaff, like Arthur, does not last: he is made to disappear by King Henry's cruel words, 'I know thee not, old man' (V, v, 47). Perhaps the seeds of Falstaff's rejection lie in this affinity with Arthur: a defeated leader, rendered powerless, who now sleeps away eternity. Falstaff is dismissed by Henry as a dream ('I have long dreamt of such a kind of man, … But being awak'd I do despise my dream' (V, v, 49–51)), and he dies in the mists of the Hostess's memory: 'I saw him fumble with the sheets and play wi' th' flowers, and smile upon his fingers' ends, … and a' babbled of green fields…' (*Henry V*, II, iii, 13–16). Perhaps, in the light of Falstaff, Old King Arthur too ceased to be a credible political figurehead. Despite Campion's cursory attempt to revive Arthurian symbolism, Arthur was not invoked as a significant model either for James or for the union. Spenser's comprehensive reinvention of Arthur had unfortunately coincided with the failure of the Tudor line, and Arthur was, once again, history. When the scepticism inspired by Polydore Vergil's *Anglica Historia* returned, Arthur was not even afforded the dignity of history, and in less than fifty years Merlin's prophecies were regarded merely as 'old wives' tales'.[19]

The decline of Arthurian unionism was also abetted by the unpopularity of the union of the crowns. Parliaments on both sides of the border appointed commissions to report on the question of formalizing the relationship of the two crowns in a legislative union recognizing James's title as King of Great Britain. The Scottish Parliament was the more enthusiastic of the two, and on 11 August 1607 actually passed an Act of Union, which was conditional on the English Parliament doing the same. The House of Commons in England was, however, very reluctant to do so, and in fact rejected the proposal: 'We should lose the ancient name of England, so famous and victorious, let us proceed with a leaden foot.'[20] Clearly, the national parliaments were acutely aware of their own identities within a greater British community, and in any case, the creation of James's Great Britain would, by dissolving the three nations, unfortunately dissolve all of their laws and treaties as well.

Although a formal Act of Union was not ratified until 1707, James nevertheless proclaimed the name Great Britain on coins and, despite parliamentary objections, he achieved a degree of economic union and some recognition of joint citizenship. His policy did have standing in common law, and so the two kingdoms were effectively, if precariously, united through much of the seventeenth century – which was itself a considerable achievement following hundreds of years of ireful feuding and outright warfare.[21] And neither was the symbolic impact of the union confined to coins and to language: on 12 April 1606, James I of Great Britain flew the first Union Flag.

Since James's accession, British ships had been obliged to fly two flags: the crosses of both St George and St Andrew. But two flags flying from one mast indicated that a military engagement had taken place, with the victor's flag hung at the top – hence flags flying at half-mast are in mourning because they have been vanquished by the invisible flag of death.* Following the union of the crowns, English sailors flew St George in the victorious position, while Scots flew St Andrew. Such sniping hardly contributed to the great ideal of marrying the two countries together; James was obliged to address the matter.

The king commissioned the Earl of Nottingham to design the first Union Flag, or 'Flag of the Great Union' as it was later described. Nottingham was faced with a difficult problem: by the laws of heraldry it is not possible to give equal prominence to different elements within a design, and each part of the flag and its overall layout are indicative of relative status and significance. Various designs were made, trying to balance the two countries equally: the St Andrew in the upper canton of St George, or in each corner, or the two imposed in different ways. The two options that most clearly drew on recent heraldic traditions

---

* Flags flying at 'half-mast' in fact traditionally fly one flag's width shy of the top of the pole; they are hoisted to the top and then lowered to this position without pausing.

were either quartering the crosses of St Andrew and St George (placing the crosses in alternating quadrants), or impaling them (placing them side-by-side). But both options inevitably gave precedence to one or other of the countries – effectively making one the dominant male line and the other the female.

This image of marriage was, of course, part of the rhetoric of the union already. It also seems to have influenced Nottingham's own endeavours, as he described his favourite design, the impalement of St Andrew, as a 'marriage': 'In my poure opinion, this wyll be the most fetest [fittest] for this is leke man and wyfe w[i]t[h]out blemesh on to other'.[22] But which was the man and which the woman? The sexual image of 'impalement' of one by the other had embarrassing overtones, implying an unequal power relationship and a dominant partner. If the Scottish royal pedigree was arguably longer than that of the English, England was a far larger and considerably more prosperous country.

The design that was eventually adopted moved out of the arena of sexual politics and attempted to balance the priority of the two elements; it was also the most ingenious of the designs and forms the basis of the Union Jack we have today. As *Boutell's Heraldry* remarks, 'From the heraldic viewpoint the [Union] flag is interesting because it represents a return to the earlier practice of compounding insignia.'[23] The imposition of the cross of St George over that of St Andrew might suggest the supremacy of England over Scotland, but the canton (the upper quarter nearest the hoist) is the most honourable situation of a flag, and in this design was occupied by the colours of St Andrew. The design elegantly squared the circle of precedence; it also proved far too subtle for those not versed in the protocols of heraldry.

The design was first ordered in an Admiralty letter of 1 April 1606, which stipulated that the new Union Flag was to be flown by all royal and merchant vessels, and this was proclaimed on 12 April 1606:

WHEREAS some difference hath risen betweene our Subjects of South and North Britaine travayling by Seas, about the bearing of their Flagges: For the avoyding of all such contentions hereafter, Wee have with the advice of our Councell ordered; That from henceforth all our Subjects of this Isle and Kingdome of great Britaine and the members thereof, shall beare in their Mainetoppe the Red Crosse, commonly called St Georges Crosse, and the White Crosse commonly called S Andrewes Crosse, joyned together according to a forme made by our Heralds, and sent by us to our Admirall to bee published to our said Subjects: And in their Fore-toppe our Subjects of South Britaine shall weare the Red Crosse onely as they were wont, and our Subjects of North Britaine in their Fore-toppe the White-Crosse onely as they were accustomed.

Wherefore wee will and command all our Subjects to be conformable and obedient to this our Order, and that from henceforth they doe not use to beare their Flagges in any other sort, as they will answere the contrary at their perill.

Given at our palace of Westminster the twelfth day of April, in the fourth yeere of our Reigne of Great Britaine, France and Ireland, &c.[24]

There was no provision for land flags: the directions were solely for use at sea. This emphasis on maritime rather than terrestrial use effectively set the tone of subsequent flag legislation, which is almost solely concerned with naval regulations.

The Scots straight away objected, because they believed that the design gave prominence to the flag of St George and chopped up the silver saltire into four pieces. Complaining to the king on 7 August 1606, they proposed further drafts for the flag:

A greate nomber of the maisteris and awnaris of the schippis of this your Majesteis kingdome hes verie havelie complenit to your Majesteis Counsell, that the form and patrone of the flaggis of schippis, sent doun heir and commandit to be ressavit [received] and used be the subjectis of boith kingdomes, is very prejudiciall to the fredome and dignitie of this Estate, and will gif occasioun of reprotche to this natioun quhairevir the said flage sal happin to be worne beyond sea, – becaus, as your Majestie may persave, the Scottis Croce, callit Sanctandrois Croce is twyse divydit, and the Inglishe Croce, callit Sanct George, haldin haill and drawne through the Scottis Croce, whiche is thairby obscurit, and no takin nor merk to be seene of the Scottis Armes. This will breid some heit and miscontentment betwixt your Majesteis subjectis; and it is to be feirit that some inconvenientis sall fall oute betuix thame, for oure seyfairing men cannot be induceit to ressave that flag as it is set doun. They haif drawne two new drauchtis and patronis as most indifferent [fair] for boith kingdomes, whiche thay presented to the Counsell and craved our approbatioun of the same; bot we haif reserved that to your Majesteis princelie determinatioun, – as moir particularlie the Erll of Mar, who wes present and hard thair complaynt, and to whome we haif remittit the discourse and delyverie of that mater, will inform your Majestie, and latt your Heynes see the errour of the first patrone and the indifferencie of the two new drauchtis.[25]

Although the new drafts mentioned here do not survive (they were probably consumed by the fire at Whitehall in 1618 that destroyed over a decade's worth of state papers, including the heralds' original design for the Union Jack), a compromise was reached that tended to undermine the whole principle of the union. Two designs became acceptable: an English version and a Scottish version, to be flown by the ships of each respective country. The Union Flag for England emblazoned the cross of St George over that of St Andrew, whereas the Union Flag for Scotland reversed the priority and imposed St Andrew over St George, 'the flagis of St Androw and St George interlaced'.[26] The Scottish version of the Union Flag survived up to the time of Queen Victoria, whose Scottish Great Seal carries the crosses in this way.[27]

This compromise was little better. Twelve months later, in response to Scottish ships which were flying this version of St Andrew imposed over St George, the Earl of Salisbury received a communication from the West Indies, complaining that

Besides the disorders amongst the younger and most ungoverned sort of merchants, here is many times disorders amongst the mariners and sea faring men, in such sort that great quarrels are many times likely to arise through their wilful follies; and principally betwixt the Scottish masters and the English touching the wearing of their flags, which now are made with both the red cross and St. Andrew's cross joined in one; and the Scot wears the English cross of St. George under the Scottish, which breeds many quarrels, and were very fit it were decreed which should be worn uppermost, for avoiding contention.[28]

Such flag-wrangling was indicative of the immediate problem facing the union: the two kingdoms could not be equal partners, and any attempts to impose unity and harmonization on the three nations of Great Britain were likely to be divisive and could even foment rebellion. As the Scots feared, the seat of power was in the south and James tacitly confirmed this by only returning to Scotland once in his life after he had been crowned in England. 'Scotland sank into the long sleep of union,' one commentator has dourly remarked, 'an ancient nation become little more than the province of a new empire.'[29]

As is clear from parliamentary objections to James's union, there was also a fear that English identity would be profoundly threatened by too close a relationship with the Scots. The old proverb 'When Hempe is spun / England's done' was interpreted as being prophetic for the fate of England following the Tudors. The first names of these kings and queens formed an acrostic: **H**enry, **E**dward, **M**ary and **P**hilip, and **E**lizabeth. England was indeed done on the death of Elizabeth as James VI of Scotland succeeded to the throne and formed Great Britain, announcing the new union with a flag made – appropriately enough – of spun hemp.[30]

It was the navy that took most interest in the new flags. By 17 April 1607, the Lords of the Admiralty had, however, begun to lobby against all British subjects flying the new Union Flag 'except it be when they are under his Majesty's pay, or employed in his Majesty's immediate service'.[31] They came up with their own designs, and by 1623 were using the rejected quartered design as a ship's jack. Serjeant Knight, the son of an arms painter who remembered this episode, recalled to Pepys that it was a 'cobled Banner'.[32] But by hoisting the Union Flag, merchantmen were posing as His Majesty's vessels and in doing so avoiding habour and piloting charges. Royal vessels felt that they required further protection. On 7 April 1634, Sir John Pennington, 'Admiral of the Narrow Seas', made a specific request for guidance with respect to ships' colours, and on 5 May, Charles I responded with a proclamation declaring that only the King's own ships could fly the Union Flag:[33]

A Proclamation appointing the Flags, as well for Our Navie Royall, as for the Ships of Our Subjects of South and North Britaine

WEE taking into Our Royall consideration that it is meete for the honour of Our owne Ships in Our Navie Royall, and of such other Ships as are, or shall be imployed in Our immediate Service, that the same bee by their Flags distinguished from the Ships of any other of Our Subjects, doe hereby straitly prohibite, and forbid that none of Our Subjects, of any of Our Nations and Kingdomes, shall from henceforth presume to carry the Union Flagge in the Maine toppe, or other part of any of their Ships (that is) S. Georges Crosse, and S. Andrewes Crosse joyned together, upon paine of Our high displeasure, but that the same Union Flagge bee still reserved as an Ornament proper for Our owne Ships, and Ships in Our immediate Service and Pay, and none other.

And likewise Our further Will and pleasure is, that all the other Ships of Our Subjects of England, or South Britaine bearing Flags, shall from henceefoorth carry the Red-Crosse, commonly called S. George his Crosse, as of olde time hath beene used; And also that all the other Ships of Our Subjects of Scotland, or North Britaine shall from henceefoorth carry the White Crosse, commonly called, S. Andrewes Crosse, whereby the severall Shipping may be distinguished, and We thereby the better discerne the number and goodnesse of the same; Wherefore Wee will and straitly command all Our Subjects foorthwith to be conformable and obedient to this Our Order, as they will answere the contrary at their perills.[34]

Other vessels were identified by their nationality, flying either the bloody cross or the silver saltire. This proclamation is the first recorded citation of the term 'Union Flag', although it was evidently in common naval usage by the time.[35]

The return to national flags came at a time of renewed antagonism between north Britain and south Britain. In the same year as the proclamation prohibiting the free use of the Union Flag, partisan broadsides were published, such as the pro-Scottish *A Comparison between St Andrew and St George* (1634). Another broadside, *The Thrissels Banner* (1640), depicted the cross of St Andrew over that of St George. The saltire has the acrostic:

WHEN ONLY THRISSELS KING OUR FAYTHFUL STEWARD BORN,

S. ANDREWS CROS ENJOY'D BY TRUETH'S PLANTATION.

The lines on the cross of St George read as follows:

BUT SINCE THE DOUBEL CROS OF BRITTANS CHIEF WAS WORN

WORLDINGS DID EVER CROSS OUR PEACE AND REFORMATION

St Andrew therefore remained strongly associated with Scotland, and, identified by his cross, he appeared on coins struck by the Stuarts, and later became the patron of the Order of the Thistle, established in 1687.* But St Andrew appears very little in art or literature, and never shared the popular appeal of St George or St Patrick. St Patrick's feast day (17 March) was in 1632 belatedly recognized by the Roman calendar, and in Limerick in 1642, St Patrick was re-enlisted as an anti-English prophet. Catholic rebels venerated the saint by recalling the promise he wrested from God during their forty-day struggle together on Croagh Patrick that the English would be ejected from Ireland.[36] Later, at the Siege of Duncannon Fort in 1645, the Irish Catholic force marched beneath the red saltire, further encouraging its identification with St Patrick.

But it was the renown of St George that rose most spectacularly during the period. King James had taken to the cult of St George with considerable gusto, creating more Garter and Bath knights in four months than Elizabeth had in forty-four years, and entertaining his knights at sumptuous feasts; his successor Charles I explicitly adopted the saint, although by this time the celebrations had become more

* The order lapsed in 1688, but was reinstated by Queen Anne in 1703.

measured affairs. Shakespeare, too, mentions the popular celebrations of 23 April (St George's Day) in *Henry VI (Part 1)*: 'Bonfires in France forthwith I am to make, / To keep our great Saint George's feast withal'.[37] But it was the runaway success of Richard Johnson's *Famous Historie of the Seaven Champions of Christendome* (1596–7) that really established the popular conception of St George and his exploits in the public imagination. The adventures of *The Seven Champions* in general, and of St George in particular, circulated as broadside ballads, chapbooks, and impromptu dramatizations, and they may have been another source for mummers' plays, which cannot reliably be dated back beyond the seventeenth century. An account of a play staged in Dublin in 1685 describes:

> the drollest piece of mummery I ever saw in or out of Ireland. There was St George and St Dennis and St Patrick in their buffe coats and the Turk likewise and Oliver Cromwell, and a Doctor and an old woman who made rare sport till Beelzebub came in with a frying pan upon his shoulder and a great flail in his hand.[38]

As the mention of Cromwell here suggests, such festivities were not so much nonsensical pantomimes as coded political allegories. At their core, they were oblique ways of presenting the tumultuous events of recent history. War had swept across the kingdoms, a republic was established, the king executed, and eventually a monarch was restored. These turbulent times reinvented national heroes and anti-heroes, from St George to Oliver Cromwell, and so too the signs with which they were identified. A profusion of flags and emblems attempted to describe variously the monarch, the union, the Commonwealth, and the different nations of Great Britain. There were redesigns, new designs, and reversions. It was as if the innovation of the first Union Flag had fired the symbolic imagination – as if here was a device that could express the complexities of national identity and political allegiance within the multiple kingdom.

The years of turmoil even began with a flag: the unfurling of King Charles I's royal standard at Nottingham Castle, on 25 August 1642: 'about six of the clock in the evening of a very stormy and tempestuous day'. The event was recorded by the king's friend Edward Hyde, later Earl of Clarendon:

> The king himself, with a small train, rode to the top of the castle-hill, Varney the knight-marshal, who was standard-bearer, carrying the standard, which was then erected in that place, with little other ceremony than the sound of drums and trumpets: melancholy men observed many ill presages about that time … The standard itself was blown down, the same night it had been set up, by a very strong and unruly wind, and could not be fixed again in a day or two, till the tempest was allayed. This was the melancholy state of the king's affairs, when the standard was set up.[39]

The hapless attempts to strike the royal standard at Nottingham were the symbolic start of what is erroneously described as the 'English Civil War'. Bearing in mind that the hostilities raged across the whole of Britain, this conflict is more properly called the *British* Civil War (if that is not a contradiction in terms) or, better still, the War of the Three Kingdoms, or even Four Nations. On the mainland, the wars lasted from 1642 to 1651; in Ireland, however, they had begun in 1641, with a Catholic rebellion against Protestant settlers from England and Scotland, and continued sporadically until 1653.

In the course of these conflicts, those loyal to the crown mustered to the royal banner and the standards of lords and noblemen, while those loyal to Parliament – at least initially – mustered to the overtly Christian devices of the crosses of Sts George and Andrew or ensigns of St George and St Andrew. In general, Parliamentarian 'Roundheads', the new English crusaders, rode to battle under the cross of St George.[40] The adoption of the bloody cross by the Parliamentarians was a significant replacement of royal with national insignia, of the personal with the communal, and so the cross became identified as the ensign for the entire Commonwealth.[41] Interestingly, as a depiction of crucifixion the emblem could be seen as breaking the second commandment – 'Thou shalt not make unto thee any graven image, or any likeness of any thing that is in heaven above, or that is in the earth beneath, or that is in the water under the earth' – but evidently this possibility did not concern contemporaries.[42] The 'idolatrous Cross' at Cheapside was, for instance, pulled down on 2 May 1643 by crowds happy to carry St George ensigns while they were about their business.[43] The bloody cross was the people's flag, not a symbol of impiety, popery, and tyranny.

Yet Parliamentarian interest in St George extended no further than appropriating his emblem. Popular enthusiasm for a papist saint – and one profoundly associated with the monarchy to boot – encouraged the Puritans to outlaw St George's feast day, and in 1645 the Directory for the Public Worship of God put paid to observing the event in any fashion. Henceforth, there could be no 'beating of drums or sounds of trumpets; no snap-dragon, or fellows dressed up in fools' coats and caps; *no standard with the George thereon*, nor hanging of tapestry cloth, nor pictures in any of the streets' (my emphasis).[44] And yet the flag survived: the idea was somehow to separate the saint from the red cross, and just four years later (on 23 February 1649) Parliament re-established the cross of St George as the national flag. The navy was ordered by the Council of State that 'Ships at Sea in service of the State shall onely beare the red Crosse in a white flag'.[45] This ambiguity, in which the standard remained but the hero was enticingly absent, allowed the Royalists to exploit the legends and iconography of St George and the dragon, using them as a metaphor for an exiled king battling against a monstrous Parliament.[46]

Parliamentarian adoption of the bloody cross was also determined by the relationship with the Scotland. In 1643, the English Parliament joined with the Scottish Parliament to form the Solemn League and Covenant, effectively a Protestant military treaty allied against King Charles. But by 1647 this had broken down and the Scots had switched their allegiance to Charles, sending an army to help reinstate him. This Scottish invasion was destroyed at Preston (17–19 August 1648) by the New Model Army, led for the first time by Oliver Cromwell. Charles I was executed less than six months later; Cromwell, a Member of Parliament and Lieutenant-General (second-in-command) of the parliamentary army, was the third man to sign the death warrant. Meanwhile, Charles's son, Charles II, was crowned at Scone, the last king to be so, on 1 January 1651.

The Scots being in rebellion and hence outside the Commonwealth, the cross of St Andrew was now outlawed and prohibited from all Parliamentarian ensigns. Shortly after the beheading of the king on 30 January 1649, Parliament decreed on 23 February that henceforth all British ships should fly the cross of St George:

> Council of State to the Navy Commissioners. Sir Hen. Mildmay reports your desire to be informed what is to be borne in the flags of ships in service of the State, and what upon the stern, in lieu of the arms formerly there engraven. The Council resolve that they shall bear the red cross only in a white flag, quite through the flag; and upon the stern, the red cross in one escutcheon, and the harp in another, being the arms of England and Ireland; both escutcheons joined according to the pattern sent herewith. Flags are to be provided with expedition for the ships for the summer guard, and their engravings altered.[47]

The royal arms displayed at a ship's stern were replaced by a pair of shields, one bearing the bloody cross, the other the harp of Ireland. The paired shields were described as 'the Armes of England' on 5 March and formed the basis of the flags of seniority flown by admirals: these bore the two shields, encircled, in the case of a full admiral, by a laurel wreath.[48] In contrast, Royalist ships flew the impaled version of St George and St Andrew as a jack.

Ireland, too, was in rebellion. Cromwell was now made Lord Lieutenant of Ireland and sent there in August, where he fought a suc-cessful if bloody campaign for ten months and effectively placed the country under martial law, before he was recalled and sent back to Scotland, leading the New Model Army. He invaded on 3 September 1650, and defeated Charles II's Scottish army, which had advanced south to Worcester, a year later to the day. Commonwealth union was therefore imposed on Scotland forcibly, although the English 'Rump' Parliament did seek Scottish representation; indeed, the new Parliament was to represent the entire Commonwealth – England, Scotland, Ireland, and Wales, as well as 'the Isles of Jersey, Guernsey, and the town of Berwick-upon-Tweed'.[49] In contrast, the Irish settlement of 1652 was criminal. One hundred thousand Irish Catholics were condemned to death, many had their land confiscated, and they were forbidden from living in counties such as Ulster; moreover, any Catholic found within a mile of the coast or of the River Shannon would face the death penalty. This policy has been attributed to Cromwell, who became Lord Protector (head of the Commonwealth) in December 1653, though there is little evidence that he was directly responsible.

With the installation of Cromwell came a new parliamentary constitution, and a new flag. Scotland was formally reunited with England by the Commonwealth Parliament on 12 April 1654. During his Scottish campaign, Cromwell had a registry made of some 223 Scottish flags he encountered. This indicates the overwhelming prevalence of the saltire in the country – at least 150 of the standards featured saltires, often in the canton – and so the device was retained.[50] The new flag of the Commonwealth was in fact based on one of the designs originally suggested in 1606: the cross of St George quartered with that of St Andrew. To this was added the harp of Ireland in the third quadrant, with

Cromwell's white lion on a black shield imposed in the centre.*

Commonwealth ensigns had already been designed for the navy, and they have become the ensigns that survive to this day. Ensigns were originally signals flown to enable ships to group rapidly into squadrons. They had been introduced in 1574 as striped flags with the crosses of St George or St Andrew either in the canton or superimposed; the stripes were sometimes red and white, sometimes green and white, matching the Tudor livery colours. These designs began to be superseded from 1621 onwards, and in 1633 the first Red Ensign was flown. Its popularity rapidly increased in 1634, when Charles I designated the Union Flag solely for royal use. The striped red and white design was subsequently taken up by the East India Company in the second half of the century.

The Commonwealth ensigns were introduced in January 1653 by Generals-at-Sea Robert Blake, Richard Deane, and George Monck. Each ensign consisted of a solid field of colour in red, white, or blue, with the cross of St George in the canton, and the Irish harp in the fly; some also had a shield bearing St Andrew's cross added to the middle of the flag, and could be superimposed by Cromwell's white lion. The White Ensign was redesigned, possibly for reasons of clarity, as a cross of St George with the Union Flag added in the upper canton (the old White Ensign nevertheless survived into the middle of the eighteenth century). The order of precedence of squadrons was fixed as being, in the order red, white, and blue: the Red Ensign, later known as the

* The new Great Seal quartered the St George cross with St Andrew's cross and the Irish harp, whereas admirals' flags had original superimposed flags with the harp added at the centre.

'Ensign of England' (red being the national colour of England) identified 'Admirals of the Red', the highest-ranking vessels, the 'White
Squadron' indicated the second rank, and 'Admirals of the Blue', the
third. But because of the difficulty in recognizing at sea the patchwork
quartered design of the Commonwealth Union Flag, a revised version
of the Union Flag of James was introduced in May 1658: 'Jack flags for
the flag officers of the fleet and for the General ships of war of His
Highness [Cromwell] be the Arms of England and Scotland united,
according to the ancient form, with the addition of the Harp'.[51]

The complexity of these negotiations is an indication of the extreme
importance attached to expressing the Commonwealth and its dominions in appropriate vexillological terms, and contemporaries were
acutely aware of the nuances. On 15 August 1660, a British ship flying
the old Union Jack arrived in Jamaica. For Colonel William Beeston,
this was the first intimation that the Commonwealth had fallen: 'His
Majesty's ship...arrived from England, with the union jack flying,
which gave all people great hopes his majesty was restored to his throne,
and was confirmed when the ship came into the harbour'.[52]

The house of Stuart had indeed been restored some weeks earlier
when, on 29 May, the exiled Charles II had arrived back in London.
One way in which the new king could quickly establish his rule was by
effacing the symbols of Parliamentarian power. At Cromwell's funeral,
the shield of St George and the harp had been used as the national
colours (interestingly, St Patrick's cross had also been used to represent
Ireland).[53] This design had been formally reintroduced by Parliament.
But with the Restoration, Ireland now reverted to being a kingdom,
meaning that the harp could appear on the royal coat of arms (Charles

was King of England, Scotland, and Ireland), but union with Ireland had not been proposed in the same way as it had been with Great Britain, and representation was not acceptable on the national flag.

In March 1660, new flags were ordered from the Navy Commissioners – the new flag being the old Flag of Great Union. On 1 May, the Restoration vote was passed and there was a frenzy of flag-making to provide ensigns, jacks, and royal standards. Samuel Pepys noted in his diary (13 May 1660), that

> the taylors and painters were at work cutting of some pieces of yellow cloth into the fashion of a crown and C.R. and put it upon a fine sheet, and that into the flag instead of the State's arms; which, after dinner, was finished and set up – after it had been shown to my Lord ... In the afternoon a council of war, only to acquaint them that the Harp must be taken out of all their flags, it being very offensive to the King.[54]

Charles II therefore reverted to the first Union Flag with St George predominating; he also, incidentally, remodelled the Irish harp as it appeared on currency so that it bore a topless female torso.*

Charles's brother, the Duke of York (later James VII and II), was made Lord High Admiral and was responsible for flags at sea, proclaiming on 19 November 1660 that flying the Union Flag was to be confined to His Majesty's ships.[55] Ships in the Royal Navy were to fly the restored Union Flag, and merchant ships the Red Ensign, with St

---

* Variations of the harp have been dictated by which design fits best on to either a shield or a standard.

George in the canton (and without the Irish harp). James's subsequent proclamations on the conduct of the navy included raising the Union Flag from the main topmast to identify the Commander of the Fleet and to indicate when ambassadors or foreign dignitaries were on board (1668–9).[56] Charles reiterated this limitation to the St George Red Ensign in *A Proclamation for Regulating the Colours Worn on Merchant Ships* (18 September 1674). The proclamation prohibits merchantmen from hoisting

> any Jacks made in imitation of his Majesties; or any other Flags,
> Jacks, or Ensigns whatsoever then those usually heretofore worn on
> Merchants Ships, *viz.* The Flag and Jack, white with a Red Cross,
> (commonly called, *Saint George's Cross*) passing quite through the
> same; And the Ensign Red, with the like Cross in a Canton White,
> at the upper Corner thereof next to the Staff.

Charles laid particular emphasis, however, on a particular flag, insisting that 'from henceforth they [merchant ships] do not presume to wear his Majesties Jack, (commonly called, *The Union Jack*) in any of their Ships or Vessels'; the emphasis is Charles's own.[57]

So by 1674, the flag was already commonly called the 'Union Jack' in official documents, and was also known as 'his Majesty's Jack'.[58] There are various theories as to why it is called a 'Union *Jack*'. It may be in reference to King James VI and I, who was known as Jacques or Jacobus (hence Jacobean), but the most persuasive theory is that the design is named after 'jacks' or '*jacques*': padded leather or armoured jerkins emblazoned with livery colours or the emblems of patron saints, such as the 'George *jacque*' or the 'Andrew *jacque*' – the modern 'jacket' is derived from 'jacque'. Ironically, of course, these surcoats had had their heyday in the Anglo-Scottish wars. But whatever its origin, the name quickly caught on. By 1627, small Union Flags were being flown at sea from a mast on the bowsprit and these were referred to as 'the Jack', 'Jack flag', or 'the King's Jack'. In the eighteenth century a special upright spar on a ship's bows was designated the 'jackstaff' from which to fly the Union Jack, and in the Royal Navy, the Union Flag is today simply referred to as the 'Jack'.

The Restoration could, of course, have been an opportunity to revoke this flag and propose a new national imagery, but as with his other policies dealing with the Interregnum (the period between the kings), Charles wisely chose to let sleeping dogs lie and was not tempted to make radical political statements. Changing such recognizable colours could be catastrophic in an era of teetering national stability, and in any case, the Scots had no desire to lose their distinctive silver cross again: it had been confirmed by Act of Parliament and recorded in the Lyon Register.

St George had remained a Royalist emblem, but here the associations were more tangled. The return of the Stuarts witnessed a restoration of Georgist symbolism – both Charles and his brother James II were crowned on St George's Day, and Thomas Lowick's verse, *The History of the Life & Martyrdom of St. George, the Titular Patron of England* (1664), was dedicated to Charles II:

> For in my judgement never *English* King
> Had greater cause than You, to honour Him:
> Heroic force and Martial form withal,
> Twixt King and Patron were collateral,

And that bright Orb where *Mars* is stellifi'd

Did equal influence 'twixt you both divide ...[59]

But in the popular imagination, the cross of St George remained firmly associated with Republican Puritanism. Years after the Restoration, the frontispiece to Edward Pettit's *Visions of the Reformation* (1683) showed a presbyter painting over the royal Stuart arms with the bloody cross. Pettit feared that, by undermining royal authority, Dissenters were effectively supporting Catholic aspirations to the throne, and the identification of the cross of St George with the Commonwealth was made explicit in the accompanying explanatory verse:

The Royall Armes doth Presbyter deface:

To Paint the Common Wealth's upon the place

Thus to Reform from Popery, he draw's

A Cross; the Common Seal to th['] good Old Cause;

Thus when the Kingdom turns a Common wealth

The Imperiall Crown will be the Popes by Stealth.

Such a strong identification of this cross with Parliamentarian politics may be one of the reasons for the profound submersion of eighteenth- and nineteenth-century English identity into the idea of Britain and the British Empire, and into the composite Union Jack flag. For decades after the Commonwealth, the cross of St George was a stark reminder of civil war and republicanism, whereas the first Union Flag had no such associations. In other words, by reinventing itself as British under the Union Jack, England was able to distance itself from the bloodshed of the immediate past without cutting itself from its long and illustrious history.

This may also help to explain the decline of Georgery. While the cross of St George remained on the Union Jack, the old remnants of medieval pageantry were considered to be too anachronistic in the modern commercial and civic society of the eighteenth century, and they gradually fell away. Ironically, it was finally in the eighteenth century that Pope Benedict XIV officially declared St George to be the patron saint of England. By this time there was a George on the throne (George III), being satirically – if fondly – caricatured as 'Farmer' George, as well as appearing incongruously portrayed as the national saint.[60] Likewise, King Arthur became an even more nugatory and risible figure, a cuckold shadow of his former mighty self, considered to be entirely irrelevant to the rhetoric of union. But one national figure of union did, however, re-emerge: Britannia.

Britannia has been recognized as a national symbol since the first century AD, when the figure was used by the Romans as a personification of Britain – a spirit of the place – and to identify the united Celtic tribes. She was initially represented in sculpture as an Amazon being cast to the ground by the Emperor Claudius (AD 41–54), who named the British territory 'Britannia', a name that, as we have seen, obviously owes something to the ancient British word '*Priteni*'. But Britannia also perhaps evolved from the Celtic goddess Brigantia: an ancient deity later associated with St Bride; a goddess of healing, fertility, and the forge; and the patron of the extensive tribal federation that occupied the north of England when the Romans invaded. Britannia is also identified with the Roman Minerva and the Greek Pallas Athena: goddesses of sovereignty and protectors on the battlefield – indeed, Britannia is often depicted with Athena's characteristic armour, and is similarly associated with the sea and with maritime power.[61] By the second century, Britannia was appearing on coins – something that continues to this day – and was very much characterized as a Briton: in tunic and breeches, brandishing a spear and shield, and sitting among rocks, alert. Later – and particularly in the eighteenth century – images of Boudicca were modelled on Britannia, further conflating the historical and mythological figures of ancient Britain.[62]

After the decline and fall of the Roman Empire, the figure of Britannia slipped into obscurity until the sixteenth century. Elizabeth became identified with her and another Roman goddess, Astraea, who was associated with justice and fertility,[63] and the resurrection of these female divinities may have been in compensation for the collapse of worship of the Virgin Mary following the Reformation. John Dee included Britannia on the frontispiece of *General and Rare Memorials portraying the Perfect Art of Navigation* (1577), imploring the Virgin Queen not to neglect her navy, and William Camden revived not only the name but the whole concept of 'Britannia' in his capacious tome of cultural and historical unification, *Britannia or, A Chorographicall Description of the Most Flourishing Kingdomes of England, Scotland, and Ireland, and the Ilands Adioyning, out of the Depth of Antiquitie* (first published in 1586).[64]

Camden's *Britannia* is a crucial text in the formation of modern British identity. Written, significantly, when the Society of Antiquaries was founded, it embodied a more archival and archaeological attitude towards the past than had hitherto been the case with accounts of indigenous cultural and geographical history. *Britannia* was a sort of illustrated national epic: describing regional topography and the folk customs of local communities, meshing myth with place to explain, for instance, the significance of Glastonbury as an actual site within the legendary Arthurian cycle. This proved to be a pioneering way of reimagining the British landscape, saturated as it was with centuries of enigmatic ruins and remains, and it marked a major shift in the nation's attitudes towards its past. Camden's treatment of the nation's legendary heroes was antiquarian rather than prophetic, communal rather than heroic; indeed, Camden stressed the importance of the society and the unity of the country even in ancient times, among the barbarian peoples:

> So far am I from working any discredit unto them, that I have rather
> respectively loved them alwaies, as of the same bloud and stoke, yes,
> and honoured them too, even when the kingdomes were divided:
> but now much more, since it hath pleased our almightie, and most
> mercifull God, that wee growe united in one Bodie, under one most
> Sacred head of the Empire, to the joy, happinesse, welfare, and
> safetie, of both Nations.[65]

Moreover, in 1610, Philemon Holland translated the text of *Britannia* from Latin into English, thereby turning it into an important declaration of independence from the world of classical learning, and the very next year the King James 'Authorized Version' of the Bible was published, also in English – another instance of linguistic autonomy.

By the time Michael Drayton's mystical and topographical verse epic *Poly-Olbion* appeared in 1612, Britannia was represented as a deity of the landscape, swathed in a map of – significantly – England and

Wales, although here she is called Albion. Britannia is, in other words, yet another example of the irksome and perennial English confusion of England with Britain; in later allegories, for example, Britannia was sometimes shown with the maidens Scotia and Hibernia (as well as America), as if she represented only England.[66]

Britannia first took up a trident, as opposed to a spear, in the seventeenth century: commemorative naval medals depict her as a guardian of the seas and possibly allude to a classical myth that Neptune had granted her dominion over the oceans. Britannia has sometimes been represented borne through the surf in a chariot of shells, and by 1682 the Royal Navy had named a man-of-war after her. Charles II introduced Britannia onto coins in 1665, and in 1672 commissioned John Roettier to redesign her figure, allegedly having her modelled on one of his royal mistresses.* In 1694, Britannia was adopted by the Bank of England for its seal, and since then she has appeared on various sterling notes and other coins of the realm.[67] The trident permanently replaced her spear in 1797, in celebration of naval victories, and she donned a helmet in 1825. As a personification of the territory of Great Britain, imperial seapower, and the economy, Britannia was to become a key image of Britishness in the following century, and she fittingly bore the Union Flag on her shield. Britannia and the Union Jack was a marriage of two highly potent symbols, and by the end of the seventeenth century they had become internationally recognized emblems, respected and feared in equal measure, in war and trade alike. They would be fitting symbols for the next century.

---

* Charles also issued Irish coins minted with harps and Scottish coins with thistles.

The next century would be more than a new century; it would also be a new epoch. It was a Stuart who had joined the crowns of England and Scotland and first created the Flag of the Great Union and Stuarts who ruled as the figure of Britannia arose as a new symbol of unity, yet the return of the Stuarts did little that was practical for the union of Great Britain. In fact, the union was in danger of becoming a royalist anachronism. If Britain's international trade was to flourish and its national security be maintained in the next century, the country needed to be modernized. A marriage of crowns was not enough: the unity of the nation needed a constitutional basis agreed by Parliament. A new Great Britain was about to be created.

V SEE ALBION'S BANNERS JOIN...

The British *Navy thro' the Ocean vast*
Shall wave her double Cross, t' extreamest Climes
Terrific, and return with odorous Spoils
Of Araby *well fraught, or* Indus' *Wealth,*
Pearl, and Barbaric gold...

John Philips, *Cyder* (1708), II, 653–7

THE HISTORY OF the flag in the eighteenth century goes hand-in-hand with an emerging sense of Britishness. The concept of 'Great Britain' was reiterated in the 1707 Act of Union and the identity of 'Britons' re-established. The Union Flag was also redesigned. But, at least initially, there was little appetite for this new British identity.

Parliamentary union was required because of fundamental changes in the nature of government during the previous hundred years. In the seventeenth century, Parliament's comprehensive refusal to accept an absolute monarchy had resulted in the king being beheaded and the establishment of a Republican Commonwealth. Although this Commonwealth lasted little over a decade, it nevertheless presented the opportunity for a classic English compromise between king and Parliament. The royal Stuart dynasty was restored and Charles II crowned, but his powers were greatly curtailed. The Stuarts might have adapted had Charles had a legitimate male heir, but his sons were a muddle of bastards, and so on Charles's death in 1685, his brother took the throne as James VII and II. This succession precipitated crisis after crisis: James was by this time a firm Catholic and seemed to have hoped to revive Roman Catholicism as the state religion, attempting to return the monarchy to the old, pre-Commonwealth days of divine absolutism, and to closer ties with Papist countries such as France – all of which was most alarming to the Protestant majority in Britain. The last straw was the purported birth of a legitimate male heir, James Francis Edward, in 1688. James's two surviving daughters by his first wife had both married Protestant princes, but since converting he had in 1673 married the Catholic Mary of Modena. To the old king, the birth of a son was nothing less than divine providence, miraculously promising the continuation of the Stuart line; to others, it was a sham. Sceptics argued that, following several miscarriages in the first years of her marriage, the queen was past child-bearing and that a convenient baby boy had simply been smuggled into her bed to pose as James's heir (the infant had allegedly been conveyed there concealed in a warming pan). The threat was that the child would be raised and crowned a Catholic, creating the possibility of a shift in the power relations of northern Europe and the likelihood of a new Anglo-French Catholic power bloc. This prompted the Dutch Protestant, Prince William of Orange, to invade England in 1688. This 'invasion', however, met with virtually no resistance. Instead, James VII and II was 'bloodlessly' deposed. William was invited into London, fêted, and assumed the throne.

Parliament allowed William to become king on a number of conditions. So as to reduce the impression that the crown had been seized by an invader backed by a 21,000-strong army, William was to rule together with his wife, Mary. Mary was James's eldest daughter and had been heir to the throne before the appearance of the 'warming-pan baby'. The joint monarchy of William and Mary would ensure that there was no suggestion of dynastic change, and extended to making Mary's sister, Anne, next in line to the throne, ahead of William and Mary's own children – although William too had Stuart blood, being a grandson of Charles I through his mother (in other words, William and Mary were cousins). William had to accept that, despite being king, he had no legal right to rule, and that oaths of allegiance to him would reflect this. Parliament also made a Declaration of Rights, which supposedly limited his powers – although it was painfully apparent that if William returned to the Netherlands, the country would descend into chaos.

So successful was this constitutional strategy to accommodate King William that his invasion is seldom considered to be an invasion at all; rather it is a described as a rebellion, a revolution against Papist tyranny by the will of the people: the 'Glorious Revolution', or 'Bloodless Revolution'. In fact, the Glorious Revolution was not at all bloodless outside England and Wales. To avoid creating another Stuart martyr like his father, James was allowed to escape to France, where Louis XIV promptly armed the exiled king and sent him over to Ireland in order to reclaim his crown. James succeeded in gaining the support of the Dublin Parliament, as well as enlisting many Catholic Irishmen, but his French and Irish troops met defeat at the hands of William's English, Dutch, and Danish army just outside the city on 1 July 1690 at the River Boyne. Yet although the Battle of the Boyne lives on in the memory of Northern Ireland – it is the source of Protestant folklore and traditions such as Orangemen parades – it was not, as some claim, a decisive victory, and Irish resistance to William continued for the next two years; even the French remained in Ireland until 1691, fighting for King James.

In Scotland, too, pockets of support remained for the old Stuart monarchy – particularly in the Highlands. Many clans were bound by oaths supporting James, and although William instructed the clans to pledge their allegiance to him, the chiefs could only do so once James had released them from their former obligations. This James left perilously late, despite William threatening the severest penalties against those who had not sworn their allegiance by 1 January 1692. The MacDonalds, by the treachery of the Campbells, found that they missed the deadline. Shortly afterwards they were massacred at Glencoe.

Resistance in Ireland and Scotland left a bloody and troublesome legacy throughout the 1690s, and it was by means of an Act of Union that William sought to pacify the mainland. The 1689 Declaration of Rights had allowed William's accession as William III and II, but in the very act of accepting the crown, William had effectively confirmed the ultimate sovereignty of Parliament. With regard to the union, this left the monarch in a peculiar position. The 'united kingdom' was precisely that: the kingdoms of England and Scotland were united under one crown, but their parliaments were not united, and it was parliaments that now held the power over monarchs. Throughout the 1690s, then, William was increasingly keen to formalize – or rather modernize –

British unification. Scotland had enjoyed free trade for fifty-six years before restrictions were introduced with the Restoration in 1660. By 1670, however, a new Anglo-Scottish trade treaty had been agreed, and this economic arrangement led in turn to proposals for parliamentary union. This was rejected at the time because it appeared that England was seeking an incorporation rather than a conjunction of parliaments, but William 'was often heard to say, That this Island could never be Easie without a Union'.[1] What the union required was a written treaty between two governments; it could no longer rely on accidents of birth.

Furthermore, the union as it stood could also be seen as an anachronistic legacy of the Stuarts, keeping sympathy for the old king smouldering away. The exiled King James – who had done nothing about uniting the countries – was by no means a spent force after his defeat in Ireland. He was holding court 'over the water' at St Germain in France and raising his son, whom Protestants still disparagingly referred to as the 'warming-pan baby'. On the death of his father in 1701, this lad was recognized by Louis XIV as James VIII and III, the rightful King of England, Scotland, and Ireland, and plans were laid for his restoration. James's supporters called themselves Jacobites after Jacobus, the Latin form of his name, and he was also known variously as the 'Chevalier de St George', 'Jamie the Rover', and, most commonly, the 'Old Pretender'.[2]

Jacobitism was a very real threat. There were Jacobite risings in 1708, 1715, and, most famously, in 1745, and invasion plots in 1720–21 and 1743, and as late as 1750 and 1759. James's dashing son and heir, Charles Edward – the 'Young Pretender' or 'Bonnie Prince Charlie' – proved to be a charismatic figurehead and continued to rally support throughout the century. Indeed, when his father, the Old Pretender, died in 1766, there were still Jacobites supporting the Young Pretender's claim to the throne as Charles III.

The principal Jacobite aim was to restore the male Stuart line and thereby re-establish a Catholic dynasty. This could only be achieved with foreign support, and realistically this was only going to come from one place: from England's traditional European enemy, France, against whom William was waging a ceaseless campaign. But Jacobitism was not just a threat to Protestantism and parliamentary government, it could also undo the integrity of Great Britain. Jacobites tended to be separatists, seeking independence from the union by asserting Scotland's 'ancient rights' – in spite of the fact that it was a Stuart king, James VI and I, who had first united the crowns. Such a separation of Scotland from England would throw the bruised English succession into yet another crisis.

In the early years of the eighteenth century, British parliamentary union was therefore presented as a compromise that could defuse the potentially catastrophic intervention of France in restoring the house of Stuart for a second time. In the meantime, the English Parliament endeavoured to prevent any possibility of a future Catholic monarchy with the 1701 Act of Settlement. This barred Roman Catholics from the succession and declared Sophia, the Electress of Hanover, the royal heir. Sophia, a granddaughter of James VI and I, was fifty-eighth in line to the throne; the previous fifty-seven claimants were all Catholics.

In addition to the Jacobite challenge, there were also major economic reasons for securing a union. Despite settling Nova Scotia in 1621, the Scots had more recently looked to Central America to launch a

Caledonian empire.* The Company of Scotland had been formed in 1695 to enable Scottish merchants to trade in Africa and India, and sent two expeditions to settle the Darien isthmus in Panama – the land joining Central to South America – which was a crucial trading route. The colonists founded a town, New Edinburgh, and erected the Fort St Andrews defences, but fever, inadequate supplies, and an attack by the Spanish finished the project.

English and Dutch speculators had originally been involved in the Darien venture, and Scottish investment was vast, but William could not condone the enterprise. He was obsessed with his wars with Louis XIV, and in the course of these he was cultivating good relations with Spain – on whose territories New Caledonia was to be established. In any case, William had no desire for a colonial scramble with his British neighbours, and English merchants objected to what they perceived as unfair competition from Scotland. William consequently declared the Darien venture illegal, English and Dutch investors withdrew, and no English support was offered to the unfortunate settlers; they were forced to abandon New Caledonia and make the hazardous journey back across the Atlantic.

The Scottish economy was crippled by the failure of the scheme, and anti-English sentiments led to brutal some retaliations in the immediate aftermath of the affair. Captain Thomas Green, for example, was an English naval officer returning from the East Indies, who docked his ship, the *Worcester*, in Scotland. He was seized by the local populace in a

* The arms of the Nova Scotia colony were based on the St Andrew saltire reversed.

reprisal against the East Indian Company taking a Darien Company ship, and summarily executed.[3] But in the longer term, the Darien venture propelled Scotland into a far closer relationship with England and Wales. With a broken economy and thwarted colonial ambitions, Scotland was a lame-duck at the beginning of the eighteenth century. The English empire had been gradually expanding since the sixteenth century, and parliamentary union with England enabled the Scots to piggyback this huge colonial undertaking. They did so with remarkable application. In mid-eighteenth century, about 10 per cent of the British population lived in Scotland, but the composition of the East India Company was at least half Scottish, and almost half the officers in the Bengal army in 1782 were Scots. In 1787, the Scottish Solicitor-General, Henry Dundas, observed of the startling imperial success of the Scots that 'all India will soon be in [our] hands', and by the middle of the nine-teenth century, Sir Charles Dilke remarked, 'In British settlements from Canada to Ceylon, from Dunedin to Bombay, for every Englishman that you meet who has worked himself up to wealth from small beginnings without external aid, you find ten Scotchmen. It is strange indeed that Scotland has not become the popular name for the United Kingdom.'[4] Nevertheless, such a forecast could never have been made in 1700, and although William lived to see the Bill of Union eventually approved by the House of Lords, it was subsequently rejected by the Commons.

By 1702, King William was dead. Tradition has it that he was killed when his horse threw him after tripping on a molehill – hence the Jacobite toast to 'the little gentleman in the black velvet waistcoat' – although he actually died from pulmonary fever a fortnight after the fall. In line with the Declaration of Rights, William was succeeded by

Mary's sister, Anne – another Protestant daughter of Charles I, and another enthusiast for parliamentary union.

With the ever-growing threat of Jacobitism, an Act of Union – William's deathbed wish – was a politically expedient tactic. There proved to be a significant amount of political horse-trading before and during the passing of the act, resulting in what the political polemicist Tom Nairn considers a 'folk-tale of conspiracy and sell-out', in which the Scottish parliaments of 1703 and 1707 proved themselves to be archetypes of 'sleaze and cronyism'.[5] The Scots transparently attempted to wring the most advantageous economic benefits they could from constitutional union with England, both for their country and for themselves, by tactics such as threatening to disinherit Sophia and the Hanoverians from the Scottish crown in the event of Queen Anne's death. For a while, at least, this worked. Anne appointed a commission to investigate the implications of an Act of Union, and Westminster agreed to compensate Scotland 'the Equivalent' for loss of internal customs and excise duties; this sum amounted to £398,085 10s – equivalent to almost the entire capital available in the Scottish economy, and to what had been lost in the Darien venture.

The appeasement of 'the Equivalent' made the policy even more unpopular in England than it already was – it also looked to both sides like a bribe.[6] During the final debates in the House of Lords on 15 February 1706, Lord Haversham, who fully supported a federal union, doubted whether 'Two Natians [*sic*], independent in their Sovereignties, that have their distinct Laws and Interests, and, what I cannot forget, their *different Forms of Worship, Church-Government, and Order*' could be united in one kingdom. He complained that 'so many mismatched Pieces, of such *jarring* and *incongruous Ingredients*' would risk 'breaking in Pieces every Moment', and he particularly lamented the disappearance of '*the good old* English *Constitution*, justly allowed to be the most equal and best poiz'd Government in the world'.[7] Neither was there much popular support outside the two parliaments. Daniel Defoe was a more committed unionist, but noted in his *History of the Union of Great Britain* (1709) that

> The people cryed out they were *Scots* Men, and they would be *Scots* Men still; They contemn'd the name of *Britains*, fit for the *Welsh* Men, who were made the Scoff of the English after they had reduc'd them. – Scotland had always had a Name and a Fame in Forreign Courts.[8]

Rioting in Scotland preceded the act, necessitating the dispatch of an English militia to Berwick: 'the common People … would go about the Street, crying No Union'.[9]

The Scottish Parliament finally voted on 15 January 1707, carrying the Act of Union by 109 votes to 69; the Second Reading followed on 16 January and saw the decisive vote – in the words of the Jacobite George Lockhart of Carnwath, a Member of the Scottish Parliament, it was 'the last day Scotland was Scotland'; in the words of Defoe, 'Happy Day!': 'This is the Famous Day to *Scotland*, in which She set Her Signal to the Union of *Great Britain*.'[10] Full political union became a reality on 1 May 1707, Article 1 of the Act uniting Scotland with England and Wales into 'one kingdom by the name of Great Britain'. The Scottish Parliament was abolished and their MPs and Lords sat in Westminster. The settlement was generous to the Scots, giving them forty-five seats in the Commons and sixteen peers in the Lords, despite, for instance, their land tax providing a little over 2 per cent of what England contributed to the country's coffers – a disparity that continues.[11] There was free trade between north Britain (Scotland) and south Britain (England), and the English colonies were made available to Scottish merchants, traders, and settlers. Scotland retained its independence in religion, education, local government, and legal institutions, although the House of Lords was nominated its highest court of appeal. King James had envisaged one sovereign, one Parliament, one set of laws, but the 1707 Act of Union was the greatest extent to which that vision would be fulfilled. Yet the Protestant succession – the legitimacy of Queen Anne and the ensuing establishment of the Hanoverian dynasty and hence stability – seemed to have been secured.

The First Article of the 1707 Act read,

THAT the Two Kingdoms of *England* and *Scotland* [this order was reversed in the Scottish Act] shall, upon the First Day of *May* next ensuing the Date hereof, and for ever after, be United into One Kingdom by the name of GREAT BRITAIN; and that the Ensigns Armorial of the said United Kingdom be such as Her Majesty shall appoint, and the Crosses of St. *George* and St *Andrew* [reversed in the Scottish Act] be conjoin'd in such a manner as Her Majesty shall think fit, and used in all Flags, Banners, Standards, and Ensigns, both at Sea and Land.[12]

The Lords Commissioners for Scotland had proposed officially conjoining the flags, to which the English Commissioners had agreed, provided that the manner of conjoining be left to the queen.[13] On 17 March, the College of Heralds was ordered to reconsider the flag, and a committee of the Privy Council and Heralds decided by an Order in Council on 17 April 'That the Union Flag continue as at present', which was proclaimed on 28 July.[14] In practice, however, the fimbriation – the white border or edging around the cross of St George – was changed. Previously this had been very narrow, but it was increased to improve visibility at sea and to avoid confusion with the Dutch Jack, a red cross on a diagonal blue and white background.

An important change was made to ensigns. With the English and Scottish navies now united, the Union Flag replaced the cross of St George in the canton. In 1688, merchant vessels had again been required to fly the Red Ensign with either St George or St Andrew in the canton, and this use was confirmed by William and Mary on 12 July 1694 in a proclamation that repeated the prohibition of the use of the Union Flag on ensigns or elsewhere at sea, except for royal vessels, as originally stipulated by Charles I in 1634.* These laws had been repeatedly flouted, and have continued to be flouted ever since, necessitating a succession of royal proclamations and merchant shipping acts. Flying the flag fraudulently was illegal, and pirates were known to sail under counterfeit colours: in 1681, a maritime law was passed forbidding 'privateers to wear our Union flagg and jack', and Samuel Butler used the image of a naval ensign in *Hudibras* ('An Heroical Epistle of Hudibras to his Lady', 1680):

---

* Despite their prevalence, ensign flags are difficult to compose, as the rectangular shape elongates the Union Flag in the canton.

As *Pyrats* all false Colours wear,

T'intrap th'unwary Mariner:

So Women, to surprise us, spread

The *borrow'd Flags of White and Red*.

Display 'em thicker on their Cheeks,

Then their old Grand-mothers, the *Picts*:

And raise more Devils *with their Looks*,

Than *Conjurers less subtil Books*.

(III, 177–84)[15]

The act was also the first to consider the use of the flag on land, although some English regiments continued to use the cross of St George – a privilege not extended to Scottish regiments for the cross of St Andrew – as did the Royal Navy on the White Ensign. It has been pointed out that such use of Georgist insignia is not only unconstitutional but in direct violation of the First Article of the Treaty of Union, and although persistent practice over the past three hundred years would make it difficult to outlaw today, the objection is technically correct.[16] On the other hand, the Scottish Union Flag (with St Andrew predominating) continued to be recognized, and indeed survived up until the twentieth century in specialist ensigns such as the standard of the Commissioners of Northern Lights (lighthouses).[17]

The memory of 1707 has not died. The event is discussed, for instance, in Walter Scott's 1817 novel *Rob Roy*. Mr Jarvie is in favour of the act, citing the economic and imperial case for union: 'Now, since St. Mungo catched herrings in the Clyde, what was ever like to gar us flourish like the sugar and tobacco trade? Will onybody tell me that, and grumble at the treaty that opened us a road west-awa' yonder?' His companion, however, disagrees.

> Andrew Fairservice was far from acquiescing in these arguments of
> expedience, and even ventured to enter a grumbling protest, 'That it
> was an unco change to hae Scotland's laws made in England; and
> that, for his share, he wadna for a' the herring-barrels in Glasgow,
> and a' the tobacco-casks to boot, hae gien up the riding o' the Scots
> Parliament, or sent awa' our crown, and our sword, and our sceptre,
> and Mons Meg, to be keepit by thae English pock-puddings in the
> Tower o' Lunnon. What would Sir William Wallace, or auld Davie
> Lindsay, hae said to the Union, or them that made it?'[18]

More recently, Tom Nairn continues to attack the Act of Union, arguing that its main aim was to remove the threat of any future Franco-Scottish alliance and to allow England to continue its ancient feud with France. Nairn calls it 'a treaty between states, and not an act of conquest, subjugation, or colonization. Its purpose was subordination, not elimination' – an *incorporation*.[19] The ensuing accusation among present-day Scottish nationalists is that this incorporation has maintained Scotland as a 'satellite' of England: as a peripheral territory that, once acknowledged, can be safely ignored.[20] Furthermore, there was a basic difference on each side in terms of what was meant by 'union' and what was meant by 'Britain'. This fundamental mutual incomprehension continues to this day: each country expects the other to conform to their own national and cultural norms.

It is true that historians such as Linda Colley have argued that the

The armorial bearings and badges of (clockwise) Henry VI, Richard III, Henry VII, and Edward IV. The leopards of England are quartered in all cases with French *fleurs-de-lys* and are encircled by the Garter, but the supporters and badges of each monarch vary considerably (Prince Arthur's Book, before 1519).

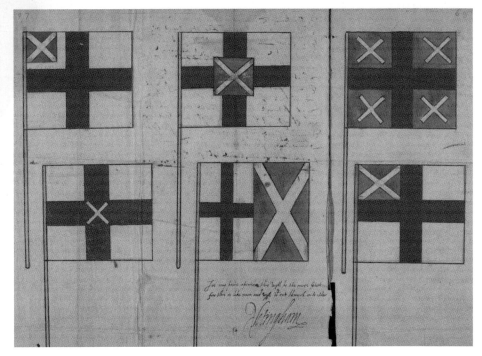

The Earl of Nottingham's designs for the first Union Flag. A further design quartering the crosses of St George and St Andrew appears on the verso. None of these were adopted, although the designs later influenced Commonwealth banners (1606).

The Grand Union Flag, the first flag of American Independence, with the first Union Flag in the canton (woodblock print attributed to Benjamin Johnson, 1776–7).

Funeral escutcheon of Oliver Cromwell. Cromwell's arms quarter the crosses of St George and St Andrew, adding the harp of Ireland and surmounted by Cromwell's white lion on a black shield; this design then impales three leopards (1658).

THE VISIONS OF THOROUGH REFORMATION.

The Royall Armes doth Presbyter deface:
To Paint the Comōn Wealth's upon the place
Thus to Reform from Popery, he draws
A Cross; the Comōn Seal with good Old Cause;
Thus when the Kingdom turns y Comōn wealth
The Imperiall Crown will be the Popes by Stealth.

'We will Reform both Church & State': the frontispiece to *Visions of the Reformation*. The royal arms are painted out by the cross of St George, by then associated with the Puritan Commonwealth (Burnford, 1683).

Benjamin West's 'The Death of General Wolfe'; the Union Jack is furled, literally lifeless (1770).

'The Mary Rose', with pennons of St George and the Tudor livery colours, and a profusion of heraldic flags (the Anthony Roll, 1546).

J.M.W. Turner's 'The Fighting Temeraire', described by the artist as 'My Darling'. This, the 'Nation's Favourite Painting', was originally accompanied by the legend, 'The flag which braved the battle and the breeze / No longer owns her' (1838).

emerging sense of Britishness in the eighteenth century was in a large part expressed as a renewal of English Francophobia – but that should come as no surprise.[21] France was Catholic, the closest point of mainland Europe, an imperial competitor, and the refuge of the Jacobite Pretender to the throne. In any case, the Act of Union did not dissolve the two countries entirely into one Britain: Scotland retained its legal system and its own Church, and continued to control many aspects of its own bureaucracy. And yet nationalistic readings of British history, by creating expectations of English supremacism, inevitably generate an imagined Scottish repression, and ignore Scottish contributions to the British Empire.

These anti-unionist readings also assume a clear sense of English identity at the beginning of the eighteenth century – an identity, which, coming out of decades of civil war, republicanism, restoration, and revolution, was actually rather a fragile and intangible thing, compared with what it had been centuries before. Englishness was expressed in many ways – perhaps too many ways – to the point that satirical verses such as Defoe's *True-Born Englishman* (1701) celebrated Englishness as mongrel diversity and hybridity:

> From whose mixt Relicks our compounded Breed,
> By Spurious Generation does succeed;
> Making a Race uncertain and unev'n,
> Deriv'd from all the Nations under Heav'n.
>   The *Romans* first with *Julius Cæsar* came,
> Including all the Nations of that Name,
> *Gauls*, *Greeks*, and *Lombards*; and by Computation,
> Auxiliaries or Slaves of ev'ry Nation.

With *Hengist*, *Saxons*; *Danes* with *Sueno* came,

In search of Plunder, not in search of Fame.

Scots, *Picts*, and *Irish* from th' *Hibernian* Shore:

And Conqu'ring *William* brought the *Normans* o're ...

The Customs, Surnames, Languages, and Manners,

Of all these Nations are their own Explainers:

Whose Relicks are so lasting and so strong,

They ha' left a *Shibboleth* upon our Tongue;

By which with easy search you may distinguish

Your *Roman-Saxon-Danish-Norman* English.

(IV, 171–94)

If English identity was unsure of itself, its relationship to the larger community of Britain was also fraught and indeterminate. In the early eighteenth century, the word 'Briton' was associated with the Welsh, and the antiquarian and naturalist Edward Lhuyd (1659/60–1709) remarked, 'I don't propose to be an Englishman, but an old Briton.'[22] As general terms, the words 'Britain' and 'British' were derided and ridiculed. They were a reminder that the English, Welsh, and Scottish remained separate and distinct national identities, and also that the creation of the institution of Great Britain was to some degree a political convenience. Indeed, fifty years after Queen Anne's Act of Union, Britishness was still being heartily mocked by the aggressively English, outrageously anti-Scottish journalist and radical celebrity John Wilkes.[23]

Although Wilkes was a peculiar case and served as the self-mythologized focus for a variety of extreme, if popular, opinions, the level of anti-Scottish feeling at this time in particular should not be underestimated. The Scots appeared to be running the government and there were scurrilous rumours that the Prime Minister, John Stuart, third Earl of Bute – who was also Scottish and seemed to exercise an inexplicable influence over King George III – was allegedly having an affair with no less a personage than the queen herself. Hence the Scots were perpetually scorned in the popular opposition press, and perceived to be sapping the resources of England and the Empire – either as starving Highlanders taking jobs or as perfidious politicking Lowland bureaucrats sitting in Westminster and ruining the country. Among the less objectionable attacks of this time is a satirical coat of arms for England, supposedly designed by a Scot, which is charged with various instruments for restraining and chastising slaves: wooden shoes, fetters, halters, muskets, a gallows, and so forth.

This imagined threat to the English way of life might have a familiar ring to it, but the Jacobite Rebellion of 1745 was a recent memory, and Wilkes brilliantly timed his most scathing attack in *The North Briton* to appear in issue number 45. It ensured that the number became a perpetual irritant to the government and a talismanic figure for radical dissent.[24] Wilkes also kept up a campaign arguing against the use of the term 'Great Britain' and 'British', insisting on 'England', as did John Horne Tooke, whose 1765 *Petition of an Englishman* urged against reducing 'the English name…down to Briton'.[25] George III, the first Prince of Wales to be born in England for over a century, was criticized for declaring in his accession speech that his patriotism was for Britain rather than England, and the historian Colin Kidd comments that 'By the middle of the eighteenth century Britishness had become associated with Scottishness, but not with a united Anglo-Scottish identity.'[26] Wilkes ultimately blamed the Scots for the

American War of Independence in 1775: 'The ruin of the British empire is merely a SCOTCH QUARREL with English liberty, a SCOTCH SCRAMBLE for English property.'[27] The loss of America was indeed perceived as a major defeat by the English, although perhaps there was some consolation in the fact that at least it was a still Protestant rather than a Catholic nation that had triumphed across the Atlantic.

But in contrast to all this Anglo-Scottish, anti-British antagonism, there was a concerted rival effort to promote a sense of Great British identity and community. A recurrent feature of English identity has been the belief that the country is guided through history by divine providence; this elect status was now shared with the union, and national destiny became a feature of Britain rather than solely of England. Isaac Watts, for instance, substituted 'Great Britain' for 'Israel' in his best-selling translation of the psalms, helping to revive this belief, and it was evident, too, in Handel's composition of the anthem 'Zadok the Priest', played at every coronation since that of George II in 1727 (Zadok was the priest who anointed King Solomon). The most influential expression of this national faith, however, was in 'Rule, Britannia', an anthem that extended the providential role of Great Britain to its imperial project.

'Rule, Britannia' is one of two anthems that literally gave voice to the possibilities that the creation of Great Britain presented to the world. It was written in 1740 by James Thomson, a Lowland Scot, who has been described by his biographer as 'a child of the Union, and perhaps the first important poet to write with a British, as distinct from a Scots or English, outlook'.[28] Thomson composed the piece as 'A Grand Ode in Honour of Great Britain' for David Mallet's dramatic masque on

Alfred the Great, the unionist king and traditionally the founder of the Royal Navy. In the revised version of 1754, Alfred and his queen Eltruda perform a duet on the anthem:

> When *BRITAIN* first, at Heav'n's Command,
>
> Arose from out the azure Main;
>
> This was the Charter of the Land,
>
> And guardian Angels sung this Strain:
>
> Rule, *BRITANNIA*, rule the Waves;
>
> *BRITONS* never will be Slaves.[29]

Hence 'Rule, Britannia' celebrates the growing Empire, defining Britain as an offshore identity ('rule the waves') in a global economy ('Britons never will be slaves'). As we have seen, the Scots had much to gain from the colonial adventure, but it could only be realized in concert with England and Wales as part of Great Britain. Nevertheless, Thomson did have to remind a fellow Scot that 'Britannia includes our native kingdom of Scotland, too.'[30]

The anthem was by no means the first to celebrate Britannia in this way. The lively ditty 'A Health to the Union' had appeared in 1716, complete with music, in the collection *The Merry Musician; or, A Cure for the Spleen*. The words, by a Mr Herbert, celebrated the recent victories of the War of the Spanish Succession, the defeat of the Jacobite Rising of 1715, and the accession of George I. They may lack the poetry of Thomson's, but do share the same resounding sentiments:

> Come, a Health to our Empress *Britannia* the great,
>
> *Britannia, Britannia, Britannia* the great,

Whose Conquests, whose Conquests,

Whose Conquests at Home, as abroad, are compleat;

Suppressing the servile most barbarous fashion,

That Badge so long pinn'd on the Sleeves of this Nation.

The Union adds Laurels to those that did grow

On the banks of the *Danube*, the [*Nile*], and the *Po*;

To crown all her Triumphs, we will plant on the Sein

A new Flag of Union this approaching Campaign;

The Red and Blue Colours in uniting, create

The Purple Imperial for our new *British* State.[31]

'Rule, Britannia', based on the legendary and evergreen spirit of Britain, had, in contrast, a more timeless appeal to this rollickingly topical chorus. But the other renowned anthem of the period was in fact, like 'A Health to the Union', written for a particular monarch at a particular time. 'God Save the King' was a Protestant, loyalist, unionist hymn popularized in 1745 in response to another advancing Jacobite army, this time led by the Young Pretender, Bonnie Prince Charlie. The Jacobites, marching under the royal Jacobite standard – a gold St Andrew's cross on a blue field – had just defeated the Hanoverian army at Prestonpans, near Edinburgh, and in order to rally the country 'God Save the King' was sung one night after a performance at the Theatre Royal in Drury Lane, London.* *The Gentleman's Magazine* for

---

* Ironically, the royal Jacobite standard recalls the banner of the English proto-martyr, St Alban. Jacobite supporters also adopted the white cockade, which was worn in their hats; supporters of the Hanoverians wore a black cockade.

October 1745 then printed the words and music, it was sung in theatres and churches, and quickly became traditional.

> GOD save great George our King,
>
> Long live our noble King,
>
>   God save the King;
>
> Send him victorious,
>
> Happy and glorious,
>
> Long to reign over us,
>
>   God save the King.[32]

Like 'Rule, Britannia', 'God Save the King' may have been written by a Scot too: James Oswald. Admittedly, there are various claimants for the authorship and composition. Henry Carey, for example, supposedly performed it in public in 1740 to celebrate Admiral Vernon taking Portobello, and it might have been printed in 1743 in a collection called *Harmonia Anglicana*, but no copies survive. Earlier versions of the music exist, one attributed to a Dr John Bull, who also wrote an air celebrating James VI and I, and there is a Scottish tradition that it is based on the seventeenth-century carols 'Remember O Thou Man' and 'Franklin is Fled Away'. The phrase originates from the Coverdale Bible (1535), and was a familiar blessing, used as a naval watchword – 'God save the King', to which the friendly response was 'Long to reign over us' – and in the concluding verse of the popular ballad 'Time's Alteration', which begins 'God save our gracious King, / And send him long to live'.[33] Yet the anthem has never received official recognition in Britain in the form of an act of Parliament or royal proclamation, despite inspiring a fashion for national anthems and providing the tune for many of them, including 'America' ('My country 'tis of thee / Sweet land of liberty'). It was not until the nineteenth century that 'God Save the King' was christened the 'national anthem', a term that may also have been invented by the British.[34]

'God Save the King' also shows how the Jacobite Rebellion presented a whole alternative culture by pervading every aspect of life, including areas such as popular song. A rebel version of the King's anthem, 'God Bless our Lord the King', was sung in 1745 when the Bonnie Prince landed in Scotland. It included the verse

> God bless the prince, I pray,
> God bless the prince, I pray,
> > Charlie I mean;
> That Scotland we may see
> Freed from vile Presbyt'ry,
> Both George and his Feckie.
> > Even so, Amen.[35]

'Feckie' was the unappealing nickname given to George's son Frederick, Prince of Wales. It is perhaps unsurprisingly that the anthem continued to be appropriated and subverted. The radical political and pamphleteer Thomas Spence, for instance, also rewrote 'God Save the King' as a 'Jubilee Hymn', a call for social renewal:

> HARK! how the trumpet's sound
> Proclaims the land around
> > The Jubilee!
> Tells all the poor oppress'd
> No more they shall be cess'd

Nor landlords more molest

Their property.[36]

But despite the Jacobite challenge and radical English antagonism, Protestant Scots were considering themselves to be British more and more. It was in very few interests to maintain a myth of separatism: the Empire was growing, and the Scots had become integral to its workings and were enjoying the benefits of free trade with the colonies. Moreover, after the crushing defeat of the Jacobites at the Battle of Culloden in 1746, the new British identity was emphatically imposed to curtail any Jacobite revival and to incorporate further the Scots into the mechanics of Empire: basic industries were subsidized, the English language replaced Gaelic in schools, and tartan was outlawed, except when worn by Scottish regiments in the British Army.

There was some further reorganization of that army. The first detailed regulations for its flags were issued in 1747, prescribing two flags: the king's colours (a square Union Flag with the regimental badge in the centre*) and the regimental colour (the regimental badge with the Union Jack in the canton).[37] The introduction of a British military standard had far-reaching effects. After Culloden, the British Army would be fighting its battles abroad. This not only made war and colonization a distant, even exotic, activity, it also encouraged a vicarious interest and even pleasure to be taken in it. In other words, war could be enjoyed as entertainment, and the aesthetics of the military clearly had affinities with the stage in the dazzling theatricality of military parades, uniforms, and regimental flags.[38]

* Because this flag is square, it emphasizes the counter-changing between the saltires.

The loyalist Hanoverian campaign was not only confined to singing 'Rule, Britannia' or 'God Save the King', or to delighting in military and maritime glory under the colours of the Union Jack. The ideology of the Hanoverian union remodelled the landscape, both in the city and in the country. New roads made it easier for government to extend its writ and move troops about the country if necessary. Towns were rebuilt in the characteristic Georgian style and gardens and parks introduced fashionable new flora from far-flung corners of the globe, making a flower bed a microcosm of the Empire. One of the most enduring physical embodiments of Scotland's economic renewal in the second half of the eighteenth century and a direct consequence of its participation in harvesting the fruits of the British Empire was Edinburgh New Town, designed by James Craig as 'a celebration of *British* patriotism, and as an assertion of Scotland's and the city's importance in the Union'.[39] Among the city's street names are Prince's Street, George Street, Queen Street, Hanover Street, and Frederick Street, as well as a St Andrew's Square and a St George's Square.* Nor did British patriotism stop there, but went for ever more colossal statements, leaving its mark on countryside in the most explicit ways. The massive white-horse chalk images on English hillsides at Westbury and Pewsey, for example, are in the main modern monuments incised during this period: gigantic instances of loyalist propaganda, celebrating the white horse on the Hanoverian coat of arms.[40]

A burgeoning sense of British identity followed the defeat of

---

* St George's Square was later renamed Charlotte Square, to honour George III's queen.

Jacobitism, then, although this identity remained largely economic and architectural, institutional and constitutional. Events such as parliamentary elections, for example, were avowedly British occasions: patriotic songs were sung, free beer was served, the Pope could be burnt in effigy (itself a not uncommon event, taking place on various Protestant anniversaries throughout the year, such as Guy Fawkes's Day and Queen Elizabeth's birthday), and, of course, above all the festivities the Union Jack flew. It is also evident from addresses and directories that the 'Union Flag' was a popular name for public houses.[41] But at the same time there was also profound interest in researching and assessing the independent cultures of, respectively, England, Scotland, Ireland, and Wales – indeed, far more attention was given to these cultural revivals than to the rather austere proclamations of a new Great British identity, such as the founding of the British Museum (1753) and the establishment of the *Encyclopaedia Britannica* (by a 'Society of Gentlemen in Scotland', 1768–71).

The philosopher Roger Scruton has consequently challenged the theory that a recognizable community of Great Britain arose in the eighteenth century, in opposition to historians from Hilaire Belloc to Linda Colley, by insisting that 'there never was a British nation' – the parts remained separate. Scruton maintains that the argument has been presented back-to-front: the idea of Britain did not emerge from the need to maintain Protestantism against continental Catholicism, but rather, as English national identity expanded over the whole of Britain, one way in which it could be consolidated was in terms of a shared Protestantism. Nathan Bailey, a member of a radical dissenting sect, spelt this out in 1727 by uniquely defining the Union Flag 'of *England*' [*sic*] as a red flag charged with the motto 'FOR THE PROTESTANT RELI-GION AND FOR THE LIBERTY OF ENGLAND'.[42] But even such an explicit statement of identity could still mean little to a vague and ill-informed populace. Defoe commented on the ignorance of English, who, along-side their love of liberty, have 'a kind of natural Aversion' to Popery:

> 'tis the universal Scare-crow, the Hobgoblin, the Spectre with which the Nurses fright the Children, and entertain the old Women all over the Country, by which means such horror possesses the Minds of the common People about it, that I believe there are 100000 stout Fellows, who would spend the last Drop of their Blood against Popery, that do not know whether it be a Man or a Horse.[43]

Any perplexities created by attempting to articulate Britishness within the nation were not, however, reflected abroad. Everywhere else, Britain was confidently and recognizably defined. The imperial foreign policy and the military campaigns fought against France and Spain were all clearly British endeavours. The Welsh had always been well represented in the forces, but during the Seven Years' War (1756–63) the army recruited heavily in Scotland for the first time. The war itself created an economic boom as Britain won huge territories in India, America, and Australasia, as well as humiliating the union's principal competitor, France, and the Empire grew under the Union Jack – a symbol of Britain, Protestant Christianity, capitalist commerce, constitutional monarchy, and industry.

By end of the century, the almost constant military activity was engag-ing the country at every level. When, in 1793, war was declared against

France, the nation's women became thoroughly involved in making ensigns for regional military units, and within a few years, almost a hundred different women presented regional militias with battle colours, suitably embroidered with local and national symbols and mottoes.[44] This patriotic enthusiasm was mirrored by their men joining up to fight against Napoleon. Units such as the Union Volunteers, formed in 1798 in Wapping, adopted the Union Jack for their breast-plates and buttons, and the flag was flown wherever there were soldiers, ministers, or the royal family.[45] At Maidstone on 1 August 1799, scores of volunteer associations congregated to welcome the king and celebrate the course of the war,

> with drums beating and colours flying, accompanied by the bands in full tune. All the volunteers wore oak-boughs in their hats, rendering the whole a very interesting scene… The royal standard was raised on the town-hall and the church, and the union flag displayed from many windows in the streets of the town.[46]

There were naturally some tensions created by the nature of a union-ist army, and for every tableau of heroes dying beneath a furled Union Jack, surrounded by a cross-section of loyal troops, there were punch-ups between rival regiments, even within small units.[47] In 1746, for instance, the Shropshire Fusiliers brawled when their Welsh troops planted leeks in their hats on St David's Day. But national pride did not always lead to brawling, and by 1766, English soldiers were prepared to undertake guard duty so that their Irish comrades could celebrate St Patrick's Night. Indeed, the first record of a St Patrick's Day parade in

New York was inspired by the presence of the British Army: a company of Irish soldiers marched to their celebration behind their regimental band and beneath their regimental colours.[48] Ireland was not at that stage formally part of the union, but the respect and camaraderie afforded by the action suggests that deeper British loyalties did exist. It was a dual rather than a divided loyalty. Campaigning during the Peninsular War (1807–14), Colonel Cadogan kept order among his troops by observing 'that the courage of the British soldier is best called forth by associating it with his [own] country'.[49]

Such a loyalty was also apparent in 1775 among the rebellious American colonies. In his 'Birthday Ode' to George III (1775), the poet laureate William Whitehead addressed his verses 'To Britain's sons in every clime' – in other words, expressing the common view held at this time that the American colonists were essentially British, despite the North American colonies having neither a hereditary aristocracy nor an established Church. America had originally been settled on the assent of the monarch, although there never had been any American representation in Westminster; hence, allegiance tended to be to the king rather than to Parliament. Neither was there any mention of the American states in the 1707 Act of Union – 'there is not one word about America in that Act', announced John Adams, later to be President of the United States, in 1775: 'Acts of Parliament have been passed to annex Wales…but none passed to annex America'.[50] Americans questioned the right of the British government to tax them, and rose in rebellion.

This distinction was reflected in their insignia. The first American Flag of Independence, the 'Grand Union' or 'Cambridge' Flag of 1776, was hoisted in General Washington's camp on 1 January 1776 in protest against British rule. This flag carried the familiar thirteen red and white stripes to indicate the thirteen American states, but in the canton was not the famous ring of white stars that was later adopted, but the Union Jack of Great Britain. The rebels declared their loyalty was to the king while asserting their independence from the British government. Likewise, the captain of a British merchantman docked in Boston Bay reported on 17 January 1776 that, 'I can see the American camp very plain, whose colours a little while ago were intirely red; but on receipt of a certain speech (which they burnt) they have hoisted the union flag, which is here supposed to intimate the union of the Province.'[51] But the king who had, for instance, ordered the settling of Massachusetts in 1630 had been Charles I – a monarch whose relationship to Parliament was profoundly different from that of George III, to the extent that it had eventually cost Charles his head.

The positioning of the Union Flag of Great Britain in the most prestigious quadrant of the first American Grand Union Flag is, then, another example of political complexities being expressed vexillologically – and all the more telling for that. Neither was it the sole example: the flag of the Federal Colonies was a Red Ensign with St George in the canton, and in the canton of St George a golden globe; and similarly the flag carried by the Americans at Bunker Hill (1775) was a blue ensign with St George in the canton, and in the canton of St George a black pine tree (the pine tree became the flag of the American Navy, 1776–81). Consequently, on a number of occasions during the American Revolution, such as at the Battle of Newtown in 1779, both sides fought beneath Union Jack ensigns. In consequence, some contemporary images of Britannia depicted her with a shield emblazoned solely with the cross of St George, a reference to George III emphasized in one illustration by adding with the motto 'George for Ever'.

Britannia, in fact, developed into an important focus for British sentiment during the century, guarding the shores of the 'Blest isle'. She was represented in a range of eighteenth-century paraphernalia – from broadside prints to medals, from regimental badges to ceilings – and she often appeared in the company of the British lion, itself derived from the useful heraldic similarity between the three crouching lions of England and the rampant lion of Scotland.* Britannia was a symbol of unity: in the frontispiece to William Guthrie's *General History of Scotland* (1767), for instance, she stands in between an English baron and a Scottish warrior, 'with the Cap of Liberty and the Union-Flag, in the action of reconciling the two Chieftains'.[52] Britannia also celebrated victories and heroism and she mourned the triumphant dead, from General Wolfe at Quebec (1757) to Admiral Lord Nelson at Trafalgar (1805), where she weeps like the Virgin of the Tears.[53] She was persistently alluded to, invoked, and reinvented as an allegorical representation of Great Britain and its people. Britannia was sober, dignified, and robust, but it is worth emphasizing that she was by no means always a figure of victory. Thomson himself had earlier described her forlorn suffering in *Britannia: A Poem* (written 1727, published in 1729):

* In 1707, the Royal Norfolk Regiment were granted a badge depicting the figure, in honour of their deployment in the War of the Spanish Succession; during the Peninsular War they became known as 'the Holy Boys', possibly because the emblem was mistaken for the Virgin Mary.

As on the sea-beat shore Britannia sat...

Bare was her throbbing bosom to the gale,

That, hoarse, and hollow, from the bleak surge blew;

Loose, flowed her tresses; rent her azure robe.

(1–6)[54]

She was often shown at the time being ridden, beaten, dismembered, and sexually abused.

Britannia was not, though, the sole personification of the British people in the eighteenth century. Throughout that time she vied with a character somewhat less sober and dignified, if comparably robust: John Bull. This gentleman was invented by the Scriblerian satirist John Arbuthnot in *The History of John Bull* (1712), published during the War of the Spanish Succession. The character began as an English trader involved in a lawsuit featuring characters such as Nicholas Frog (a Dutchman), Lewis Baboon (French), Sister Peg (Scottish), as well as his wife, the second Mrs John Bull, and combined a number of traditional English characteristics: he was of portly stature, plain speech, and splenetic irascibility, and he was bovine and boozy. But by the end of the eighteenth century John Bull was being represented as being more generally British in his garb, often accompanied by Britannia or the first Union Flag, and he later appeared resplendent in a Union Jack waistcoat. As such, he lasted well into the twentieth century.

Other generic figures also emerged.* Tommy Atkins was the typical

---

* Sawney Beane, sixteenth-century clansman and cannibal, was more a figure of fear and loathing, invoked at the time of the first Act of Union (and allegedly dating to the time of James VI and I), and embodying fears of that the Scots were barbarians preying on the English.

English soldier, replacing figures such as Thomas Lobster, whose name alluded to the red military coat. It has been claimed that Atkins was a real soldier who was fatally wounded at the Battle of Boxtel (1794). When approached by the young Lieutenant-Colonel Arthur Wellesley (later Duke of Wellington), Atkins dismissed his wounds as 'all in a day's work' and then promptly expired. The name was subsequently used to illustrate army pay books. He survived well into the Second World War, and remains a figure in military adventure stories.[55] The regional organization of the British Army into local regiments tended to encourage immediate national loyalties in the shape of Tommies, Jocks, and so forth, but there were no such distinctions in the navy and its 'honest' Jack Tars. Tar was a popular, salt-of-the-earth figure, probably named after his tarred sailor's coat and hat. In *Humorous and Diverting Dialogues* (1755), Monsieur Baboon, a French dancing master with an excruciating accent, constantly berates 'honest' Jack Tar (one of the 'stoutest and gallantest cocks upon earth'), and consistently addresses him as 'Mr. *Inglishman*'.[56] But by the Napoleonic wars at the end of the century, Jack Tar had become a popular British rather than simply an English figure. A broadside such as *The Toast* (*c.* 1800) features a group of Britons, among them Jack Tar, watched over by Britannia. Similarly, *The Naval Songster, or Jack Tar's Chest of Conviviality* (*c.* 1798) opens with a version of 'Britannia, Rule the Waves', celebrating Sir John Jervis's victory over the Spanish fleet at the Battle of Cape St Vincent in 1797. This new anthem begins,

> When Britain *late* at Heaven's command,
> > *Rode mistress of the subject main;*
> Her guardian angels hand in hand,

Sung this melodious joyful strain:

Rule, Britannia; Britannia, rule the waves;

Thy Hearts of Oak shall ne'er be slaves.[57]

The song includes the exhortation,

Ye British tars to you 'tis giv'n,

This mighty truth to tell the world:

Through you th' avenging hand of Heav'n

'Gainst treach'rous Spain the bolt has hurl'd.[58]

Jack Tar was to be typically found, then, serving beneath a union ensign.

It was at sea that the Union Jack was most prolifically flown, and throughout the eighteenth century the Laws of the Sea were restated. Admirals were identified by their flags and colours, as they had been in the previous century: Admiral of the Fleet (a Union Flag), then admirals of, respectively, the Red, White, and Blue.[59] The Union Flag was used to communicate between ships and to make a vessel's intentions clear: battle order at sea was signalled by the Admiral of the Fleet raising the Union Flag on the mizzen-peak, which would be answered by the admirals of the other squadrons responding likewise; the order to sail was made by the admiral raising a White Ensign.[60] The hoisting of the Union Flag from different masts was also used to position squadrons in relation to the admiral's ship and the wind.[61] These instructions were usually accompanied by a cannon shot to alert commanders to the signal, and power was given to change these signals regularly. They became increasingly sophisticated: in 1746, signalling protocols covered sixteen flags and 144 signals, by 1780 about fifty flags could give over

330 signals, and in the Trafalgar signal book there were over 400 flags alone.[62] The encounter between French and Spanish ships and the British and Dutch in the Mediterranean at the Battle of Vélez-Malaga (13 August 1704), during the War of the Spanish Succession, gives a flavour of how squadrons were arranged and identified:

> Their Fleet consisted of Three Squadrons; that which bears the White Flag, with a Red Cross, was Commanded by Admiral *Shovel*; and was in the Van; the Second Squadron, which carried the Union Flag in the Main-Top, was commanded by Admiral *Rook*, and was placed in their Center; and the 3d, consisting of all the *Dutch* Ships, under Admiral *Callemberg*, as we are told, was in their Rear.[63]

Such signals were also used on land. Edward Cooke describes being besieged in the town of Guayaquil, Ecuador, by Spaniards, and how on 27 April 1709, the men 'took down our Union Flag and hoisted a Flag of Truce, firing a Gun, for a Signal that the *Spaniards* might come into the Town, and that no Hostilities should be committed on either Side', although if artillery was landed by a naval vessel, it would be accompanied by the Union Flag.[64] Courts martial also began with the striking of the Union Flag:

> At half past eight o'clock the Union flag was hoisted on a rope, on board the Sandwich, in Portsmouth Harbour, representing the larboard mizen shrouds, signifying a Court Martial was to be held, and the royal standard was hoisted on a rope, placed for the starboard mizen shrouds, signifying the Court Martial was to be held on an Admiral.[65]

The laws governing merchant ships remained as they had been for a hundred years or so. They were 'restrained from wearing the King's Colours, commonly called the Union Jack' and confined to flying the Red Ensign, with the cross of St George as their jack.[66] These instructions are repeated in many eighteenth-century books on maritime conduct.[67] The Red Ensign was also designated for privateers, with a smaller version of the ensign as the jack, also referred to as the 'Budge' or 'Bugee' flag.* The Scottish Ensign was still flown in the eighteenth century (a red flag with the cross of St Andrew in the canton), and the Irish Ensign was a green flag with St George in the canton and a gold harp in the fly.[68]

Flying the Union Jack at sea was not confined to warships and traders. The eighteenth century witnessed a great expansion in the British Empire, with explorers and adventurers claiming land across the globe, and the claim was usually staked by planting a Union Jack on the new territory. For example, the explorer Captain Edmund Halley recorded that on 17 April 1700 he landed on an island off St Helena, which he settled with livestock to provide future provisions, and then claimed for King William:

This morning we moored in 18 fathom on the W. side of the Isle, the North part bearing ENE, the South part SE, and the high steep Rock like a Ninepin ESE. While the Longboat brought more water aboard I went ashore and put some Goats and Hogs on the Island for Breed,

* In 1687, Pepys mentioned the 'Budgee' as the Red Ensign; by the nineteenth century the 'burgee' meant the small identifying flag flown by a yacht.

as also a pair of Guiney Hens I carried from St. Helena. And I took possession of the Island in his Majesty's name, as knowing it to be granted by the King's Letters Patent, leaving the Union Flag flying.[69]

British navigators likewise took possession of many lands for King George III by virtue of planting a flag, and accounts of the expansion of the Empire, of lonely Union Jacks flying on remote shores, punctuate travel accounts of the period. The Falkland Islands, for instance, were claimed by John Byron, to prevent the Spanish taking them:

On the twenty-third of January [1765], the Commodore with the Captains of the Dolphin and Tamer, and the principal officers, went on shore [the Falkland Islands], where the Union Jack was erected on a high staff, and, being spread, the Commodore named the whole his Majesty's isles, which he claimed for the crown of Great Britain, his heirs and successors. The colours were no sooner spread, than a salute was fired from the ship. They were very merry on the occasion, a large bowl of arrack punch being carried on shore, out of which they drank, among several loyal toasts, success to the discovery of so fine a harbour.[70]

Byron subsequently declared that the King George Islands in the South Pacific, and other territories such as Prince Frederick Island had been christened with the names of the royal family. Likewise, Queen Charlotte's Sound was claimed by Captain James Cook:

I took a post to the highest part of the island, on Tuesday, January 30,

1770, and after fixing it firmly in the ground I hoisted upon it the union flag, and honoured this inlet with the name of QUEEN CHARLOTTE's SOUND, at the same time taking formal possession of this and the adjacent country in the name and for the use of his Majesty King George the Third. We then drank a bottle of wine to her Majesty's health.[71]

At such colonial outposts, governors and generals were in 1726 permitted to fly the Union Flag, and lesser officers could fly the cross of St George.[72] John Hunter, Governor of Norfolk Island, had a large (20' x 36') Union Jack made and hoisted outside his house that was used as a rallying point when he imposed martial law on the convict colony: 'every person, beginning with the lieutenant-governor, passed under the union flag, taking off their hats as they passed it, in token of an oath to submit and be amenable to the martial law'.[73] The ubiquitous flag could also turn up in the unlikeliest of places. Robert Drury, who married a Madagascan after being shipwrecked on the island in 1702, describes the traditional dress of native women as being long cotton dresses:

Those of the better Sort embellish it with Beads, in a very neat Manner, more especially on the Back; where they are rang'd in Rows, and cross one another; and as they are of different Colours, they form a large double Cross, so like a Union-Flag that One would imagine they coppy'd after it.[74]

It is as if he is instinctively reading the sign of the British Empire into the fabric of Madagascan culture.

Yet despite being such a potent and international symbol, the flag was also open to ambiguity, and there was, perhaps surprisingly, confusion over the national components of the Union Jack. In one set of satirical engravings from 1781, for example, *Saint George for England* is represented with the traditional red cross in his hat, but *Saint Andrew for Scotland* is identified not with the silver saltire but with the Union Flag itself, incongruously included amid a profusion of stereotypical Scottish motifs such as a unicorn, tartan, thistles, oatmeal, haggis, bagpipes, and so forth. Moreover, eighteenth-century prints revel in a variety of different designs for the first Union Flag. It seems that the most striking and recognizable feature of these flags was the geometry of the crosses, and that this was developed to produce an unmistakable design that contrasted with French and Spanish ensigns. This means that in many hand-coloured prints the pattern of St Andrew is reversed, so that the cross of St George is imposed on a blue saltire against a white field, and fimbriation varies. In James Gillray's *Light Expelling Darkness* (30 April 1795), for instance, the shield is shown as the first Union, but with the Scottish colours reversed; more complicated versions appear in *Britannia between Death and the Doctors* and *Phantasmagoria*, in which Britannia's shield displays the white saltire of St Andrew itself superimposed by a further blue saltire. This demonstrates that the concept of further imposition was already acceptable just a few years before union with Ireland.[75] Although admittedly Gillray did not colour these prints himself and the choice of tones may simply have been the result of the colourist's ignorance or imagination, they nevertheless suggest the flexibility of the Union design.[76]

Public and popular verse of the period sought to iron out these confusions – at least in terms of restoring the symbolism and values of Great Britain to the flag. James Ogden's epic *The Revolution* (1790) celebrated the anniversary of the Glorious Revolution and the succession of William III and II:

> Loud acclamations, then, through Britain ring,
>
> And echo all around, GOD save the King;
>
> Towr'd steeples high, the union flag display,
>
> Illuminations, turning night to day,
>
> While towns and cities emulative vie,
>
> The public gratitude to testify.[77]

For Ogden, the Union Jack meant British Protestantism. Samuel Bishop's 'Epigram' 246 (1796), on the other hand, was more topically (and ecstatically) patriotic, braiding together Britannia and George III with the national flag:

> BRITAIN has known, in many a well-fought day,
>
> Her UNION FLAG to victory lead the way.
>
> Yet never did that UNION FLAG avow
>
> A more expressive Type of Her, than now!...
>
> Oh! long! long! sacred, may that Banner stand!
>
> Glory, at once, and Emblem of her Land!
>
> Still may She boast – and still the Nations see –
>
> Freedom so loyal! Loyalty so free! –
>
> For Worth so thron'd, such popular Union shown! –
>
> And popular Union's zeal, perpetuate such a Throne![78]

A sense of British communality had, then, emerged by the end of the eighteenth century. It would not, however, last. Before long, Britain and England would once again be confused, and the Union Jack be described as the flag of England. But there was also in the meantime a far more serious threat to the union. The course of the relationship between England (and Wales) and Scotland within the parliamentary union might not have been smooth, but there was no serious attempt to undo what the MPs had joined together. Not so with Irish union, which lasted little over a hundred years, bedevilled nineteenth-century British politics, and would periodically degenerate into violence and rebellion.

From the middle of the eighteenth century there were calls for an Act of Union with Ireland, inspired by the success of the union with Scotland. In 1751, for example, Wills Hillsborough, first Marquess of Downshire, called for 'a complete and perfect Incorporation of the two Kingdoms, inseparably and perpetually united', arguing that Ireland would turn Protestant by the irresistible economic advantages to be gained from British trade opportunities.[79] He was swiftly answered by a satirical reversal of his arguments in 'A Proposal for Preserving the Kingdoms of Great Britain and Ireland Disunited', that simply re-presented his entire argument as the case for 'a compleat and perfect Disjunction of the two Kingdoms, inseparably and perpetually disunited'.[80] The idea rumbled on through the century. In 1759, there was an anti-union riot in Dublin, although for his part, Hillsborough was still recommending an Irish Act of Union in his last speech to the House of Lords in 1786. But it was not until the French threat once again became tangible under Napoleon Bonaparte that serious attempts were made to unite Ireland with Great Britain. The French Revolution (1789) inspired the Irish Rebellion of 1798, a rebellion for a united Ireland, free of any English influence. The rising was supported by Napoleon, who actually landed an army at Co. Mayo in August 1798. Britain had already been at war with revolutionary France for five years, and the prospect of a new front opening up on the western shore was an unwelcome development – indeed, so desperate was the Prime Minister, William Pitt, for soldiers after the many years of campaigning against Napoleon that captured Irish rebels were offered military service in the West Indies rather than being transported to Australia.[81]

Pitt engineered a constitutional union with Ireland. The proposal was to abolish the Irish Parliament in Dublin and revoke Irish legislative independence (which it had enjoyed for less than twenty years); Irish MPs and Lords would thenceforth sit in Westminster. The Bill was given its first reading in 1799. It was at first opposed by the Irish Parliament, but subsequently passed in January 1800, with the promise of equal rights for Catholics and Protestants. The House of Commons passed the Bill in April, and the Act of Union with Ireland became law on 1 January 1801, to form the 'United Kingdom of Great Britain and Ireland'.* The act did not, however, facilitate Catholic emancipation, which was promptly rejected by George III as contravening his coronation oath, and Pitt was forced to resign. Consequently, the Act of

---

* The subsequent independence of the Republic of Ireland created the 'United Kingdom of Great Britain and Northern Ireland'; note that the Channel Islands and the Isle of Man are not part of the United Kingdom but are Crown Dependencies.

Union proved very unpopular in Ireland and provoked the 'Irish Question' of Home Rule that was to dominate domestic British politics for the next century, and has subsequently contributed in no small way to the political situation in Ireland today. But on New Year's Day 1801, the flags were out: according to the patriotic *Union Magazine*, 'The Royal Union standard was hoisted on the Tower...the Union Jack on the Parade.'[82] It was a new union, with a new Union Jack. Where did the second Union Flag come from?

The Union Jack was already an emblem of unity and the Empire. Its very name, *Union* Jack (or Flag), and its ingenious design that combined the red cross of St George with the silver saltire of St Andrew, was symbolic of the 1707 Act of Union – presented as a combination and compromise of different elements that maintained and balanced the distinct identity of the two kingdoms. Any Irish component added to the flag would have to do so too, and a number of possible Irish symbols were available. The Irish Ensign was green, with St George's cross in the canton and a harp in the fly. The colour green had been long identified with Ireland, but was rejected on the grounds that it was a colour associated with independence. The harp was another possibility. This device had been imposed on Commonwealth flags by Oliver Cromwell, but for the new Union Flag created problems of hierarchy and eminence in terms of where it could be positioned. On this occasion, the harp was added to the royal crest, and when engaged in Irish affairs, shamrocks too sometimes appear in the field on which the shield stands. So the second Union Flag neither incorporated a green quadrant, nor was charged with either a harp or a shamrock. Instead, another saltire was woven into the design: the diagonal red cross on white of St Patrick.

Although the red saltire originally derived from the arms of the Geraldines of Kildare, it had, as we have seen, been recognized as a flag of Ireland since at least the sixteenth century. In fact, the cross of St Patrick had been flown by Lord Edward FitzGerald, one of the Kildare dynasty, as recently as 1798 – in support of the rebellion. But in contrast, William Robert FitzGerald, second Duke of Leinster, had in 1783 granted permission to the Knights of the Most Illustrious Order of St Patrick the right to use the red saltire in their regalia. This order had been instituted by George III, so if by the time of the Act of Union the symbol did have associations with rebel Geraldines, it had also been used in sympathy with the king. Since 1801, the cross of St Patrick has continued to also appear independently in Ireland on the badges of the Catholic Boy Scouts of Ireland, the Irish Guards, the Irish Freemasons, and the arms of Queens University, Belfast.

So the choice of the red saltire for the new Union Jack was not merely opportunistic: the device did have a strong association with Ireland, if not actually with St Patrick, and it could be elegantly incorporated in the existing design. Moreover, with a little manipulation, the red saltire could be added to the flag in a way that provided an instant history of the evolution of the British union.

The Act of Union received royal assent on 2 July 1800. As with the Act of 1707, the First Article dealt with the question of flags:

That it be the first Article of the Union of the Kingdoms of *Great Britain* and *Ireland*, that the said Kingdoms of *Great Britain* and *Ireland* shall, upon the first Day of *January* which shall be in the Year of our Lord one thousand eight hundred and one, and for ever after, be united into one Kingdom, by the Name of *The United Kingdom of Great Britain and Ireland*; and that the Royal Stile and Titles appertaining to the Imperial Crown of the said United Kingdom and its Dependencies, and also the Ensigns Armorial Flags and Banners thereof, shall be such as his Majesty, by his Royal Proclamation under the Great Seal of the United Kingdom shall be pleased to appoint.[83]

With the 1801 Act of Union, George finally abandoned the title 'King of France' and consequently confined his coat of arms to the badges of England (first and fourth quarters), Scotland (second quarter), and Ireland (third quarter), with the arms of Hanover placed on a smaller shield in the middle.* It was, however, mooted that the significance of the union with Ireland should be elevated by styling the monarch 'Emperor of the British Isles and their Dependencies', rather than simply 'King of the United Kingdom and Ireland', and by naming the new flag the 'Imperial United Standard'.[84] This would have avoided treating Ireland merely as an addition to the United Kingdom and would emphasize that the 'Emperor' (*Imperator Britanniarum*) united different thrones and peoples – '*Tria Juncta in Unâ*,' (three joined in one, the Irish motto, alluding to the shamrock) – just as did his close neigh-

---

* 'That the arms or ensigns armorial of the united kingdom shall be quarterly; first and fourth, England; second, Scotland; third, Ireland: that there be borne therewith on an escutcheon of pretence the arms of his majesty's dominions in Germany, ensigned with the electoral Bonnet [the crown of the Electorate of Hanover]'.

bour and detested enemy, the emperor Napoleon. In the event, however, George was content to be *Georgius Tertius, Dei Gratia, Britanniarum Rex, Fidei Defensor* ('George the Third, by the Grace of God of the United Kingdom of Great Britain and Ireland King, Defender of the Faith'), and the flag continued to be called the Union Jack.

The account of the new flag was ordered by George III on 5 November 1800. The Admiralty Office issued a directive on 15 November, instructing that from 1 January 1801 it should be flown from 'all His Majesty's Forts and Castles' in the United Kingdom and Crown Dependencies, 'on board His Majesty's Ships', and at dockyards and naval yards, and military hospitals, although no provision was made for private displays.[85] On the same day, the king's proclamation was published, which announced the birth of the new Union Jack. The news was reported in the *London Gazette*:

> That the union flag shall be azure, the crosses saltires of St Andrew and St Patrick quarterly per saltire, counter-changed argent and gules: the latter fimbriated of the second, surmounted by the cross of St George of the third, fimbriated as the saltire.[86]

As with other proclamations, the relationship between power and its heraldic representation is extraordinarily intimate.

In this description, the second Union Flag is formed by laying a red saltire over the white saltire of St Andrew; the cross of St Patrick was not, however, placed exactly upon that of St Andrew, as this would have effectively effaced Scotland's membership of the union. Instead, the red saltire was narrowed and set slightly lower: this established the precedence of Scotland, the senior member of the union, over Ireland. Interestingly, however, the orders of 5 November 1800 for the second Union Flag do not describe the Union Jack familiar today. The blazon, or heraldic description of the flag, stipulates that the cross of St George should be 'fimbriated as the saltire' – in other words, that the white border around the central red cross should be no wider than the narrowest border between the crosses of St Patrick and St Andrew: a return to the style of the seventeenth century. Although the British army initially followed the recommended blazon in the flags it carried, the admiralty continued to use the broad border version introduced by Queen Anne because it had a much greater definition at sea, and eventually this style took precedence on land as well. This involved increasing the fimbriation and narrowing the saltire of St Patrick, and fixing the proportions of the flag at 1:2, the length being twice the dip, or depth.* These adjustments are retained for maritime and civil use today, and the flag also keeps to the naval tradition of displaying the cross of St George effectively imposed on a broad white cross, which is then imposed on the crosses of St Patrick and St Andrew.

There are other peculiarities in the royal proclamation: as noted, the red cross of St Patrick is necessarily made narrower than the saltire of St Andrew – otherwise St Andrew would be obliterated and only white fimbriation would remain – but the diagonals are also 'counterchanged' (or asymmetrical) so that, on each half, one diagonal cross is higher than the other. This asymmetry avoids the implication that the Irish saltire is placed above the Scottish, and also allows the flag to be

* The army makes its flags in the proportion 3:5.

flown upside-down, which is a signal of distress. It is also a convenient heraldic rule that in counter-changing, the metal (white) has precedence over the colour (red). Such subtleties confirm the status of St Andrew's cross, which still occupies the upper hoist canton, or first and most prestigious quarter, and it is the position of the Scottish colours that indicates that the flag is flying correctly. According to *The Manual of Seamanship*:

> the white cross of St. Andrew, that is the broad white stripe, is always above the red cross of St. Patrick in that part of the flag nearest the staff; the broad white stripe is below the red stripe in that part of the flag farthest from the staff.[87]

This marriage between Sts George, Andrew, and Patrick did not go unremarked by the Irish. The design for the new flag was known from 1800, and was greeted with a rough satire *Saint George and Saint Patrick: or, The Rival Saintesses* (published in Dublin, 1800). In this so-called 'Epic Poem of the Eighteenth Century', St Patrick, alarmed at the prospect of union, demands a meeting with St George, which takes place on the planet Mars. George is described as '*Great Britain*'s Saint', to whom 'Saints ANDREW and DAVID were born your tools'; Patrick offers to cut off his nose.[88] Meanwhile, George's wife, Britannia, is pining away and resolves to cuckold the George by St Paddy, as an apt reward for the union:

> If I'm discontented, there's nothing strange in it,
> ST. PATRICK can kiss his wife three times a minute.[89]

The anxiety of being subsumed into a Greater England is a familiar one, and a return to 'Anglo-Britishness' did accompany the union. This is not to say that public poets such as the agoraphobic Poet Laureate Henry James Pye (or, as Francis Douce called him, 'Goose-Pye') did not endeavour to make the new union that of a new Britain, and in between poems on hot-air ballooning and partridge shooting, Pye penned a seldom-read six-book epic on Alfred the Great.

Pye's *Alfred* was published in 1801 – a propitious year for Pye, who had already insisted that the new century began not in 1800 but on 1 January 1801, the day on which the United Kingdom and the second Union Flag came into being. *Alfred* is consequently a millennial nation-alist epic. The poem's contemporary resonance is revealed, for example, in the insignia of the Dark Ages armies. The lines teem with banners on the battlefield, but the poem's heraldry is of an idiosyncratic sort:

> The snow-white steed in Saxon banners flies,
> There Cambria's griffin, on the azure field,
> In snaky volumes writhes around the shield;
> And Scotia's lion, proud, erect, and bold,
> Rears high his irritable crest in gold.
> Gold too her harp, and strung with silver wire,
> Erin her arms displays with kindred fire,
> And Britain's sister isles in Alfred's cause conspire
> (IV, 728–35).[90]

The insistence in the passage on 'shields', 'crests', and 'arms' makes this imagery emphatically heraldic. But rather than depicting the golden dragon of Wessex, described as the standard of Alfred in sources as accessible as Camden's *Remains*, or even the crouching lions of England, Pye makes the Saxon standard the white horse, and ties the image to the equine chalk figures carved into the English landscape.[91]

Alfred, then, symbolically unites the four nations in the conflation of their heraldic devices. The Scottish king predicts:

> 'So, at the eve of some victorious day,
>
> When in mix'd folds the British ensigns play,
>
> Either unconquer'd nation shall embrace,
>
> In deathless amity, a kindred race,
>
> Each shall protecting Alfred's glory claim,
>
> And hail him monarch, in Britannia's name.'
>
> (II, 194–9)[92]

The 'mix'd folds' of the 'British ensigns' described here are the national badges of the Saxon heraldic white horse, the griffin (rather than the dragon) of Wales, the rampant lion of Scotland, and the harp of Ireland. In other words, the design is a prototype of the Hanoverian Royal Coat of Arms, whose characteristic charge was, of course, the white horse.*

Pye was not content with his myth of the new royal armorial bearings, however, and also suggested the Alfredian formation of the Union Jack, for which the coat of arms was a sort of precedent. There is a second Druidic prophecy at the end of the poem:

---

* *Hanover: tierced per pale and per chevron: I. gules two lions passant or; II. or a semy of hearts gules a lion rampant azure; III. gules a horse courant argent; overall an escutcheon of pretence gules charged with the crown of Charlemagne.*

Now learn events, yet unreveal'd that lie

In the dark bosom of futurity. –

As my delighted eyes, in yon firm line,

With friendly folds see Albion's banners join,

I view them, in prophetic vision shewn,

United subjects of a mighty throne;

See Cambria's, Caledonia's, Anglia's name

Blended, and lost in Britain's prouder fame.

And ye, fair Erin's sons, though Ocean's tide

From Britain's shores your kindred shores divide,

That tide shall bear your mingled flags unfurl'd,

A mutual barrier from an envying world;

While the same waves that hostile inroad awe,

The sister isles to closer compact draw,

Waft friendship's intercourse, and Plenty's stores,

From Shannon's brink, to Humber's distant shores.

Each separate interest, separate right shall cease,

Link'd in eternal amity and peace,

While Concord blesses, with celestial smiles,

THE FAVOUR'D EMPIRE OF THE BRITISH ISLES.

(IV, 531–50)[93]

The emphasis here is no longer on shields, crests, or arms, but explicitly on *flags*: 'That tide shall bear your mingled flags unfurl'd'. It is a vision of the Union Jack: a symbol of union realized by George III, the millennial heir of Alfred the Great, traditionally the first *English* king, but here emphatically reinvented as the first British king.

At the opposite end of the reading spectrum, however, another writer was also invoking Alfred in 1801, the year of the Act of Union. The radical poet Thomas Campbell was responsible for 'Ye Mariners of England', one of the most popular verses of the nineteenth century, destined to be reprinted in magazines, on broadsides, and ultimately in Palgrave's *Golden Treasury* in 1861.

Campbell's poem is a celebration of specifically *English* jolly Jack Tars. But his verses begin with a resounding invocation of the Union Jack, oft-quoted and alluded to in the next hundred years by writers of the British Empire. He imagines it as a maritime beacon, first raised by Alfred the Great – traditionally the father of the senior service, the British navy:

> Ye Mariners of England
>
> That guard our native seas,
>
> Whose flag has braved a thousand years,
>
> The battle and the breeze –
>
> Your glorious standard launch again
>
> To match another foe![94]

Campbell imagined the distinctive triple-cross Red Ensign as a shooting star, blazing across the firmament, ominous and propitious:

> The meteor flag of England
>
> Shall yet terrific burn...[95]

So England here resolutely stands for Britain, the United Kingdom, and the Empire. This insistent use of 'England' as an umbrella term for 'Britain', which becomes common during the nineteenth century, may be irritating today, but perhaps it needs to be stressed that it was Thomas Campbell – the 'Scottish Milton', a *Glaswegian* – who blended the two together in 'Ye Mariners of England', and that in this he had the support of his countrymen. In the words of a Scottish MP in 1805:

> We commonly when speaking of British subjects call them English, be they English, Scotch, or Irish; he, therefore, I hope, will never be offended with the word English being applied in future to express any of His Majesty's subjects, or suppose it can be meant as an allusion to any particular part of the United Kingdom.[96]

Another Scotsman, Sir John Moore, said before his death at the Battle of Corunna (1809), 'I hope the people of England will be satisfied. I hope my country will do me justice'; Charles Wolfe, the poet who elegized him in the famous 'Burial of Sir John Moore after Corunna', was Irish.[97] Admiral Lord Nelson's famous signal before the Battle of Trafalgar, 'England expects that every man will do his duty', was not only hoisted but actually suggested by Pasco, a Scot, who recommended the formula 'England expects...' in place of 'Nelson confides...'[98] Just as Scots such as James Thomson, author of 'Rule, Britannia', had encouraged the development of a British identity, it was now writers such as Thomas Campbell who were encouraging 'British' to be succeeded by 'English'. In the very year of the Act of Union, and despite the long-winded efforts of the Poet Laureate, the English were already generally regarded as being synonymous with the British, and with the Union Jack. National identity had, once again, entirely turned around.

VI AN ENGLISHMAN, AN IRISHMAN, AND A SCOTSMAN

Unite the Empire; make it stand compact,
  Shoulder to shoulder let its members feel
The touch of British brotherhood, and act
  As one great nation – strong and true as steel.

Henry Newbolt, from Baden-Powell's *Scouting for Boys* (1908)

BY THE NINETEENTH century, the Union Jack was everywhere – whether flown across the globe as the 'red duster', the Red Ensign of the Merchant Navy, or sported by fashionable gents, who could purchase Union Jack handkerchiefs from the Burlington Arcade. The Union Jack and the Royal Navy ensigns became the most widely recognized trading and military emblems in the world, and symbolized both the high idealism and the high-handed cruelty of empire. In fact, the story of the Union Jack in the nineteenth century is predominantly the story of the British Empire, the Empire on which the sun never set. At its greatest extent, this covered about a quarter of globe's land territory (12.7 million square miles), one in five of the global population lived and worked under British rule (444 million people), and three-quarters of the world's shipping sailed under its flag. In 1897, the year of her Diamond Jubilee, the *St James's Gazette* claimed that Queen Victoria ruled over 'one continent, a hundred peninsulas, five hundred promontories, a thousand lakes, two thousand rivers, ten thousand islands'.[1] Sir John Seeley – who, incidentally, preferred the term 'Greater Britain' to 'British Empire' – expressed the sense of disorientation that accompanied this huge expansion: 'We seem, as it were, to have conquered and peopled half the world in a fit of absence of mind.'[2]

What could all these peoples possibly have in common? The victories over France, culminating with Waterloo in 1815, had given support to the belief in the destiny of Britain, and the union and its dominions were again regarded as the bearers of divine providence, their primacy confirmed by military victories and the stretch of Empire. But by the second decade of the nineteenth century, British identity needed rethinking both at home and abroad. The country had now lost its old enemy, and the two countries would henceforth go to war as allies. Moreover, Catholic Ireland had joined the union. Defining British identity at home as anti-French and anti-Catholic had been possible in the eighteenth century, but was no longer a credible option.*

There was, as ever, an attempt to unify Britain and the Empire in celebrating military victories, whether on the battlefield or at sea. At the beginning of the century, Felicia Hemans eulogized the new British union by invoking Arthur in her poem on the spectacular victory at the Battle of Vimiera (21 August 1808), during the Peninsular War:

---

* Catholics were given equal rights in 1829.

> Bright in the annals of th' impartial page,
>
> Britannia's heroes live from age to age ...
>
> From doubtful Arthur, hero of romance,
>
> King of the circled board, the spear, the lance;
>
> To those whose recent trophies grace her shield,
>
> The gallant victors of Vimiera's field;
>
> Still have her warriors borne th'unfading crown,
>
> And made the BRITISH FLAG the ensign of
>
> renown.[3]

The inclusiveness of the diverse British union was meanwhile cultivated explicitly in popular ballads such as 'The Battle of Vittoria' (1813):

> The English Rose was ne'er sae red,
>
> The Shamrock waved where glory led
>
> And the Scotch Thistle raised its head
>
> And smiled upon Vittoria.[4]

Here, both Britain and British nationalities are identified. Even Ireland seemed to have accepted the union. Thomas Daniel Cowdell identified the characteristic bunting of the Union Jack with King George in his loyalist 'Evening Hymn' from *The Nova Scotia Minstrel* (1817). It is a poem about the city of Dublin:

> We hail the joyful morn at hand,
>
> When Jubilee throughout the land,
>
> His matchless reign shall tell to all,
>
> From Nova Scotia to Bengal:

The isles, the colonies shall ring,

And ocean shout 'long live the king.'

Deep cannon sound the fiftieth year,

Tell it sweet bells, both far and near.

Let not the church enjoy it least,

Nor afterwards the sober feast;

And when the sun withdraws his ray,

Light up an artificial day:

Brilliant devices crown the night,

Be George the subject of the light!

Let Nelson's pillar hold the same,

Surround the hero with a flame;

By night, behold him from afar,

And on his breast a blazing star!

Adorn with lamps of various hue,

But don't forget red, white, and blue.

Festoon the railing round his feet,

Let loyalty and victory meet.

On such a subject light to throw,

Will make a most exalted show![5]

These poems describe and then gloss the flag, embroidering patriotic meaning into the fabric – a particularly *British* patriotism at that. Not only did the flag fly as the ensigns of the Royal and Merchant Navies, at military camps and imperial outposts, but it also fluttered in the streets. Free flags were distributed at George IV's coronation in 1821 and at other royal pageants, indicative of a trend towards mass celebrations and flag-waving.[6] A Welsh mining community in the Parys Mountains celebrated the coronation with a banquet in a marquee over which flew the Union Jack, and by 1857 popular celebrations in the area involved covering the local hotel with flags.[7] In the 1830s, the flag was prominent during the turbulent passage of the Great Reform Bill, the first major overhaul of electoral practices. Demonstrators carried Union Jacks and images of Britannia and Admiral Nelson.*

If one thing could be said to have bound nineteenth-century Britain and the British Empire together, it was the instantly recognizable Union Jack. Throughout the century, popular ballads and patriotic verse repeatedly returned to the flag – in Thomas Campbell's words, as they were frequently adapted, 'The flag that's braved a thousand years / The battle and the breeze' – to inspire the necessary loyalty, strength, and courage needed to maintain the vast imperial territories. In many cases, Campbell's stirring lines were used directly. 'The Flaunting Flag of Liberty', for example, a popular ballad of the mid-century that survives in several different versions, adopted Campbell's lines as a refrain:

> The Flaunting Flag of Liberty,
>> Of Gallia's sons the boast,
> Oh never may a Briton see
>> Upon his native coast.
> The only flag that freedom rears,
>> Her emblem on the seas,
> Is the flag that's braved a thousand years
>> The Battle and the Breeze.

---

* Admittedly, in Scotland they carried St Andrew saltires and images of William Wallace and Robert the Bruce – champions of British freedom.

To aid the trampled rights of man,
    And break oppression's chain,
The foremost in the battle's van,
    It never floats in vain.
The mariner whene'er he steers,
    In every clime he sees,
The flag that braved a thousand years
    The Battle and the Breeze.

If all unite, as once we did,
    To keep that flag unfurled,
Old England still will fearless bid,
    Defiance to the world.
But fast will flow its nation's tears,
    If lawless bands should sieze [*sic*],
The flag that's braved a thousand years
    The Battle and the Breeze.[8]

Anne Grant, in contrast, also quoted Campbell in her topical epic *Eighteen Hundred and Thirteen* (1814), and its lament over the American Revolutionaries of 1776:

The flag that braved triumphant o'er the seas
'A thousand years the battle and the breeze,'
Seem'd faintly fluttering in the inconstant blast,
Or feebly clinging round the stedfast mast,
While Britain's day a double gloom o'ercast,[9]

just as Thomas Jefferson Monkman was to do some seventy years later
in 'Unconquer'd on the Deep' (1885):

> 'The flag that's braved a thousand years
>> The battle and the breeze,'
> Shall still maintain its glory,
>> As mistress of the seas;
> Our tars all valiant seamen,
>> Unsullied they shall keep
> Our Union Jack triumphant,
>> Unconquered on the deep.[10]

R. M. Ballantyne took the line to title a novel (*The Battle and the Breeze;
or, The Fights and Fancies of a British Tar*, 1869), while J. M. W. Turner's
painting *The Fighting Temeraire* (which he referred to as 'My Darling'
and refused to sell) had shown a veteran of the Battle of Trafalgar being
scrapped; it was first exhibited at the Royal Academy in 1839, accompanied by lines based on Campbell:

> The flag which braved the battle and the breeze
> No longer owns her.

Aside from Campbell's definitive lines, there were also scores of
other popular invocations of the flag: ballads such as 'The British Flag
Flies at the Main'; 'The Red, White, & Blue'; and 'Nelsons Last Sigh'.[11]
'Under the Union Jack' is typical, concluding with a rousing crescendo:

> What though our wooden walls are gone,
>> Our tough old hearts of oak;

We'll run our flag, and hold our own,

  In midst of the battles smoke.

The British flag is a brave old flag,

  Whate'er our foes may say,

And when the guns crack, then the Union Jack,

  Will be nailed to the mast that day.[12]

The talismanic qualities of the Union Jack and White Ensign for seamen, particularly those associated with Admiral Lord Nelson, is evident from the scenes at Nelson's funeral, after his death at Trafalgar on 21 October 1805. His sailors tore a strip from the White Ensign from HMS *Victory* as it was laid on his coffin and ripped it up for souvenirs. The scene was described by the wife of the captain of HMS *Orion*, who attended the service at St Paul's Cathedral, as being somehow characteristic of the dead hero: 'That was Nelson: the rest was so much the Herald's Office.'[13]

Later in the century, in addition to broadside ballads, dozens of music-hall songs later in the century took the Union Jack as their theme. They could be sung while the family gathered around the pianoforte: 'Our Union Jack of Liberty' (*c.* 1873), 'Our Glorious Union Jack' (*c.* 1893), 'Floats the Union Jack' (*c.* 1896), 'Beneath the Union Jack' (*c.* 1899), 'The Good Old Union Jack' (*c.* 1906), and 'The British Union Jack' (*c.* 1909) were all favourites. Dan Lipton and T. W. Thurban's 'My Girl's a Union Jack Girl' (*c.* 1914) is typical, combining the romance of the flag with wistful memories of a patriotic sweetheart:

My girl's a Union Jack girl,

She's British thro' and thro'.

> Red are her lips, teeth pearly White,
>
> Eyes of a heavenly hue, true Blue.
>
> And I'll live or die for the colours;
>
> Gladly I'll play my part;
>
> Always be true to the Red, White and Blue
>
> In the Empire of my heart. (*Chorus*)

Such lyrics indicate the degree to which the flag filled the imagination. It was omnipresent, subtly informing all aspects of everyday life. It suffused the century; it was the spirit of the Empire. This response lies behind 'My Dream of the Union Jack' (1909), a meditation that offered a century of Union Jack-inspired history, which was determinedly British:

> I saw Nelson fight at Trafalgar Bay,
>
> Wellington at Waterloo.
>
> And the gallant charge of the Light Brigade,
>
> Charlie Beresford's brave deeds too,
>
> I saw Bulldog Butler in the Boer war
>
> Good old Bobs and Fighting Mac
>
> And they all fought for our liberty,
>
> In my dream of the Union Jack. (*Chorus*)

These British heroes came from all three kingdoms: Nelson was born in Norfolk and Wellington in Dublin; Beresford, commander of the *Condor* at Alexandria in 1882, in Co. Louth; Sir William Butler, commander of the British forces in the Transvaal and a Catholic Irish nationalist, in Co. Tipperary; Sir Hector Macdonald, 'Fighting Mac', who was instrumental in securing victory at the Battle of Omdurman (1898), in Ross-shire; and Earl Roberts, 'Sir Bobs', Commander-in-

Chief of the British Army and a hero of the Boer War, in Cawnpore, India, to Irish parents.

Children had the Union Jack whether at home or at school. *Union Jack*, subtitled *Tales for British Boys*, was established in January 1880. It was published weekly and sold for sixpence a month. The magazine featured imperial adventure stories, and included helpful advice on how best to run away to join the navy or what chest measurements were required for various regiments. Despite its title, the first issue of *Union Jack* featured a very poorly drawn flag on the masthead, and an inaccurate account of its history in the editorial. Following a torrent of complaints, the masthead had been redesigned by the next month, and a page was devoted to pictures and verses about the flag:

> IT's only a small bit of bunting, –
>
> It's only an old colour'd rag: –
>
> Yet thousands have died for its honour,
>
> And shed their best blood for the flag.[14]

Originally edited by W. H. G. Kingston, the magazine was taken over by the ultra-patriotic writer George Alfred Henty when Kingston retired in May. Shortly afterwards, Henty redesigned the masthead again, making it more nautical – and ironically reverting to the erroneous flag design. *Union Jack* folded in 1883, but Henty had by then established himself as a prolific writer of adventure stories for boys and was producing an average of three novels a year, including *Under Drake's Flag: A Tale of the Spanish Main* (1883), *St. George for England: A Tale of Cressy and Poitiers* (1885), and *True to the Old Flag: A Tale of the American War of Independence* (1885).

Capitalizing on the success of the Kingston–Henty venture, *The Union Jack Library* was published in twelve parts in 1888, consisting of short paperbacks selling for a penny each, and containing stories with titles such as 'The Handsome Hussar' and 'Larry the Lancer'. This was followed by *The Union Jack: Library of High-Class Fiction*, published weekly from 1894 at a ha'penny a copy, and it was here that the detective Sexton Blake first appeared. The original style of this magazine was derived from Henty's rope lettering for his *Union Jack* magazine, although printed on poorer quality paper, and the editorial for the first issue also echoed Henty's sentiments:

> We have chosen our title because it is a name with which the whole world is familiar, and one that will appeal to every British heart. Many brave deeds have been done beneath the Union Jack, and as a recital of such deeds of bravery will appear in our pages, a more appropriate title it would be impossible to find.[15]

This *Union Jack* differed from Henty's in one important respect, however – it ran for considerably longer, and both Sexton Blake and the magazine continued well into the 1930s.

Another growth area was military toys. From the mid-nineteenth century, lead soldiers began to be produced for boys, and by 1893 these were being mass-produced by the appropriately named William Britain and Sons. Within a few years Britains had over fifty regimental sets available, as well as special commemorative packs such as the 1897 Jubilee issue.[16] Many came with national and regimental standards, and all the uniforms were accurately painted. War and colonization were once more part of the leisure industry, offering a miniaturized connection with the expeditions and battles between the Empire and its enemies. The connection was almost literal: movingly, during the Great War, soldiers and sailors invalided out of the forces were recruited to make such toys.

A schoolboy could also find himself being taught from *Cassell's Union Jack Series* (1893–4). These were five little books for a patriotic education, including such useful ditties as

> Under the Union Jack,
>
> White, and brown, and black
>
> Strive, with one accord.[17]

Rather more elaborate was W. Lane Frost's patriotic operetta for children *The Birth of the Union Jack* (c. 1900), in which Great Britain Ltd [*sic*] is formed by the three patron saints marching about and singing choruses about flags. There is some knockabout humour – St Patrick, for instance, suggests a quartered flag bearing Bass Ale, Guinness Stout, Scotch whisky, and an empty quadrant 'that represents the teetotallers' – and interestingly, in terms of the dimensions of the flag, Britannia makes a special point of mentioning that the cross of St George lies on a white cross 'which has no name'.[18] Lane Frost is also sensitive to the Welsh: when Dame Jones complains that Wales is not directly represented on the flag, Britannia points out that England and Wales are closely tied by virtue of the Prince of Wales being the heir to the throne. There were also many Union Jack marches, some scored for full marching bands, and even a Union Jack polka and a quadrille.[19] By the end of the century, S. R. Redman had composed a 'New National

Poem', *The British Flag* (1892), which consisted of thirty-eight lines of
Union Jack doggerel:

> Beneath the British Flag what glorious victories
>> have been won?
> Beneath this flag what noble deeds of daring
>> have been done?[20]

What deeds indeed?

The Great Exhibition of 1851 had included ceramics bearing images
of Britannia and the Union Jack, and the design decorated commodities
from biscuit tins to handkerchiefs.[21] Charles Dickens in his
'Uncommercial Traveller' essays (written from 1863) later described
how 'Down by the Docks...the pawnbroker lends money on Union-
Jack pocket-handkerchiefs'; in the same decade, Charles Digby Harrod
was packaging groceries in Union Jack wrapping paper.[22] Patriotism
was a popular national hobby. Union Jacks were a favourite embroidery
pattern across the Empire and schoolboys idled away their time doo-
dling Union Jacks on their exercise books.[23] The clerk Wemmick in
Dickens's novel *Great Expectations* (1860–61) lives in a diminutive Gothic
Revival castle in Walworth: 'Wemmick's house was a little wooden
cottage in the midst of plots of garden, and the top of it was cut out and
painted like a battery mounted with guns.'[24] Wemmick fires a cannon
every evening at nine and on Sundays 'I run up a real flag'; when Pip
visits one Sunday he finds the Union Jack proudly flying.[25]

The Union Jack was ubiquitous. It inspired nonce phrases such as
'Union Jackery', 'Union Jackist', and 'Union Jackite' – coinages that the
press loved. The *Pall Mall Gazette* (3 July 1886) noted that 'At

Nottingham...the Tory party is locally known as the Union Jackists',
while the *Spectator* (7 March 1896) condemned 'The national outbursts
of "Union-Jackery" in the courts and music-halls'.[26] The flag was a
piece of modern magic: in Gilbert and Sullivan's supernatural melo-
drama *Ruddigore* (1887), the wicked plans of the cursed baronet Sir
Ruthven Murgatroyd are foiled by Richard Dauntless brandishing a
Union Jack and declaring,

> Here is a flag that none dare defy [*all kneel*], and while this glorious
> rag floats over Rose Maybud's head, the man does not live who would
> dare to lay unlicensed hand upon her![27]

But perhaps the most remarkable instances of all this Union Jackism,
however, are the occasions when it was literally built into the land, like
a gigantic maker's mark stamped onto a colonial territory, reminiscent
of the chalk impressions of the Hanoverians. The Sudan city of
Khartoum lost by General Gordon was, for instance, rebuilt in 1898 by
Lord Kitchener on the plan of the Union Jack – in part because he
thought it would be easier to defend – and Faisalabad, the third largest
city in Pakistan, still has a marketplace at which eight bazaars meet; this
too was designed by the British on the pattern of the Union Jack.

Despite all of this persistent Union Jack chatter, the incessant appropriation and trivialization, regulations concerning the manufacture,
handling, flying, and disposal of actual Union Jack flags and naval
ensigns became more strictly codified. The Union Jack was far more
than a military banner or a naval standard, and in its weft and weave
there was more than just Yorkshire bunting. It could be flown on certain
circumstances, such as 'Union Days' or royal anniversaries, but also

remained 'the distinctive flag or mark of an Admiral of the Fleet, when displayed at the main-top-gallant-masthead'.[28] The queen's colour, based on the king's colours of the eighteenth century, now required a 'colour-party' on parade, consisting of two lieutenants, two sergeants, and two privates. Great care was taken at sea when raising and lowering the Union Jack: the flag was carefully unfolded and folded, and was never supposed to touch the deck. Nor was it flown before sunrise or after sunset. Disgracing the flag became a criminal offence. Faded and frayed Union Jacks were shredded and disposed of as rags – they were not permitted to be used as decorations – and flags that had seen active service were framed and retained on board while ships remained in service, and subsequently lodged in museums or churches.[29]

Every activity surrounding the flag was pregnant with meaning. A popular verse, 'Hoist the Flag', was written on the departure of the fleet for the Crimea and featured in the *Illustrated Crimean War Songbook* (1854) – hoisting the flag was, of course, the prelude to war, and, it was assumed, inevitable triumph.[30]

The Union Jack was, in the nineteenth century, very definitely a flag of union: the flag of the United Kingdom. During this period, the Celtic Fringe was dominant in British public life, and even towards the end of the First World War, John Hay Beith famously recorded:

Today, a Scot is leading the British army in France [Field Marshal Douglas Haig], another is commanding the British Grand Fleet at sea [Admiral David Beatty], while a third directs the Imperial General Staff at home [Sir William Robertson]. The Lord Chancellor is a Scot

[Viscount Finlay]; so are the Chancellor of the Exchequer and the Foreign Secretary [Bonar Law and Arthur Balfour]. The Prime Minister is a Welshman [David Lloyd George], and the First Lord of the Admiralty is an Irishman [Lord Carson].[31]

Indeed, if the first British Empire of the eighteenth century was powered by the Scots, the Irish played a similar role in the Empire of the nineteenth century. Irish recruits made up 43 per cent of British servicemen in 1830, and between 1825 and 1850 nearly 48 per cent of the Bengal army, and gunboat diplomacy was most enthusiastically pursued by Foreign Secretary and later Prime Minister Lord Palmerston, an Irishman.

The Irish predominance in the second British Empire is evident today in the almost worldwide observance of St Patrick's Day, which was spread by Irish soldiers stationed in colonies, and by Irish settlers migrating to America, Australia, and elsewhere. These celebrations began as loyalist events, but became significant declarations of independent Irish identity following the American War of Independence, the 1798 Rebellion, and the Union of 1801. In New York today, the St Patrick's Day parade is joined by 100,000 people, with another million spectating and drinking specially dyed green beer.[32]

In Ireland, St Patrick's Day parades are now celebrated by both Catholics and Protestants, and ecumenical services have been held at Downpatrick, traditionally the resting place of St Patrick, St Columba, and St Brigit. But this is a comparatively recent development. Since at least the seventeenth century, Irish men and women had been sporting a shamrock, green ribbon, or a cross on his feast day of 17 March, which they commemorated with 'the drowning of the shamrock' and drinking 'St Patrick's pot'. The celebrations were at this time, however, split between Catholics and Protestants, and each community conducted them in very different ways and at a very different social level. By 1795, the Orange Order was founded and set about observing a variety of potentially divisive anniversaries, such as that of King William's victory at the Battle of the Boyne. But some Protestants argued that St Patrick's Day should be seen as a common holiday. *The Dublin Evening Post* for 15 March 1825 called upon 'the Orangemen of Ireland' to consider 'however divided we may be in sentiments, in politics, in religion, let us never forget that we are one nation…We shall all celebrate on Thursday next, the anniversary of our national saint.'[33]

That call went unheeded, but four years later the Viceroy of Ireland donned a shamrock and appeared before the revellers in Dublin, thereby joining high Protestant culture with popular Catholic culture. This small but symbolic union was also recognized thereafter by regular performances of 'St Patrick's Day' and 'God Save the Queen' on 17 March.[34]

St Patrick continued to be reinvented throughout the nineteenth century. Following the death and suffering during the Great Hunger (*An Ghorta Mhór*: the Irish Potato Famine of 1845–8), the saint became an increasingly political symbol and developed once more into a figure of Irish separatism who could lead the Irish Catholics, the 'true Irish', out of the long night of English and Anglo-Irish oppression. There was considerable support for independence, even if it could only be achieved violently. In 1848, the Year of Revolutions, what is now the Republic of Ireland's Tricolour of green, white, and orange was first flown, identifying the Young Ireland movement, which later led a rebellion at Tipperary. Tricolour cockades had been popular following the French Revolution of 1830, but the colours did not appear as a flag until first raised by Thomas Francis Meagher on 7 March 1848. The colours are popularly supposed to symbolize a united Ireland, representing the Catholics or older Gaelic tradition and the Protestants or Orangemen, joined by peace – the white flag being the traditional sign of amity and goodwill, rather than of surrender.

But violent dissent continued throughout the century. In 1861 the National Brotherhood of St Patrick was founded in Dublin as a social club, but was soon taken over by the Fenians, who strongly opposed the union with Great Britain, and who became the Irish Republican Brotherhood. The seemingly innocuous St Patrick's Day parades also became opportunities for both the Irish and the colonies to express their dissatisfaction with Britain and the Empire. After a series of disturbances in Melbourne, for example, the colonial administrators were forced to pass the Party Processions Bill in 1847 to keep the peace and discourage militants from wandering the streets armed with hurley sticks. Similarly, in the early twentieth century the Melbourne parade in 1918 featured what were called 'Sinn Féin banners' (the Tricolour*), and in 1920 loyalists complained that the Union Jack was too small (12″ x 15″, compared with the St Patrick's Society banner, 10′ x 12′). The following year, a Union Jack was seized and doused with petrol.[35]

Just as interest in St Patrick revived, so it did in St George as well. Throughout the nineteenth century, folk customs and traditions were

---

* Known as the Sinn Féin flag in the republican song 'Johnston's Motor Car'.

being resurrected and invented in order to provide the Isles with a continuous cultural history of its people. St George appealed in several ways. He reminded the English of their Englishness, he was a folk hero with a Merrie Englande aspect as the hero of various mummers' plays, and he was also a Christian martyr. Furthermore, St George was a fitting warrior saint for the Empire and its attendant conflicts – particularly by the mid-nineteenth century, when the nation, the Church, and soldiering had been forged together to produce muscular Christianity, typified by Sabine Baring-Gould's hymn 'Onward Christian Soldiers'.[36] Mummers' plays were revived and collected, and old institutions were newly revered – as early as 1805, the installation of the Garter knights at Windsor on St George's Day was a lavish affair costing over £50,000.[37]

St George was also adopted by early socialist movements. In 1871, John Ruskin established the Guild of St George ('my St George's Company') as an agricultural society. It met for the first time in 1879. Ruskin reinvented the George-and-the-dragon struggle as Christian socialism confronting industrial capitalism: 'the Lord of Decomposition, the old Dragon himself'.[38] Likewise, the image of the warrior saint vanquishing the dragon appealed to Walter Crane of the Arts and Crafts movement, who saw the struggle as an allegory of socialism and capitalism:

> Our patron saint in full armour upon a white horse with red
> trappings, charging the dragon, behind which was a gloomy
> landscape with factory chimneys dark against lurid bars of sunset,
> and to the left a stretch of seashore, and a neglected plough in the
> middle distance – perhaps not an obscure allegory.[39]

Other institutions were founded. The Society of St George was established in 1894, supported by Rudyard Kipling, and in 1896 Queen Victoria became patron; her son Edward VII later appointed the Society the Royal Society of St George. The flag of St George was both literally and metaphorically flown at Queen Victoria's Diamond Jubilee in 1897, for which Edward Elgar wrote *The Banner of St George,* with words by Shapcott Wensley:

> Where the strong the weak oppress,
> Where the suffering succour crave,
> Where the tyrant spreads distress,
> There the cross of George must wave![40]

St George was also celebrated by less conventional writers such as the eroto-occultist Hargrave Jennings, author of *The Rosicrucians, their Rites and Mysteries* (1870), who in 1853 commented gnomically on the mystical migrations of the rosy cross:

> his goodly cross of red, which shone a very beacon in the conflicts
> with the Paynim, hath, of itself, passed, and been eagerly transmitted
> from land to land, and hath served as the rallying light for a hundred,
> (but for it), to all Christian and humane tendencies, benighted
> generations.[41]

Throughout the century, cathedrals were dedicated to St George across the Empire – in Cape Town and Madras, for example, Kingston (the Windward Islands) and Georgetown (British Guiana), and even in Jerusalem. Many churches, too, were consecrated to him, and by 1899 there were almost two hundred dedicated to the saint in England alone. St George's feast day, 23 April, was once again a popular holiday, with children being released from school, flags flying, and special services conducted.[42] Robert Baden-Powell made St George the patron saint of the Boy Scout movement, and in *Scouting for Boys* (1908) he is prominently presented as the patron of chivalry: on his day, 'all good scouts wear a rose in his honour and fly their flags'.[43]

Against this separatism, the Union Jack was supposed to stand clearly for solidarity in diversity, for a common purpose, and for imperial unity. There are many references to the credo 'one flag, one people' throughout the century, although it often seemed to mean 'one Union Jack, one England'. There was, for example, considerable interest in both legendary and historical monarchs of union. King Arthur was depicted in many Pre-Raphaelite paintings and became the principal subject of Tennyson's romance of power and Empire, *Idylls of the King* (1856–74).[44] Attention was also renewed in Alfred the Great, whom poets attempted a second time to reinvent as a hero of British unionism. John Fitchett's sprawling epic *King Alfred: A Poem* (1841) advocates unification in the image of the 'Union wreath', a garland that encircled badges on ensigns, when an Irish prince hopes for

> friendly league and endless union
> 'Twixt lesser Erin and Britannia's isle,
> Allies by nature, were at length fulfill'd!
> How would the shamrock, twined with England's rose,
> And Scotland's thistle to the world present
> A badge and emblem of united power
> Pure proof against decay, or rude assault.[45]

Similarly, Martin Farquhar Tupper's patriotic play *Alfred* (1858) concludes in Glastonbury Abbey with 'crowds of Danes and English, as in amicable union of the two nations, their flags and emblems mixed', before the National Anthem is sung (recalling James Thomson's King Alfred duet, 'Rule, Britannia', in the previous century).[46] The emphasis was very much on balancing the union. In the year he became Poet Laureate, Alfred Austin wrote the play *England's Darling* (1896), in which Alfred advised,

> In this Island there must be one lord,
>
> One law, one speech, one bond of blood between
>
> Saxon and Briton, and that Wales must be
>
> Not more or less than England but the same,

and the appropriately named Alfred Lord Tennyson wrote a comparable verse for the 'Opening of the Indian and Colonial Exhibition by the Queen' (1886).[47] This poem, composed 'at the Request of the Prince of Wales', concludes:

> Britain's myriad voices call,
>
> 'Sons, be welded each and all,
>
> Into one imperial whole,
>
> One with Britain, heart and soul!
>
> One life, one flag, one fleet, one Throne!'
>
> Britons, hold your own![48]

The verse was set to music by Arthur Sullivan; the exhibition was visited by five and a half million people.

Other invocations were, however, often risibly anachronistic. In

Little Red Robin: Or, The Dey [sic] *and the Knight* (a 'burlesque extravaganza', written by Vivian Matthews and Alice Manley and published in
1900), Robin Hood's Merry Men rather rashly enlist to follow King
Richard to the Crusades. The Lionheart somehow marches under the
Union Jack, rather than under the cross of St George:

> For our swords they swing and our spurs they ring,
>
> As we ride in the train of our Soldier King;
>
> Whether by land, or whether by sea,
>
> Or who is the foeman, what care we?
>
> 'Here's to the hearts that are brave and true!'
>
> We sing in a rousing chorus;
>
> 'Here's to the Red and the White and the Blue
>
> Of the flag that's waving o'er us!'[49]

Equally fatuous is Eliza Winter's drawing-room play *The Making of
Our Union Jack: 1707–1801*, privately printed in Ontario in 1911. In
this, Winter imagines the first Act of Union in a fantasy sequence set
in 1706 – presumably under the misapprehension that the first Union
Flag was introduced in 1707. A Welsh peer declares that the two flags
will unite many factions – English Whigs and Tories, the Welsh, the
Scots, and the Jacobites – and the play concludes with the six colonies
– Newfoundland, Australia, New Zealand, India, Canada, South
Africa – devoting themselves to the flag. We learn along the way that
the Welsh support St George because his cross is a Christian symbol,
and that the Union Jack is symbolic: red for freedom, white for purity
and honour, blue for truth, and red again for the blood of our fore-
fathers.

At the end of the nineteenth century, identifying such symbolism became a pastime for cranks, invariably those hoping to identify Britons with any or all of the tribes of Israel. This way of reading the flag is summarized in a strange pamphlet by one M. Bloxam, in which all of the symbolism is scrupulously referenced to Ferrer Fenton's translation of the Bible (1903). The red, white, and blue symbolize the shedding of the sacred Blood, purity, and 'Service in Holy Things, on *behalf of the people*', as well as the Son, the Spirit, and the Father, respectively. The cross of St George is not the 'rosy cross' identified by the Rosicrucian mystic Hargrave Jennings, but rather its two arms show 'Redemption for Divorced Israel, and salvation from Sin for all the world', while the crosses of Sts Andrew and Patrick variously sacrifice and purity (again). The three crosses form a star, 'and are symbolic of the promises of God to our forefather Abraham, of multitudinous Seed "as the stars"', and also make eight spokes of the wheel of Ezekiel's vision; meanwhile, eight is the number of the name Jesus Christ in Greek. The crosses furthermore symbolize addition (+) and multiplication (×), and 'these three crosses *crossed*, are the monogram of the name of Christ – the Alpha and Omega – the first and last', conforming to the first and last letters of the Hebrew alphabet, *Aleph* and *Tau*. The double-cross is apparently mentioned in Ezekiel (9:4–6) – although not in the Authorized Version, the King James Bible.[50]

This leads Bloxam to argue the Union Jack is 'the Mark of God's Seal on Israel Britain': 'The Union Jack – or Union of the sons of Jacob, gathered in their appointed place'. The Saxons were really the Isaacsons, descended from the Ephraim (one of the Twelve Tribes of Israel), and moreover 'the symbols of our ancient heraldry were chosen and inspired by Divine direction'.[51] Britain therefore has an inherent right to use the heraldry of Israel. Bloxham then turns his attention to the royal coat of arms, whereupon his reading becomes farcical. The lion is, he declares, self-evidently the lion of Jacob, but Bloxam then has to equate the standard of the Ephraim (an ox or a bull) with the unicorn. Unperturbed, he simply concludes that the unicorn is really an ox or a bull as seen in profile.

Although the union of 'one flag, one people' was a dominant strain in the nineteenth century, and was invoked by writers from Charlotte Brontë (*Villette*, 1853) to Oscar Wilde (*The Picture of Dorian Gray*, 1890), the idea did, however, experience practical problems.[52] There was not just one flag: there were literally hundreds of British flags and ensigns, covering the various civil and military offices of Empire. The Union Jack featured in the majority of the British Empire's flags, which multiplied spectacularly with the introduction of Colonial flags in 1869. Most of these were based on the public seal of each colony combined with a Union Jack or an ensign, but there were over a hundred British dominions, colonies, protectorates, and other variously administered territories that adapted the Union Jack for their colours: Sierra Leone, for example, had a Union Jack with a badge in the middle showing the first Union Flag on a shield together with a freed slave and a palm tree. Union Jacks were frequently sent over to African tribes as gifts; in at least one case, they were cut up and made into a suit, which was then returned to Britain.[53]

Among these sibling flags, the flag of Hawaii is a unique anomaly. It, too, has a Union Jack in the canton, but Hawaii has never been a British colony. A Union Jack was presented to the king, Kamehameha the Great, by Captain George Vancouver, who had accompanied Captain James Cook when he first landed on Hawaii in 1778. Vancouver visited the islands again in 1792–3 and in 1794, during which time the archipelago was being unified under Kamehameha, and he offered British protection in return for the islands ceding to Britain. The Union Jack was raised on 25 February, and the islands claimed for George III, but the cession was never ratified. Nevertheless, the Union Jack was flown by Kamehameha until 1816, when it was replaced by the Hawaiian flag of eight stripes (one for each island) with the Union Jack in the canton. This had been designed in about 1809, possibly by a British sea captain – either Alexander Adams or George Beckley. By the 1830s, the British government had decided to launch a complete takeover, but despite a brief interlude in 1843 when Union Jacks were raised over all the islands, Hawaiian independence was instead restored and confirmed by Britain. The Hawaiian flag flew again, and the Union Jack remained in the canton: it stood for the close, if not precisely imperial, links between the two countries.

The Union Jack flown by the Royal Navy and the British Army over hundreds of territories was a symbol of imperial military might and effectively the trademark of British merchantmen. But there were problems with the design. It had never been standardized in dimensions or colour, and what was being flown was an adaptation of the 1801 heraldic blazon. Unlike the flags of other other countries, the proportions of the Union Jack have never been codified in law. Naval flags are in the proportion 1:2 because square flags do not fly as well those that are twice as long as they are wide, but army flags are made either in the ratio 3:5 or square; other variations are also possible. During his second tenure as Secretary to the Admiralty, Samuel Pepys recorded in 1687 that the flag should be based on the golden ratio, 1:1.6180339. But flags were measured by the standard measurement of a 'breadth', based on the width of hemmed bunting for the stripes. Since the seventeenth century, this breadth has gradually reduced from eleven inches to nine inches, and these changes in the width of bunting over the years have consequently distorted the golden ratio to 1:2.

These problems with the heraldic blazon led the admiralty to develop their own formula, in which the red of the cross of St George should be a fifth the depth of the flag (if the flag is 45" deep, this comes to 9"); the fimbriation of the white border of the St George cross a third the width of the cross (3"); the red of St Patrick the same width (a third the width of the St George cross: 3"); the narrow fimbriation of St Patrick a sixth the width of the red of St George (1½"); and the broad white of the saltire of St Andrew half the width of the red of St George (4½").[54]

Finally, flags also changed their meaning. On 18 October 1864, for example, an Order in Council abolished the three-squadron system of Royal Navy ensigns, formally adopting as the imperial standard the insignia deployed by Admiral Lord Nelson at the Battle of Trafalgar in 1805, when he ordered all British fighting vessels to fly the White Ensign. As had become traditional, the Red, White, and Blue Ensigns designated variously the Merchant Navy, the Royal Navy, and the Naval Reserve: the Merchant Navy had the affectionately nicknamed 'red duster'; the Royal Navy the White St George Ensign; and the Naval Reserve and other designations sailed beneath the Blue Ensign. Previously, admirals had been ranked by the colour of their squadrons (in order of seniority: red, white, and blue); they now flew the cross of St George from the main, the fore, or the mizzen mast, indicating full, vice, and rear admiral, respectively. Only the Admiral of the Fleet was permitted to fly the Union Flag from the main mast, although others could do so if the monarch was aboard. Military vessels flew the Union Jack from the bowsprit; merchantmen and the reserve flew an adapted Union Jack with a broad white border.[55]

In effect, by the middle of the nineteenth century, the Union Jack was less a flag than a whole culture. It also had its detractors. Objections to the uses of the Union Jack were, for instance, aired in 1853, with the establishment of the National Association for the Vindication of Scottish Rights. This nationalist group rightly pointed out that the Royal Navy's White Ensign depicted the cross of St George with a Union Jack in the upper hoist, which, as indicated by the 1707 Act of Union, was unconstitutional. Objections were also made about the colours of the flag, as the blue of St Andrew was progressively deepened during the nineteenth century. The azure field of St Andrew was originally meant to represent the sky, but on Victorian Union Jacks was dyed almost black in order to withstand the effects of wind and rain at sea. Despite attracting some five thousand sympathizers to a public meeting in Glasgow, the campaign came to nothing. The problem of St Andrew's blue persisted well into the next century and the grumbling continued. In 1937, a flag-making company sought Admiralty advice for the correct shade in the coronation flags it was manufacturing. The Scottish Office, which had consulted the Lyon King of Arms, recommended azure (sky-blue) in place of the old blue-black dye.

The Union Jack may have quite clearly been a flag of union, of the United Kingdom, but as we have already seen, there was a growing tendency to elide 'England' and 'Britain', treating the Union Jack as the flag of the English. The chorus of 'The Union Jack of Old England' is typical:

> The flag that guides the sailor on his way,
>> The flag that fills all foes with dismay,
> The flag that always carried the sway,
>> The Union Jack of Old England.[56]

By 1845, the working-class poet and progressive journalist Eliza Cook could see in the Union Jack the freedom, liberty, courage, and honour that made it unmistakably 'the flag of an *Englishman*' (my emphasis). The second stanza of 'The Englishman' runs:

> There's a flag that waves o'er every sea,
>> No matter when or where;
> And to treat that flag as aught but the free
>> Is more than the strongest dare.
> For the lion-spirits that tread the deck
>> Have carried the palm of the brave;
> And that flag *may* sink with a shot-torn wreck,
>> But never float over a slave;
> Its honour is stainless, deny it who can;
> And this is the flag of an Englishman.[57]

Even these 'lion-spirits that tread the deck' recall the three lions: the heraldic device of the English monarch.

There were advantages to this Anglicization. Abroad, questions of British identity carried profound implications. Should all British subjects share similar human values, rights, and opportunities? Were all British subjects equal, or were some Britons now slaves? Slavery was already illegal in England, and Lord Mansfield had famously declared in 1772 that the air of England was too pure to be breathed by a slave: any slaves who set foot on English ground were instantly freed. The sentiments were celebrated by the abolitionist poet William Cowper in *The Task*:

> Slaves cannot breathe in England; if their lungs
> Receive our air, that moment they are free;
> They touch our country, and their shackles fall.
> (II, 40–2)

Such declarations helped abolitionists in their attempts to extend English values over the Empire. Nineteenth-century Britain swiftly withdrew from the slave trade (1807), and in 1833 finally freed slaves on its West Indian plantations.

British identity became irrepressibly annexed by and then modelled on English identity. The fact is that the English had submerged far more of their own national character, culture, and history into the British Empire than did the other partners in the union, to the extent that today England lacks basic institutions such as a national library or museum, having built instead the *British* Library and the *British* Museum, while simultaneously supporting, for example, the National Libraries of Scotland, Ireland, and Wales. This British identity needed to be capacious to include not just the United Kingdom, but all the colonies as well. Britons needed to be multifarious and hybrid, moderate and liberal, as well as capitalist and, ideally, Protestant Anglican – believing themselves to be blessed by providence. All of this is reminiscent of the characteristic English mongrel identity. Not only was England by far the biggest and most industrially advanced of the four nations, capable of making the largest investments in colonial trading and thereby standing to reap the biggest rewards, it also believed it could offer the basis of a national character.

Given the massive economic, social, cultural, and psychological investment that the English made in the union in the nineteenth century, England and Britain are unlikely ever to become wholly separable. The historian James Bryce commented in 1887 that 'An Englishman has but one patriotism because England and the United Kingdom are to him practically the same thing', and a few years later Robert Baden-Powell had to revise *Scouting for Boys* before it went to press, replacing each reference to 'England' in his manuscript with 'Britain'.[58]

On the other hand, the merging of English with British identity meant that it was the English who received most criticism for the gigantic tub-thumping that often accompanied extravagant outbreaks of patriotism, and who were blamed for the crimes of colonialism. Cook's 'The Englishman' was an unequivocal declaration of all-round superiority, and thereby a justification for maintaining and enlarging the British Empire. It was frequently reprinted and its persistent popularity is indicated by the fact that it was still being parodied over thirty years after its first publication.

On 9 November 1878, *Punch* printed 'The Jingo-Englishman'. The first two stanzas followed Eliza Cook's original poem closely, demonstrating how effectively the imagery of the Union Jack could be inverted by making the verse effectively a call of distress:

> There's a Land that's Cock of Creation's walk,
>   Though it is but a tiny isle,
> And to hear its brag, and its tall tall talk,
>   Might make e'en *Bombastes* smile.
> It holds itself holiest, first in fight,
>   Most brave, most wise, most strong,
> And will n'er admit what it fancies right
>   Can by any chance be wrong.
> 'Tis the pink of perfection, deny it who can,
> The Home of the Jingo-Englishman!
>
> There's a Flag that floats o'er every sea,
>   And claims to control the brine;
> And if any dare hint that it makes too free,
>   The result is a deuce of a shine.
> For the bouncing boys who walk the deck
>   Deem the Ocean their own little lot,
> And if foreign fools at their pride should check,
>   They will catch it exceedingly hot.
> Right-divine's in its bunting, deny it who can,
> Is the Flag of the Jingo-Englishman!

The unedifying and facile reduction of the British Empire to these bullying tones of English national prejudice made a favourite topic in *Punch*. The magazine particularly derided 'Jingo-ists' – supporters of bellicose military action. Jingoism was typified by the Prime Minister,

Benjamin 'Dizzy' Disraeli (by then Lord Beaconsfield), who had recently deployed the Royal Navy to Constantinople to halt Russian advances in Turkey. The name derived from G. W. Hunt's blatant music-hall song:

> We don't want to fight,
>
> But by Jingo if we do,
>
> We've got the ships,
>
> We've got the men,
>
> And got the money too.
>
> We've fought the Bear before,
>
> And while we're Britons true,
>
> The Russians shall not have Constantinople.

The feigned reluctance disguising barely repressed enthusiasm to go to war was also apparent in the popular song 'Don't Wake the Lion of Old England!', which warned that although 'We don't want a bother, we don't want to fight, … We expect to have a finger in the pie, / Before many weeks are gone'. The conflict was similarly stylized as the British lion savaging the Russian bear:

> The Russians will soon hear the British Lion roar,
>
>   If they meddle with the flag of Old England.[59]

This was the darker side of the Union Jack. For many, it was already menacing and grim, a herald of strife, a flag of death. The satirist Robert Williams Buchanan made a scathing attack on the late-Victorian scramble for Africa, evoking the image of the flag as an ominous threat, a threat posed explicitly by England. The enterprise was being managed through private companies, and his poem 'The Charter'd Companie'

(1899) includes the Devil reciting the following stanza:

> 'The Flag of England still doth blow
>   and flings the sunlight back,
> But the line that creepeth now below
>   is changed to a line of black!
> Wherever the Flag of England blows,
>   down go all other flags,
> Wherever the line of black print goes,
>   the British Bulldog brags!
> The newspaper, my dear, is best
>   to further such work as mine, –
> My blessing rest, north, south, east, west,
>   on the thin black penny-a-line!
> For my work is done 'neath moon or sun,
>   by men and not by me,
> Now I've changed myself, in the reign of the
>   Guelph, to a Charter'd Companie!'[60]

The premier banner of the Empire could not only be appropriated to condemn the perfidious English, however – it was the most obvious and often the most vulnerable target for commentators and critics. Buchanan was on the attack again in 'The Union' (1901), which cast the union of Great Britain and Ireland as being held together by nothing more substantial than 'pride and hate':

> Back rings that cry from far away
>   To fill the Motherland,
> Where 'neath the Union Jack this day

Both false and true men stand –

Hark to the foes of all things free,

    Who, arm'd in hate, intone:

    'The Union! let our war-cry be

    That word, and that alone!'[61]

Other defamations of the flag were less bitter, more melancholy. In 1900, *Punch* criticized the travel agent Thomas Cook for advertising tours of the battlefields of the Boer War. 'The Tourist and the Flag' inverts the Union Jack as a sign of unification and the spread of civilization and Christianity, and instead sees it as the occasion of so much grim litter. The poem begins,

O flag! whose benefits so fair

We would with others freely share –

Aye, forcing on reluctant nations,

At bayonet point, their own salvations,

And bidding them accept our mission

On pain of instant demolition –

and concludes,

O flag! O tourist! Powers twain

That all the world resists in vain,

When 'neath the one the other picks

The wings and legs of festive chicks,

And strews the battlefield with bones,

Newspapers, orange peel, plum stones –

Then is the reign of darkness done,

And Freedom's fight is fought and won.[62]

The Union Jack exerted itself so powerfully on the imagination, though, that the most subtle evocations of the flag were able to combine triumphalism, pride, sacrifice, and futility within the complexity of the triple cross. The poignant account of the Siege of Lucknow of 1857 is a case in point. Lucknow was one of the most celebrated defences of the Indian Mutiny and exemplified the unvanquishable spirit of the British Empire. The British held the Lucknow Residency for three months before they were relieved, and throughout this heroic resistance the Union Jack flew day and night, defying Indian attempts to shoot it down.

Lucknow became a touchstone of the imperial spirit. General Sir Henry Havelock had attempted to relieve Lucknow, but having arrived his force was too weak and he died shortly afterwards. In 1770 Benjamin West had famously depicted General Wolfe expiring beneath a furled Union Jack flag. This tableau of the national standard in mourning for a victorious but dying hero became a popular locus classicus for similar episodes, tying the image of the flag to both death and glory. Almost ninety years on, the national flag was attending to Havelock in the same way: 'England's banners o'er him wave –/ Dead, he keeps the realm he saved'.[63] Lucknow was also the occasion of several epic paintings, such as Edward Armitage's *Retribution* (1858), T. J. Barker's *The Relief of Lucknow* (1859), and George Jones's *Lucknow* (1865), which provided the templates for popular engravings of the Indian Mutiny.[64]

In memory of the defence, the flag was not lowered over the ruins of Lucknow Residency for another ninety years: the one place in the Empire to be given this privilege. Finally, at midnight on 13 August

1947, on the very eve of Indian independence, a British warrant officer led a party of soldiers to the ruins of the Residency. They quietly lowered the flag, and the next evening sappers took down the flagpole and filled in the foundations. The site had become sacrosanct, and no other flag would be permitted to fly there.[65]

The most renowned use of the motif of the ever-flying flag at Lucknow is Tennyson's poem 'The Defence of Lucknow' (1878):

> Banner of England, not for a season,
>> O banner of Britain, hast thou
> Floated in conquering battle or flapt
>> to the battle-cry!
> Never with mightier glory than when
>> we had reared thee on high
> Flying at top of the roofs in the ghastly
>> siege of Lucknow –
> Shot through the staff or the halyard,
>> but ever we raised thee anew,
> And ever upon the topmost roof our
>> banner of England blew.
>
> (1–6)

Each stanza ends with a variation of the line 'And ever upon the topmost roof our banner of England blew', wafting like a refrain through the poem. Here the Union Jack is an impossibly fragile reminder of the British Empire, where loyalty and allegiance hang by just a thread. Thirteen years later, Rudyard Kipling used similar imagery in 'The English Flag'. The four winds describe the 'Flag of

England [*sic*]' being borne to the ends of the earth by the British Empire: 'Go forth, for it is there!' The South Wind, for example, tells of its encounters with the ever flying flag:

> 'I have wrenched it free from the halliards to hang
>> for a wisp on the Horn;
> I have chased it north to the Lizard – ribboned and
>> rolled and torn;
> I have spread its folds o'er the dying, adrift in a hopeless sea;
> I have hurled it swift on the slaver, and seen the
>> slaves set free.

> 'My basking sunfish know it, and wheeling albatross,
> Where the lone wave fills with fire beneath the
>> Southern Cross.
> Where is the Flag of England? Ye have but my reefs to dare,
> Ye have but my seas to furrow. Go forth, for it is there!'
> (29–36)

Notwithstanding the vilifications of warmongers published in *Punch* and elsewhere, the public were, of course, eager to show their support for soldiers during Britain's frequent military campaigns of the period. A case in point is the Boer War (1899–1902), especially the commemoration of the Relief of Mafeking (announced on 18 May 1900), and the eventual peace (2 June 1902). The Relief of Mafeking in particular caused hysterical 'mafficking': T. W. H. Crosland, for example, described a group of Jewish immigrants at his local café singing 'God Save the King' and waving a Union Jack, and such displays of patriotic fervour provoked a lively correspondence regarding the correct use of flags.[66] Then, as now, flags were flown indiscriminately – from the Union Jack (mistakenly flown half the time upside-down) to the royal flag of Scotland and even the inverted French Tricolour, 'now displayed as a British emblem in rural districts'.[67] It became apparent that despite the ubiquity of the Union Jack in Victorian culture, very few actually knew how it was designed or supposed to be flown: 'The makers seem, as a rule, to know nothing of the matter.'[68] The medieval scholar Walter Skeat wrote a paper explaining how the flag should be constructed, paying special attention to fimbriation and to the counterchanged saltire of St Patrick; such subtleties were in fact ignored in many popular nineteenth-century depictions of the flag, in which it is presented as symmetrical.

There was also debate as to whether the Union Jack could be flown at all by citizens on land. According to the antiquarian Emanuel Green, the Union Jack was restricted to the Royal Navy and the British Army, and the White or St George's Ensign to the navy; 'there remains for general purposes the Red Ensign as the National flag, and this only should be generally and publicly used'.[69] The suggestion was confirmed by Baden-Powell, who argued that strictly speaking, only the army and government buildings should fly the Union Jack; private households should fly the Red Ensign.[70] The Merchant Shipping (Colours) Act of 1894 had perhaps inadvertently confirmed this opinion:

> The red ensign usually worn by merchant ships, without any defacement or modification whatsoever, is hereby declared to be the proper national colours for all ships and boats belonging to any British subject, except in the case of Her Majesty's ships or boats, or

in the case of any other ship or boat for the time being allowed to wear any other national colours in pursuance of a warrant from Her Majesty or from the Admiralty. If any distinctive national colours except such red ensign, or except the Union Jack with a white border, or if any colours usually worn by Her Majesty's ships, &c ... are or is hoisted on board any ship ... without warrant ... for each offence ... a fine not exceeding five hundred pounds.[71]

Some commentators described the Union Jack as 'the Standard of Empire'.[72] Baden-Powell agreed: the Union Jack embodied the imperial ethos – it was not to be raised lightly:

The Union Jack stands for something more than only the Union of England, Ireland, and Scotland – it means the Union of Great Britain with all our Colonies across the seas; and it also means closer comradeship with our brothers in those Colonies, and between ourselves at home. We must all be bricks in the wall of that great edifice – the British Empire – and we must be careful that we do not let our differences of opinion on politics or other questions grow so strong as to divide us. We must still stick shoulder to shoulder as Britons if we want to keep our position among the nations; and we must make ourselves the best men in the world for honour and goodness to others so that we may DESERVE to keep that position.[73]

Others, however, declared that the Union Jack was specifically *not* 'The flag of the Commonwealth' but 'the fighting emblem of the Sovereign'.[74]

From 1902, there was a long-running discussion on the letters page of *The Times* debating which flags could be flown on land, and by whom.[75] A congregation in Folkestone had spent £10 on a royal standard with which to celebrate the coronation of Edward VII, but the King's Private Secretary had forbidden them to fly it from the church tower, although they were informed by him that they could fly the Union Jack. This renewed the dispute about whether the correct flag to fly by civilians on land should be the Red Ensign rather than the Union Jack – a dispute which eventually reached the House of Commons. The Garter King of Arms minuted that on the question of what flag non-arms-bearing civilians were permitted to fly, 'There is no flag in existence answering to this general description', but that the royal standard and Union Jack could be displayed during periods of national rejoicing.[76] Two days later, the Prime Minister, A. J. Balfour, declined an invitation to legislate, and concluded it 'is best left, as hitherto, to the guidance of custom and good taste'.[77] It is worth noting that in the same year, Admiralty Circular 1535 declared that the terms 'Union Flag' and 'Union Jack' were interchangeable and that both were correct.

Yet significant doubt remained concerning whether citizens were obliged to fly the Red Ensign or permitted to fly the Union Jack. In 1908, following reports that the police had been removing Union Jacks, Earl Howe sought clarification from the government. He received the following reply from the Earl of Crewe:

Many of us know that there has existed in the public mind a great confusion as to what flag may be flown and what may not. At one time it was thought that the Royal Standard could be flown by

anyone and everywhere. We now know that this is not the case, and
that the Royal Standard is the personal flag of the Sovereign, and
cannot be flown without His Majesty's permission, which is only
granted when either the King or Queen is present. A very different
state of things applies to the Union Jack. A Union Jack should be
regarded as the national flag, and undoubtedly may be flown on land
by all His Majesty's subjects.[78]

The Earl of Meath observed, 'My Lords ... it is rather curious that a
British citizen is about the only one who is not quite certain under what
flag he stands as a private citizen.'

Yet even this met with objection, as the Lords Lieutenant of the
Counties flew the Union Jack as a declaration of their office as the personal representative of the monarch. In 1911, they were granted a
Union Jack with a horizontal sword. By 1917, the confusion had
reached the colonies. The Union Jack was required to be flown from
the colonial Government House, but potentially that would not now be
distinguishable from any other house. This quandary was resolved by
stipulating that colonial governors should fly their maritime Union
Jacks (to which the badge of the colony had been added) on land.

Edward VII, meanwhile, tried to restrict both the use of the royal
standard and the adoption of the Scottish royal banner as the 'Scotch
Standard', which had been popularly flown throughout the nineteenth
century. He proposed a personal version, with his cipher and crown, to
be protected by the 1883 Trade Mark Act, but the Board of Trade
demurred – its authority did not stretch so far. In 1906, the Admiralty,
the War Office, the Home Office, and the Scottish Office jointly

directed that the royal standard should only be flown when the monarch was personally present; police forces were advised to restrict its use by private citizens. However, by 1907 parliamentary discussion suggested that the police should not prosecute misuse of the royal banner over-zealously, and the Scottish Patriotic Association suggested adopting the red lion as the national flag in its 1912 pamphlet *The Lion Rampant, Whose Is It?* In the same year, Dugald Ferguson published a long poem on 'The Flag of Scotland', which described how the silver saltire and the red lion remained inspiring either as individual emblems or as constituents of the Union Jack and the royal standard:

> May still for Scotland's Lion flag in gracious love vouchsafe
> That, borne above the tides of Time, it yet may prouder wave,
> And yearly widening in range, more glorious may it soar
> As herald of the Gospel's gift to ev'ry heathen shore.
> Now intertwined with England's red and Erin's emerald green,
> The Scottish Lion rears upon the flag of Ocean's Queen;
> And, terrible in might combined, the Union Jack unfurled
> Floats everywhere, a tow'r for Truth, a beacon to the world.[79]

Britannia too remained a potent symbol of the Empire. Her image became fixed on banknotes and on stamps, a fitting emblem of imperial trade and communication. Britannia's crested helmet was usually pushed back to reveal her face, she sat beside a large shield emblazoned with the Union Jack, she carried a spear or, more commonly, a trident, and occasionally held an olive branch as well; her faithful lion was often present, sometimes curled at her feet. Indeed, in the nineteenth century, 'the Mother of Nations, / Calm-hearted and tranquil-eyed' was probably the most recognized heroine across the globe.[80] The peoples of the Empire were encouraged to identify with Britannia, and to identify Britannia with Queen Victoria, as had been the case with Queen Elizabeth some three hundred years before. For her, the Empire declared it would fight and die for the Union Jack. Britannia not only regularly appeared in *Punch*, much as she had in prints the previous century, but literally came to life. By the turn of the century, renditions of 'Land of Hope and Glory' and the celebrations on the Last Night of the Proms were led by singers dressed as Britannia.[81]

The establishment of Empire Day on 24 May 1904 gave the opportunity for annual displays of Britannic flag-waving.* In the wake of the continuing debates about the national flag, card representations of the Union Jack became popular, explaining, in the words of one, *What All Should Know About the Union Jack*.[82] *The Union Jack Explained* is typical of such ephemera: it is approximately two by three and a half inches and consists of leaves that fold out to show the three elements that made up the union – cutouts of the crosses of Sts George, Andrew, and Patrick – that could then be laid over each other to build up in turn the first and second Union Flags.[83] The Boy Scout and Girl Guide movements also provided such *Union Jack Cards*, explaining how the flag was composed and how to fly it correctly.[84] Similarly, *The Union Jack: Its History and Description* remarks of the counter-changed spacing and fimbriation, 'In cheap and carelessly made flags this important distinction is often conspicuous by its absence.'[85]

---

* Empire Day was celebrated 1904–58, and was then replaced with Commonwealth Day until 1965; it is now celebrated on the second Monday in March.

But for all their show of imperial pride, these pocket-sized lessons in vexillology were really little more than advertising opportunities: *The Union Jack Explained*, for instance, was promotional material for Palmer Tyres. These advertisements left no doubt how the Union Jack should be interpreted,

> Whenever you see a British Flag remember:–
> The pneumatic tyre was a British invention.
> The pneumatic tyre made motoring possible.
> The original pneumatic tyre was a Dunlop.[86]

Likewise, a folded souvenir card, *An Empire Day Resolution for British Soldiers & Sailors* (*c.* 1908), also made one's duty quite clear:

> On Empire Day every patriotic Briton renews his resolution to do his utmost to hold the British Empire intact, and to strengthen the bonds which bind the scattered parts of the King's Empire together.
> In no better way can he help in so doing than by becoming a subscriber to the Over-Seas 'Daily Mail'…[87]

After everything that had happened in the previous hundred years, the Union Jack had finally reached the acme of capitalism: it had become an unrivalled advertising opportunity. In the next century, the flag would be resanctified with blood as an enduring banner of hope; it would also become a design classic.

VII TWO WORLD WARS AND
ONE WORLD CUP

Draw the blinds and watch the show,
Heard it on the radio, saw it on the news today
I heard the lonely people say,
'There's a great big crack in the Union Jack.'
'There's a great big crack in the Union Jack.'

Suede, 'Crack in the Union Jack' (1999)

ON 1 JULY 1907, His Majesty the King, Edward VII, opened the Union
Jack Club, a residential club for non-commissioned members of the
British armed forces. Soldiers and sailors could refresh themselves in
the Waterloo Rooms, where there was a canteen and a bar, and in case
the serviceman 'arrived from some distant part of the United Kingdom,
and may therefore require tonsorial attention', the Club had its own
barber for the 'removal of superfluous hair either from head or chin'.[1]
The event was marked by the publication of *The Flag*, sponsored by the
Daily Mail. This ultra-patriotic souvenir includes prose by Rudyard
Kipling and verses such as 'The Flag of England' by Alfred Austin,

who was by now Poet Laureate:

> Unfurl the Flag of England,
>> And fling it to the breeze,
> Beloved by British hearts at home,
>> And those Beyond the Seas;
> The symbol, as in ages gone,
>> Of reverence for the Right,
> That leads men ever on and on
>> Through Liberty to Light.
>
> Its folds to all of Friendship speak,
>> Of enmity to none,
> Protection for the wronged and weak,
>> Wherever shines the sun.
> And when the 'Union Jack' is seen
>> Rippling o'er wave and wind,
> Men hail it, for its tidings mean
>> Peace unto all Mankind.
>
> God guard the Flag of England,
>> The Empire, and the Throne,
> And sister Nations far away
>> In every sea and zone!
> And when at freshening dawn it flies
>> Anew beneath the sky,
> Vow we once more, should need arise,
>> To strike for it, and die.[2]

Austin's verse is very much in the tradition of popular Union Jackist verse – a tradition that in the face of impending war would continue with collections such as Frederick James Johnston-Smith's oft-reprinted *Union Jack Lyrics and a Foreword concerning the Flag* (1914). 'THE purpose of this little book is the promotion of Imperial patriotism, brotherhood and loyalty,' Johnston-Smith proclaimed.[3] Most of his verses invoked the Union Jack and the flags of the Commonwealth in the familiar tones of imperial loyalty and personal sacrifice, and the volume's epigraph reminded the reader that, in contrast to countries such as America, the Empire had abolished slavery long ago. Freedom was in the very fabric of the Union Jack:

> 'TIS BUT A THING OF COLOURS –
>
> 'TIS BUT A TATTERED RAG!
>
> BUT EYES OF SLAVES GROW BRIGHTER
>
> WHEN THEY SEE THE BRITISH FLAG.[4]

The flag's popularity continued in patriotic works such Madame Henri Curchard's *The Union Jack* (1915), which included a title poem and 'The Old Flag', educational works such as Cecil Crofts's *ABC of the Union Jack* (*c.* 1915), music-hall songs ('The Dear Old Union Jack', *c.* 1917), a song for Girl Guides (which described each of the three crosses and also included the leek of St David for good measure), a pageant (*The Flag of the Free* by Una Norris, *c.* 1928*), and *The Union*

---

* *The Flag of the Free* includes the flags of the Dominions and also, bearing in mind that it was still part of the Empire, the Tricolour of the Irish Free State, and the flag of Ulster (a red hand on the first Union Flag).

Jack Bazaar Cookery Book (undated).[5] Kensitas ran a series of forty-eight cigarette cards featuring flags of the British Empire, and silk cards were produced by B.D.V. Cigarettes.

On this evidence, the status of the flag was very much as it had been at the end of the nineteenth century. The men who served under the Union Jack, who frequented the Union Jack Club, and about whom these verses and songs were written were, in the popular imagination, the same men who had served in the Boer War (1899–1902): men who mixed imperial military expertise with a maverick canniness acquired from indigenous peoples. It was this cross-bred spirit that Robert Baden-Powell captured in *Scouting for Boys* (1908), one of the most idiosyncratic and contradictory books of the period. Baden-Powell's work is a collage of conventional British soldiery and native guerrilla tactics borrowed from every corner of the Empire – tactics that had often been used against the British Army itself. The colonies are described by Baden-Powell as wellsprings of cunning ingenuity, which he welcomes as particular branches of the same imperial family: in a poster for the 1920 Great Jamboree Pageant of 'The Genesis of Scouting', Sikhs, Zulus, Aborigines, and even an American Indian were pictured dancing around a maypole from which fluttered a Union Jack.[6] Naturally the book instructed how the flag should be hoisted and saluted in the morning and how it should be properly flown, in addition to laying out such helpful advice as King Arthur's chivalric code of conduct. Baden-Powell's handbook survives to this day as a glimpse of the brotherhood of the British Empire at play, training up the next generation of chaps, keen as mustard, not knowing that they were destined for a very different sort of battlefield.

The summer before the outbreak of the Great War in 1914 was characterized by 'hysteria', as one witness put it: 'A vast procession jammed the road from side to side, everyone waving flags and singing patriotic songs.'[7] Although the war would be fought, as so often before, in France and Belgium, the enemy was now German. By the late nineteenth century, Germany had replaced France as the alien power against which Great Britain defined itself. Britain found herself in alliance with the French and the Russians against the Austro-Hungarian Empire and recently unified Germany, and despite Queen Victoria's marriage to the German prince Albert, her grandson George V would prudently change their Teutonic name, Saxe-Coburg-Gotha, to the thoroughly English appellation Windsor.

When world war did finally – perhaps inevitably – break out in 1914, the old imperial training, like the imperial adventure itself, proved of little help. The British colonial project, along with all its accompanying rhetoric and professed idealism, its hardships and sacrifices, and its huge profits, disappeared almost overnight. Indeed, the rapidity with which the massive architecture of Victorian imperial ideals vanished is indicated by the story of one officer who, encouraging his men with high talk of 'the Empire', was taken aback to find that they thought he was referring to some sort of entertainment palace. The men in the trenches on the Western Front could not afford to expend their energies on such distant, lofty ideals, and, much like their medieval forebears, they found their loyalties lay in comradeship and in reviving the old heroes.[8]

St George returned to the field of battle once more. He now extended his supernatural patronage to the British, rather than just the English, army, and in Great War posters, Britain was popularly symbolized as St

George confronting the Prussian dragon and protecting defenceless women and children. He also apparently literally appeared, as he had first done over eight hundred years before. Arthur Machen's short story 'The Bowmen', which was first published in the London *Evening News*, described how in 1914 St George had sent Agincourt longbowmen to defend the British Army during the retreat from Mons. The origin of the 'Angels of Mons' legends lies in this fiction, which was rapidly taken as fact and treated as a vestige of Britain's divinity. The raid on Zeebrugge, launched on the saint's day in 1918, began with the signal 'St George for England'. Eight Victoria Crosses were awarded for bravery that night and St George currently looks out over the cemetery where most of the 170 killed during the raid are buried. After the war, St George was commonly raised on memorials, as if attempting to dignify the slaughter of the trenches with the majesty of chivalry, and his feast day was marked with remembrance services, Boy Scout parades, mumming pageants, and by flying the flag.

The Union Jack played its part at the front, flying higher than it had ever flown before. When the First World War started, aircraft such as the Bristol Scout carried Union Jack markings on their wings and, occasionally, on the fuselage. This insignia was never standardized, however, and before long, red, white, and blue roundels adorned the wings and fuselages of British aeroplanes while vertical stripes in the same colours featured on their rudders. But bright flags were not welcome in the mud and slime of the trenches among the khaki-clad soldiers, and it was on the home front that the Union Jack was most recognizable. Perhaps for want of a more contemporary symbol of national unity, civilians focused on the flag. In August 1914, a Welsh housewife raised £10 for the National Relief Fund by selling miniature Union Jacks; shortly afterwards a Glaswegian, Mrs Morrison, proposed Union Jack Day. The campaign to 'Support the colours by wearing the colours' rapidly spread to other cities and became an established model of fund-raising during the First World War. The first national flag day was on 3 October 1914, in aid of Belgium. Flags were initially made of fabric but subsequently of paper and tended to adapt national flags, emblems, and military ensigns, sometimes with mottoes added, such as 'Bravo Belgium' or, for the Red Cross, 'Our Day'. Bandaged service-men were depicted standing before the colours, sometimes giving the thumbs-up sign. The Union Jack was obviously a popular choice for a flag day, but with the proliferation of different themes, flags were printed for different services (for example, the White Ensign for the Royal Navy), as well as for each of the separate countries of the union – both the crosses of Sts George and Andrew, and national badges such as the Welsh dragon and the Irish harp. A common figure on the flags is also a patriotic gentleman in a white-lapelled blue suit, with white shirt and red tie.

The eventual armistice on 11 November 1918 was greeted by a 'GREAT DISPLAY OF FLAGS', *The Times* announcing that the whole of London was 'beflagged': 'Never was so complete a show of really handsome bunting'.[9] But the union and the Empire were already cracking. Over half a million Scots fought in the First World War, of whom over a quarter died. Likewise the Welsh fought bravely along-side the English, as they had done for over five hundred years, and the Australians were so keen that conscription was not required. Moreover, when war began, about a third of British forces stationed in France were Indian, and over a million Indians eventually served. The first black officer in the British armed services also fought in the Great War: Walter Tull, the grandson of a Barbadian slave and a professional football player for Northampton Town. He was eventually killed in action in 1918.[10] But the Great War brought Britain's already troubled relationship with Ireland to crisis point. Lloyd George decided not to impose conscription on Ireland for the simple reason that he did not believe it could be enforced. The Irish Home Rule Bill was passed in 1914, revoking the union of 1801, although it was suspended for the duration of the war. Some Irish nationalists rallied to Britain and 140,000 joined up to die on the fields of France and Belgium.[11] Others sued for German aid in the Republican cause: Sinn Féin sent Sir Roger Casement to Germany, and the party attempted an armed coup in Dublin in 1916 – the Easter Rising. This eventually led to the Irish Free State (1922–48), which was succeeded by the Republic. The dream of union, which had existed for 1,500 years, was now ending, and the Age of Britain was entering a possibly terminal decline.

This failure of the United Kingdom was both gradual and irreversible, although it would rally one last time. The decline of the union and the collapse of Empire briefly helped to provoke another reassessment of English identity with a renewal of interest in St George in the 1930s, led by the self-proclaimed Englishness of Rudyard Kipling and Edward Elgar – who were both still active – and a generation inspired by English composers such as Ralph Vaughan Williams. But it was to be the nature of British identity that ultimately received a fresh stimulus from the next outbreak of hostilities in 1939. Much as the country had united against Napoleon in the 1790s and 1800s, so Winston

Churchill powerfully proclaimed a specifically British resistance to fascism. It was, in many ways, the last stand, and the rhetoric of heroic futility invoked by Churchill echoed the dimly remembered defences of the Britons against the Vikings, more than ten centuries before. This stand, it seemed, was the final destiny of Britain, a destiny that had been bruited for so long: the thousand years spent consolidating the union had readied Britannia for her confrontation with the Thousand Year Reich. 'This is indeed a grand heroic period,' Churchill growled from the wireless in April 1941, 'and the light of glory shines on you all.' In a sense, he was right – there was little enough resistance to Hitler in France, Stalin had signed a non-aggression pact, and America would not enter the war until December 1941, when Japan attacked Pearl Harbor. And Ireland – now Éire – was neutral.

It is conceivable that, even without the Second World War, Britain would have begun to fragment twenty-five years before it did. As it was, another war with Germany inspired a profound renewal in the idea of the fate of the nation, embracing the whole of Great Britain. This sense was bolstered by the extraordinary speeches of Winston Churchill, the deliverance of the British Expeditionary Force at Dunkirk, and profoundly symbolic images – one of the most telling being that of the apparently miraculous survival of St Paul's during the Blitz. The cathedral stood wreathed in smoke but ever steadfast, an image that became part of the stirring tapestry of 'little Britain' symbolism. The imperial sweep was made homely and domestic: St Paul's was endearingly dubbed 'the parish church of the Empire', and everyday sounds such as the peal of church bells were charged with new meaning – as the signal warning of invasion, bells were not rung from

1939 until after the Battle of El Alamein in October 1942. This was a decisive victory for the British and their allies, and so the church bells at home heralded a turning point in Britain's wartime fortunes. The army that had won the victory in Egypt, General Montgomery's Eighth Army, hoisted the flag in the desert in their own way, calling their newspaper the *Union Jack*.

Mobilization revived the economy, especially in Scotland and Wales, and social and national differences evaporated in a common British solidarity. This unity was possibly in part over-compensating for early attempts at appeasement, although, perhaps appropriately, the pre-war British-Nazi friendship badges produced in Germany depicted an upside-down Union Jack. It did not seem to matter that, in the popular imagination at least, Britain was most frequently represented by images of south-east England: St Paul's, London's East End, the South Downs, and the White Cliffs of Dover. These sites were recognized as being on the front line of the Battle of Britain and the Blitz, and, in the case of the South Coast and Downs, would form the expected beachhead and battleground of any German invasion.

Winston Churchill presented himself as the consummate Briton. He may have been born to an American mother of Iroquois descent and was often taken as the quintessential Englishman, but Churchill was committed to extolling the resilience of Britain as a whole and the British as a single people during the dark days of 1940. From the very outbreak of war, in fact, the emphasis was on *Britain* standing against Germany. No chances could be taken with other loyalties within the British Isles. On 13 May 1940, for instance, Churchill addressed the House of Commons in the sonorous tones of union and Empire:

You ask, What is our aim? I can answer in one word: Victory – victory at all costs, victory in spite of all terror, victory, however long and hard the road may be; for without victory, there is no survival. Let that be realised; no survival for the British Empire; no survival for all that the British Empire has stood for, no survival for the urge and impulse of the ages, that mankind will move forwards towards its goal. But I take up my task with buoyancy and hope. I feel sure that our cause will not be suffered to fail among men. At this time I feel entitled to claim the aid of all, and I say, 'Come, then, let us go forward together with our united strength.'[12]

There were, however, serious threats to this united strength. Nationalist groups within the union were potential fifth columnists: both Scottish National Party and Plaid Cymru members and sympathizers refused conscription and expressed their support for a Nazi invasion of England via Scotland and Wales respectively, on condition of some sort of subsequent national independence – disgracefully, the Welsh nationalists went so far as to send an official delegation to Berlin in 1940. Worse still, the IRA openly supported the Nazis and, following a declaration of war on 16 January 1939, launched a bombing campaign against mainland Britain. This – the S-Plan – killed seven civilians and wounded over a hundred others before the bombers were arrested and the ringleaders executed.

Irish history can, of course, be read as a history of continuing resistance and rebellion. The Easter Rising and the terrorism of the twentieth century (in 1920–21 in Ireland, and on mainland Britain from 1939 to 1941 and again from 1973 onwards) can be seen as part of a struggle for self-determination that has been waged since the Anglo-Norman campaigns six centuries before. Yet the overtures made to Germany in 1916 and, later, to the Nazis poison any of the more romanticized claims for liberty and independence. The Irish government referred to the Second World War merely as 'The Emergency', although 40,000 citizens of Éire defied their Prime Minister, Eamon de Valera, and enlisted to fight (shockingly, they received no official recognition until 1995). Conscription was not imposed on Northern Ireland, but 38,000 still joined up and proved among the most loyal of servicemen, with very low rates of desertion.

The Second World War, however, confirmed Éire's independence from Britain – as well as further souring relations between the North and South. Irish neutrality cost the Allies thousands of lives, as the Royal Navy was refused access to ports that would have increased the range of its ships as they sought to protect the Atlantic convoys from U-boats. And perhaps the most despicable moment was de Valera's personal visit to the German Embassy in Dublin on 2 May 1945 to 'express condolence' at the news of Hitler's death. Ireland might have been overtly neutral, but moral blindness is certainly not a condition of neutrality, and by the time of de Valera's call to the German Embassy the first Nazi death camps had already been revealed to the world. With de Valera's actions apparently almost condoning genocide, Churchill's victory speech retrospectively threatened that Ireland could (and perhaps should) have been occupied by the British government during the course of the war. This unwittingly gave de Valera the chance to respond to this threatened breach of neutrality by seizing Churchill's arguments in a way that offered no possibility of reconciliation or reunion:

Mr. Churchill is proud of Britain's stand alone, after France had fallen and before America entered the war. Could he not find in his heart the generosity to acknowledge that there is a small nation that stood alone, not for one year or two, but for several hundred years against aggression, that endured spoilations, famines, massacres in endless succession, that was clubbed many times into insensibility, but that each time on returning consciousness took up the fight anew, a small nation that could never be got to accept defeat and has never surrendered her soul?[13]

Soon after the war, in 1949, Éire became wholly independent of the British Empire as the Republic of Ireland. Despite Éire's independence from Britain, however, two million Irish citizens living in the United Kingdom remained eligible to vote in British parliamentary elections; it took the Irish government over sixty years to reciprocate the privilege (i.e. in 1984).[14]

The Germans capitalized on such dissent by setting up the pro-nationalist propaganda radio stations Radio Caledonia, Welsh Freedom Station, and Irland Redaktion, and they transmitted broadcasts by the notorious Lord Haw-Haw (William Joyce), who was heard regularly on the Reichsrundfunk's English-language service, the New British Broadcasting Station.[15] In response, the BBC fostered a sense of British and imperial unity throughout the war by deploying a range of broadcasters, from intellectuals such as E. M. Forster to singers such as Vera Lynn – hence the outburst of savage hatred against P. G. Wodehouse, who, following his capture in France, was duped into making a short series of radio talks, which the Nazi propaganda machine aired in America. Wodehouse, innocent of any collaboration, was nevertheless denounced as a traitor and did not return to Britain after the war. The Germans seemed to have annexed the inimitable post-imperial English spirit of Jeeves and Wooster, the Empress of Blandings, and the membership of the Drones Club; Wodehouse had effectively committed cultural treason.*

English nationalism posed its own problems. It was a term actively discouraged by the government during the Second World War, despite the institution of the George Cross on 24 September 1940. This medal carries an image of St George slaying the dragon, and is awarded for acts of the most conspicuous gallantry; it was famously conferred on the island of Malta in 1942 and appears on the Maltese flag.† Yet significantly, it was during the Second World War that for the first time in centuries, St George did not consistently appear in the cause of the Allies, but was also enlisted by the Axis powers. The anti-Bolshevik fascist John Amery formed the Legion of St George, enrolled from Nazi sympathizers among Allied prisoners of war; between thirty and forty joined him. The recruiting poster for this band of traitors showed the Union Jack being carried alongside a swastika banner by Aryan soldiers, above the slogan 'OUR FLAG IS GOING FORWARD TOO'. The legion was later renamed the British Free Corps and became part of the SS, identified by Union Jack and three-lion badges. This attempted Nazification of St George was a good reason for discouraging

---

* An MI5 investigation later confirmed Wodehouse's innocence.

† The George Cross is second only to the Victoria Cross, by virtue of the fact that it is awarded for acts that are not directly 'in the face of the enemy'.

expressions of a separate English identity, to the extent that a radio producer for the Home Service commented in 1943 that 'nine out of ten people haven't the least idea who St George was and don't care anyway'.[16] It was only later in 1951 that the chapel of remembrance at Biggin Hill, an RAF fighter station and a mainstay during the Battle of Britain, was dedicated to the national saint. Tainted by such Nazi associations, St George went into hibernation for several decades.

But despite threats from Scottish, Irish, and Welsh separatism, from Nazi sympathizers, and from the enemy appropriation of key icons, the unity of Great Britain was emphatically and perpetually stressed throughout the period of hostilities. Indeed, so profound was that unity that the war almost re-created the huge twelfth-century kingdom of the Angevins that had so haunted the imagination of medieval English kings. On 16 June 1940, the French and British governments merged in a Franco-British Union, which consisted of a single government and common citizenship of the two countries. This union was an attempt to keep France in the war as the Germans advanced relentlessly towards Paris, and was proposed by Jean Monnet of the French Economic Mission to Britain (significantly, Monnet later masterminded European union); Charles de Gaulle, who had arrived in London after successfully halting the Germans at Caumont (28 May), also supported this historically momentous unification. However, before British ministers could leave for France, the French government had been reconstituted and Marshal Pétain was negotiating an armistice with the Nazi leadership, which was duly signed on 22 June. Britain's break with Europe was now total: the country was left without allies, but with most of its old Empire.[17]

Great Britain's geographical as well as political isolation from Europe was a familiar position, reminiscent of military and imperial campaigns stretching back over two hundred years. Geography did save Britain from invasion, but the country also found the resolve and the resources to continue its resistance against Nazi Germany in the Empire – the slogan for Empire Day in 1941 being 'One King, One Flag, One Fleet, One Empire'.[18] Over four million Asian and Commonwealth citizens volunteered to fight for the Allies, two and a half million of whom were from India. Twelve thousand West Indians joined up and mainly fought with the RAF, and many West Indians who later arrived on the first immigration voyage aboard the *Empire Windrush* following the Nationality Act in 1948 were demobbed servicemen.

One of the more positive definitions of Britishness to emerge from the Second World War, therefore, was that the rights of black Africans, West Indians, and Asians seemed to be confirmed. In direct contrast to the disturbing racial segregation of the American armed forces, there was no colour bar in Britain, and many non-white Britons now achieved high rank and were decorated. The British government resisted American efforts to impose segregation, and the Minister for Information simply declared that the millions of the king's black subjects were, of course, 'British citizens' who enjoyed 'the same rights as Englishmen'.[19] Asked about American troops billeted locally, a West Country farmer was reported as saying about the institutional racism of their army, 'I love the Americans – but I don't like those white ones they've brought with them.'[20]

The war united Britain because it was clear to all but the lunatic nationalist fringe that there was a common enemy: it was a black-and-white issue, one subsequently confirmed in the most horrifying and unequivocal way by the discovery of the death camps. These chilling revelations completely undermined the idea that the German people had merely been the victims of an evil gang of Nazi thugs who had somehow come to power and steered the country on its fatal course. In the final stages of the war, little distinction was made between a Nazi and a German – to the extent that Churchill alarmingly recommended that all German males should be castrated.[21]

The end of the war in Europe was signalled by raising the Union Jack over Berlin, described as a 'symbolic unfurling'.[22] Victory crowds surrounded Buckingham Palace and Westminster, which were bathed in light, but one image seemed to float in the air: 'a striking and, to many people, most moving sight in that direction was the great spotlit Union Jack that floated serenely over the lofty Victoria Tower.'[23] There had been some debate over the national flag and the constitutional right of private citizens to fly it before the outbreak of war. On 27 June 1933, replying to a question about whether private citizens were forbidden to fly the Union Jack for the forthcoming Silver Jubilee of George V in 1935, Sir John Gilmour, the Home Secretary, commented, 'No, Sir, the Union Flag is the national flag and may properly be flown by any British subject on land.'[24] This is the last official pronouncement on the Union Jack. No single government department or public body has overall jurisdiction over the Union Jack or for any policy concerning it. The Union Jack may be flown at any time.

Despite the tremendous outburst of flag-waving at the end of the war, patriotism was not sustained. The American poet T. S. Eliot warned that Britain faced losing its identity in its victory and argued that it was crucial to continue to promote cultural diversity within the union by maintaining national identities: 'it would be no gain whatever for English culture, for the Welsh, Scots and Irish to become indistinguishable from Englishmen – what *would* happen, of course, is that we would all become indistinguishable featureless "Britons".'[25] What actually happened is that these national identities began to corrode the integrity of Britain. Although the 1948 Nationality Act extended the definition of British identity to all citizens of the Commonwealth, the Irish were at best semi-detached from Great Britain and Éire became a republic in 1949, and Scottish (and, to a lesser degree, Welsh) nationalism was emerging as a powerful post-war phenomenon.

In response to this dissolution, the Festival of Britain (1951) was run as an elaborate attempt to promote cultural and national homogeneity. It was, though, a profoundly insular affair, which did nothing of the sort. There was no international co-operation in this event: none from Europe, but, more surprisingly, none from the Commonwealth. The British Empire Exhibition of 1924–5 ('Walk Up, Walk Up and Hear the Lion Roar') had featured a West Indian cocktail bar, had seen the launch of the Gold Coast Cocoa campaign that boosted the sales of chocolate, displayed the Prince of Wales sculptured in Canadian butter, and even included a miniature history of the Empire in flags.[26] Not so in 1951. Instead, the festival celebrated Christian Britain's continuous history as 'the fight for religious and civil freedom [and] the idea of Parliamentary government; the love of sport and the home; the love of nature and travel; pride in craftsmanship and British eccentricity and humour'.[27]

Britannia was there, combined with the points of the compass to create the festival's logo. She had been deployed in both world wars in a minor way. During the First World War, for example, Britannia had endorsed national savings stamps and mourned on memorial plaques. The heraldic beasts, the lion and the unicorn, were also there – indeed, they had their own pavilion at the festival, for, according to Laurie Lee, these two creatures had for centuries symbolized the British character – as opposed to being heraldic supporters identifying England and Scotland:

> We are the Lion and the Unicorn
>
> Twin symbols of the Briton's character
>
> As a Lion I give him solidarity and strength
>
> With the Unicorn he lets himself go.

And Noël Coward was there, waving his little workers' flag in his wryly enthusiastic song 'Don't Make Fun of the Fair':

> Peace and dignity we may lack
>
> But wave a jolly Trades Union Jack,
>
> Hurrah for the festival,
>
> We'll pray for the festival
>
> Hurrah for the Festival of Britain![28]

Two years later, the country was celebrating what was essentially another festival of Britain, and one that was rather more successful in uniting the country: the coronation of Elizabeth II in 1953, following what was in essence the same ritual as that used to crown Edgar the Peacemaker in Bath almost a thousand years before. Against the background of increasing American influence, the erosion of the Empire, black and Asian immigration, Scottish and Welsh separatism, and reluctant European integration, the coronation provided a focus for British identity. The event stimulated what was to become the largest domestic market of the 1950s: television sets. Britain was second only to the United States in its use of the television, and by 1953 there were almost two million sets in the country.[29] As the coronation approached, another 526,000 sets were sold, and on the day, twenty million people – 56 per cent of the country's population – crowded around TVs across the country to watch the new queen being crowned; another twelve million tuned in on the radio. It was by far the biggest event in television history.

One of Lord Reith's plans for the BBC before the war had been 'The Projection of Britain' via the Empire Service (begun in 1932), including such broadcasts and the king's Christmas Day speech. The first major BBC television coverage after the war was of the victory parade in June 1946, and the continual reaffirmation of Britain on both public and commercial television continued after the war in coverage of the laying of wreaths at the cenotaph on Remembrance Sunday. Indeed, the Second World War, in both its history and its pageantry, proved to be hugely popular televisual entertainment. Over a hundred war films were screened at British cinemas in the 1950s and 1960s, often promoted by local premières involving territorials, cadets, bunting, and Union Jacks; they were then broadcast by terrestrial channels, and the 1970s saw major documentary series such as *The World at War*, as well as popular dramas such as *Colditz*.[30] This enthusiasm also reached children's comics, much as it did in the nineteenth century: *Warlord* had from its inception in 1974 a British Marine who found himself with the American Rangers in Burma; as Sgt Jackson, he was inevitably known as 'Union Jack' Jackson.

The coronation – and indeed television – proved to be a coming of age of sorts for the Union Jack. Despite fripperies such as Union Jack handkerchiefs and the popularity of red-white-and-blue borders of geraniums planted for patriotic national events, the mood towards the flag was still reverential in the 1950s, and less than a week before the coronation it had been one of the flags solemnly placed on top of Mount Everest by Edmund Hillary and Sherpa Tenzing. But among coronation souvenirs were certain garments bearing the Union Jack design. These were greeted with outrage by Tory MPs, the member for Buckingham asking Churchill to outlaw 'entirely objectionable' items such as 'Coronation ladies underwear, ornamented with the Union Jack at the rear'.[31] As the 1950s drew to a close, the critic Kenneth Allsop said,

> The collapse of our old image of imperial splendour did give a spur to
> the idea that our national vigour and imaginativeness no longer lay in
> the field of panoply or splendour. Suez was a spur: a very palpable
> spur. Suddenly there was a violent swing to the culture of the great,
> gritty, youthful *lumpenproletariat* … Every generation of kids since
> has been swayed by the sort of scepticism and derision that produces
> Carnaby Street knickers with Union Jacks on them.[32]

The sixties had begun, and bands such as the Beatles were seen as national exports, cultural colonialists, ambassadors for a new Britishness. This was an entirely different way of flying the flag, and informal and ironic patriotic gestures became the norm. When the lovable moptops collected their MBEs in 1965, the *New Musical Express* exclaimed,

> Did the Beatles deserve to be honoured by the Queen? The answer
> must be irrevocably and unquestioningly – Yeah! Yeah! Yeah!…
> Where the Beatles deserve their awards is in the field of prestige.
> Their efforts to keep the Union Jack fluttering proudly have been far
> more successful than a regiment of diplomats and statesmen. We may
> be regarded as a second class power in terms of politics, but at any
> rate we now lead the world in pop music![33]

After centuries of military and imperial grandeur, the Union Jack changed almost overnight into an ultra-fashionable design icon. The Union Jack became a touchstone of the new generation, and the pop scene emphatically embraced its colours and style. The flag not only appeared adorning girls' bums, it became the commercial trademark of British cool, and it became one of the defining commodities of the 1960s.

Pop music was, as the *NME*'s comment on the Beatles' MBEs suggests, a vibrant reinvention of British cultural identity. Teenage fashion did not begin and end in Carnaby Street, just as the Mersey Sound did not restrict its appeal to Liverpool. As the fashion bible *The Mod* warned, the movement was not confined to trendy Soho clubs:

> We're always inclined to think that the girls and guys up there
> [Scotland] walk about in kilts saying 'haggis' or 'och' with every other

word. It's not true. Seeing the photographs that they have been sending... I'd say that in some parts they are in fact just as much fashion mad go-ahead as we are in London.[34]

Pop television shows, which spread these fashions over the United Kingdom, learned to favour large bold designs for their sets: '*Ready Steady Go!* was targets, chevrons, bright colours, crisp hard edges.'[35] The quality of black-and-white TV pictures in the mid-1960s meant that they lacked the definition to capture much subtlety or over-elaboration in the graphic design of television studios, so the medium itself encouraged the use of Pop Art motifs, for dressing both the studios and the stars themselves. Jeff Nuttall describes 1960s fashions in *Bomb Culture* as 'applied art': 'As much inventiveness and creativity was employed there as in action paintings, the collages and assemblages. The colours were delirious. England had stopped being grey.'[36] The Who's drummer Keith Moon, for example, wore trendy roundel T-shirts, which encouraged their manager to market the band as ultra-Mods. They were 'Modernists' – cool, smart, arty, sophisticated, and up-to-the-minute – in contrast to Rockers, the leather-clad bikers who had evolved out of Teddy Boys. The sense of a shared and driving identity among Mods was so powerful that Pete Townshend, guitarist with the Who, remembers that

everybody looked the same, acted the same, and wanted to be the same. It was the first move I have ever seen in the history of youth towards unity: unity of thought, unity of drive, and unity of motive. It was the closest to pure patriotism I've ever felt.[37]

Mod united teenagers across the country – and appropriately enough their favourite Pop Art motif was the Union Jack.

Townshend, who had a 'huge Union Jack' adorning one wall of his tiny bedroom,[38] defined Pop Art in the *Melody Maker* (3 July 1965) as 're-presenting something the public is familiar with, in a different form', like clothes:

> Union Jacks are supposed to be flown. We have a jacket made of one. Keith Moon, our drummer, has a jersey with the RAF insignia on it … We stand for pop-art clothes, pop-art music and pop-art behaviour. This is what everybody seems to forget – we don't change off stage. We live pop-art.[39]

The Who burst through posters of Union Jacks.[40] They were photographed for an album cover in a massive bed covered with a Union Jack bedspread. Was it art? Did Mod share the same ethos as the American Pop artist Jasper Johns, who had famously painted the Stars and Stripes? The singer George Melly thought not, arguing that Carnaby Street, the centre of Swinging London, was in a totally different spirit from that artist's 'plastic researches':

> From shopping bags and china mugs [the Union Jack] soon graduated to bikinis and knickers. Americans, for whom the flag in their century of Imperialism has a great deal more significance, were amazed by our casual acceptance of our flag as a giggle. They might burn their flag in protest but they'd never wear it to cover their genitalia.[41]

Mod culture appealed more to commentators such as George Melly as a popular version of Dadaism, the art movement out of which had Surrealism emerged. The Union Jack was, in Dadaist terms, almost a 'ready-made' object: it could be completely transformed through unlikely juxtapositions, and could be reworked into other items – a jacket, for example.[42] The writer Angela Carter wondered whether the young Pete Townshend fully realized what he was doing, stealing traditional signs and objects such as smart suits and Union Jacks and placing them in new contexts: 'In the pursuit of magnificence, nothing is sacred...The pursuit of magnificence starts as play and ends as nihilism or metaphysics or a new examination of the nature of goals.'[43] But the Who did have some sense of their impact. Townshend had been a member of the Young Communist League and CND, and had even played banjo on the Aldermaston marches. Like many aspiring pop stars of his generation, he attended art school. In 1964, there was a ten-year retrospective of American art at the Tate (54–64), including works by Robert Rauschenberg and Jasper Johns: 'targets and flags and what have you'. A graphic designer of the period remarked, 'Then you'd drift off to see The Who and you'd put two and two together. There seemed to be a direct line between what was going on at the Tate Gallery and what was going on at the Marquee.'[44] The ritual destruction of luxury goods wrapped in a Union Jack was therefore a considered gesture. The band was called the Who; they wore Union Jacks or hung them over their amplifiers and then hurled guitars into them; they were enticingly ambivalent in their attitude towards the flag.[45] On the other hand, comedy bands such as the Scaffold (famous for 'Lily the Pink') were also using the Union Jack for their own eccentrically patriotic reasons, declaring it to be 'the most democratic flag in the world', and it continued to appear on the knickers of girls who had no absolutely interest in making radical modernist statements.[46]

The flag was omnipresent in 1960s culture. The 'archetypal 1966 pad' – like that of the actress Julie Christie – was decked out with Victoriana, potted plants, and a Union Jack.[47] This ubiquity may explain the enthusiasm for the Union Jack during the 1966 World Cup, hosted by England. English football fans did not carry banners of St George crosses or even standards of the three lions or the Tudor rose, but flew the Union Jack: in other words, the competition was for the fans as much a celebration of Swinging London and the sixties as it was the England football team. Two decades after the defeat of Nazi Germany by the Allies, this was history repeated as farce; VE Day became Cup Final Day, the Union Flag unthinkingly appropriated for another famous victory over the Germans. *The Sunday Express* described how,

> A blaze of Union Jacks waved, as people unashamedly gripped by emotion and patriotism danced, wept, and hugged each other... What they will tell their grandchildren in the years to come is that it was English nerve and English heart and English stamina which finally overcame the tenacious resistance of [the Germans]... No one who saw this historic World Cup Final can deny England their 'finest hour'.[48]

Union Jacks were everywhere: at Wembley, in the streets, at parties, and festooned around pubs and clubs. Kenneth Wolstenholme, who uttered the most famous words in English sporting history – 'Some people are on the pitch, they think it's all over … it is now!' – later complained, 'Sooner or later I hope it will dawn on all English fans that the Union flag is the flag of the United Kingdom and that the flag of England is the St George's Cross.'[49] But England had appropriated the Union Jack to the extent that at Wembley Stadium the winners' board for 1966 was emblazoned with the Union Jack. English football had been in the doldrums since 1953's shock defeat by Hungary, melodramatically described by *The Times* as 'Agincourt in reverse'.[50] This was its triumphant return, establishing the English as world leaders in football, as they were in pop music. Simply by waving the Union Jack on the Wembley terraces, English fans had turned the Swinging Sixties into an English rather than a British phenomenon. Most Scots, for example, were indifferent to England's success, although the Scottish Football Association shamelessly congratulated the English FA on their great 'British' achievement. For others, such as Scottish international Denis Law, the day that England won the World Cup was 'the blackest day of my life'.[51]

Law's comment indicates the extent to which national rivalries within the United Kingdom over activities such as sporting fixtures were eroding British identity. Neither was this factionalism helped by the simultaneous appropriation by the English of the Union Jack and all that went with it. The evergreen film *The Italian Job* (1969), for instance, takes it for granted that the Union Jack stands for England rather than Britain. The film is set against Swinging London, and although it mixes social classes and even includes a black man and a camp homosexual as members of the gang led by Charlie Croker (played by Michael Caine), the whole patriotic caper is resolutely

Anglo-centric, and there are no Scottish, Irish, or Welsh characters. The heist – ostensibly to help the UK's balance-of-payments crisis and masterminded by the archetypal aristocratic gangster Mr Bridger (Noël Coward) – is made under the cover of an England–Italy football match, for which the English supporters are festooned in Union Jacks. In one of the most famous car chases in British cinema, the three Minis that make the getaway through a traffic jam are, of course, painted red, white, and blue.

As had already happened in the aftermath of the Second World War, the only way was down from this peak of supreme confidence. Europe, the far right, frictions between the constituent nations, and radical popular protest all contributed, and the following decade saw an inevitable slump and a decline in the fortunes of both British identity and the Union Jack. Memories of Britain's isolated stand during 1940 were still reasonably fresh and the British people had little enthusiasm for a European union, but on 1 January 1973, the UK became a member of the EEC. In recognition of this historic event, the Union Jack flew over Brussels – upside-down.[52] Among its more unfortunate effects, membership of the EEC provoked a resurgence of extreme right-wing and neo-fascist politics. Predominantly targeting immigrants who had settled in the country, the skinhead National Front occupied the national identity vacuum left after the 1960s and hijacked the Union Jack. Throughout the 1970s, the flag remained strongly associated with the racist National Front, whose first policy was 'Stop all immigration and start phased repatriation'. The Union Jack appeared in the party's advertising – one image, for instance, showed a Union Jack 'stained' with dreadlocks – it was painted on steel-capped Dr Marten boots, and waved at marches expressly to intimidate immigrant communities.[53] Today's liberal and left-wing antipathy towards displays of the Union Jack seems to derive in part from memories of skinhead racist violence being conducted under the banner of the red-white-and-blue.

The discovery and exploitation of North Sea oil, meanwhile, reignited Scottish antipathy to England, and moreover Scotland itself went through a popular cultural renaissance akin to England's in the 1960s. The Scottish singer Rod Stewart (previously 'Rod the Mod') became an international superstar, and the tartan-clad teenybopper pin-ups the Bay City Rollers were enjoying phenomenal worldwide success; even Paul McCartney and Wings jumped on the bandwagon with the bagpipe anthem 'Mull of Kintyre', which spent nine weeks at the top of the charts in 1977. At football matches, Scottish fans booed 'God Save the Queen' and sang 'Flower of Scotland' instead – and have done so ever since.

There were, of course, positive occasions for the flag. At the same time that it was being brandished by the National Front, the Union Jack continued to deck out British athletics teams, who have always performed under the flag of the United Kingdom rather than as constituent nations, and it featured prominently at Queen Elizabeth's 1977 Silver Jubilee. The jubilee was an attempt to rekindle a sense of a united Britain: the Queen toured extensively, there was much Union Jackery in the shape of souvenirs such as milk bottle-tops and the ubiquitous underwear, and the day itself was characterized by street parties, bunting, and a blizzard of flag-waving. And the jubilee also inspired the most pungent reinvention of the flag since the Mods: the cataclysmic arrival of punk rock was under the banner of a slashed Union

Jack, raised both in ironic homage to the Swinging Sixties and in outright antagonism to the establishment.

The Union Jack was clearly a highly resonant and contested sign, and so became a favourite design for punks – an appropriation inspired by the Situationist thinking of punk impresario Malcolm McLaren and graphic artist Jamie Reid. The Sex Pistols in particular seem to have had a distinct agenda, making persistent, iconoclastic assaults on the institutions that had become the tourist traditions of British identity – the monarchy, Parliament, the Union Jack – through singles such as 'Anarchy in the U.K.' and 'God Save the Queen'. Malcolm McLaren, their manager, declared on the BBC's flagship news and opinion programme *Nationwide* (12 November 1976), 'You have to destroy in order to create, you know that.'[54] Situationism was a way of subverting, dismantling, and reassembling the world in order to undermine conventional thinking – which is precisely what Jamie Reid did to the Union Jack on the record covers he put together. For the Pistols' first single, 'Anarchy in the U.K.', Reid cut up a souvenir Silver Jubilee Union Jack flag and loosely reassembled it with safety pins, paperclips, and bulldog clips. The idea was repeated for the 'God Save the Queen' single, when a furling and inverted flag was used behind a treated version of the Queen's head, and the record sleeve was also printed in the jubilee colours, blue and silver. Danny Friedman of the Victoria & Albert Museum said of the institution's purchase of the Jamie Reid archive:

> just as the Sex Pistols were important in democratizing music, the
> designs democratized art ... All you need is a newspaper and some

scissors and an airbrush if you get a bit flash later. I mean the whole thing about photo collages, xeroxes, polaroids was really bringing Art with a big 'A' right down to where anyone could do it.[55]

The Sex Pistols and the Clash both adapted the design of the Union Jack and there were bands with names such as the UK Subs (originally the UK Subversives, who had seven Top Thirty hits and two Top Ten albums in two years) and UK Decay (whose singer coined the description 'gothic' for another emerging musical genre). Derek Jarman's edgy punk film *Jubilee* (1978) also made ambivalent figures of the flag and national icons such as Britannia, who is called 'Amyl Nitrate' in the film and played by a punk ice maiden by the name of Jordan. Punk recognized that despite the Union Jack's institutional status and its wartime and imperial history, the events of the past decade had made the flag wholly ambiguous. It was a sign determined by its context: the red-white-and-blue design on a bikini sold from a tourist stall on the corner of Oxford Street had a profoundly different meaning from that of the flag raised on Remembrance Sunday, and the Union Jack pinned to the back of a Mod's fish-tail parka was entirely at odds with the Union Jack tattooed on the arm of a Dr-Marten-booted skinhead. In addition to its formal roles, the flag could be a declaration of monarchist patriotism, a tourist souvenir, a neo-fascist banner, or a homage to the sixties, and by cutting it up and then pinning it back together again, punks could present themselves as symptoms of the degeneration and fragmentation of Great Britain.[56] Predictably, however, the slipperiness of this symbolism undermined punk's own position, and the British establishment was able to absorb these attempts to unravel the integrity of the flag.

Before long, punks found themselves alongside bobbies, pillar boxes, and beefeaters as just another patriotic London tourist attraction – as English, one is tempted to say, as the Union Jack.[57]

The Union Jack has since become a pop fetish, eternally returned to. Freddie Mercury of Queen made the flag a favourite stage prop, and even the chameleon David Bowie had a frock coat based on a Union Jack made for his Earthling phase. But it has not always been received with equanimity. Former Smiths singer Morrissey draped himself in the Union Jack in 1992 while performing at Finsbury Park and was vilified. The music press had been happy for others to take the flag: the Who, of course, were considered to be prime exponents of 1960s Pop Art, and more recently the post-punk Mod band the Jam had dressed themselves in 'Union Jackets' as a way of reclaiming the flag from the National Front skinheads. But Morrissey's handling was different. Many commented that Morrissey seemed to be embracing neo-fascist chic: unfurling the flag before a backdrop of harsh black-and-white photos of bovver boys, and performing songs such as 'The National Front Disco'. And not only were there skinheads in his audience, making Nazi salutes, but outside the venue, National Front and British Movement supporters were confronting left-wing marchers. In such a context, Morrissey appeared to be using the Union Jack as a way of flirting with racism.

For the flag at least, the storm of controversy blew over. Since Morrissey's misconceived antics, the flag has been adopted by Britpop groups as different as the Spice Girls (Geri Halliwell's minidress at the Brit Awards) and Oasis (Noel Gallagher has a Union Jack guitar and was also photographed on a Union Jack bedspread). It was further revived at the opening of the 1998 London Fashion Week by a topless model painted with red-white-and-blue stripes. All of this has helped to distance the Union Jack from neo-fascist racism, and by 1997, new Labour had spotted its opportunity. The party leadership endorsed the concept of Cool Britannia, promoted by the emblem of the Union Jack.* Peter Mandelson, in a lecture delivered in that year, declared:

> Now, together, we have reclaimed the flag. It is restored as an
> emblem of national pride and national diversity, restored from years
> as a symbol of division and intolerance to a symbol of confidence and
> unity for all the peoples and ethnic communities of a diverse and
> outward-looking Britain.[58]

The cult comic *2000AD* was quick to explode Labour's 'Cool Britannia Myth' in a special 'True Brit' issue, festooned with ironic Union Jacks, and the music collective Asian Dub Foundation subsequently criticized new Labour's opportunism with *Real Great Britain* (2000):

> Union Jack and Union Jill
> Back up and down the same old hill
> Sell the flag to the youths
> But who swallows the bill
> Murdoch she wrote
> Him have his hand in the till.[59]

* The phrase 'Cool Britannia' was popularized in the press from 1996 and became the name of an ice cream. It actually dates back to a Bonzo Dog Doo Dah Band song (1967).

Mercifully, Cool Britannia had by then fizzled out.

Attempts to rebrand the United Kingdom have always proved problematic. In 1996, the Chief Executive of British Airways, Bob Ayling, had been publicly criticized by Margaret Thatcher for replacing the stylized Union Jack on the tail-fins of BA's fleet with world art liveries: she covered up a model of a 747, saying, 'We fly the British flag, not these awful things.' Versions of the Union Jack had appeared in British civil aviation since at least 1931, when Imperial Airways had requested the adoption of the Civil Air Ensign, and the design was later adapted for aircraft livery. BA, 'the world's favourite airline', eventually returned to the traditional red-white-and-blue in 2001. By this time, Virgin had taken up the initiative, adding Union Jacks to their own planes' winglets and to their figurehead (1999). Other national icons were also redesigned. Interest in the imperial figure of Britannia has declined since the war, and indeed Cool Britannia's adherents seemed wholly ignorant of the figure. Britannia was, however, recently restyled for a postage stamp by having her figure moulded to the nation's average women's chest measurement of 36B.* Her transformation perhaps recalls that of Mrs John Bull, who in the nineteenth century was represented literally as a domestic goddess (as Britannia at home, armour neatly stowed away), but by 1928 had become Joan Bull,

---

* The 1993 £10 stamp. In July 2004, a 'Rule Britannia' set of stamps and first-day covers was issued by the Post Office, featuring Union Jack stamps and Great British icons such as milk bottles on a doorstep, a red pillar box, a deckchair, red double-decker bus, red telephone box, tea, a Union Jack umbrella, and a stick of rock.

representing recently enfranchised women. Joan Bull could be recognized by her top hat and Union Jack dress, rather than a coal-scuttle helmet hanging on a hat stand, and she later stripped off down to her Union Jack brassière (1946).[60] Her husband John Bull's Union Jack waistcoat, meanwhile, was sported by everyone from comedians (Tim Brooke-Taylor in *The Goodies*) to the royal family (as a prefect at Eton College, Prince William was permitted to customize his uniform – he did so with a Union Jack waistcoat) to dogs (in 2005, Tory MP Andrew Rosindell campaigned with his bulldog, Spike, so attired; Rosindell was elected) and to proud fathers (Shajaad Khan, the father of the British Muslim boxer Amir Khan, attended all of his son's 2004 Olympic bouts wearing a Union Jack waistcoat).

The flag has nonetheless staunchly maintained its military bearings. In 1955, for example, HMS *Vidal* was sent to Rockall, a tiny island in the North Atlantic, three hundred miles from Scotland and a mere eighty feet long, hundred wide, and sixty high. Commander Richard Connell's orders from the Queen were as follows:

> On arrival at Rockall you will effect a landing and hoist the Union
> flag on whatever spot appears the most suitable or practicable, and
> you will then take possession of the island on Our behalf… When the
> landing has been effected and the flag has been hoisted you will
> cement a commemorative plaque to the rock.[61]

All this was accomplished and the *Vidal*, named after Admiral T. E. Vidal, who had discovered Rockall in 1831, gave a twenty-one-gun salute. The importance of Rockall lay in the possibility of discovering oil or gas, and it later became strategic during the Cod War with Iceland (1975–6). Rockall's status as part of Inverness-shire is still contested by Denmark, Iceland, and Ireland.

In 1982, a considerably larger task force was to be dispatched to the South Atlantic with the express purpose of raising the Union Jack again over the Falkland Islands following their invasion by Argentina; appropriately, the warships were seen off from Portsmouth quay by bevvies of girls with Union Jacks painted on their breasts, waving and blowing kisses. Similar scenes accompanied the departure of troops to the First Gulf War (1991), and the *Daily Star* promoted red-white-and-blue T-shirts displaying the Union Jack and Old Glory, with the motto 'These Colours Don't Run'. During the Second Gulf War (2004), the *Sun* newspaper produced a grotesque coalition flag made up of the Stars and Stripes diagonally joined with the Union Jack; it seemed that this travesty was permitted to be waved solely by page-three models.*

If the post-war life of the Union Jack has been a restless one, so too have been the recent histories of the crosses of Sts George, Andrew, and Patrick, and also that of the Welsh dragon – indeed, the Welsh have acquired an admirable degree of recognition for their once unofficial standard. The Welsh flag had, of course, been a standard of Henry Tudor, and was based on the medieval Welsh dragon. As Henry VII,

---

* In stark contrast, the artist and anti-war campaigner Peter Kennard produced *Decoration* in 2004, an exhibition profoundly influenced by the invasion of Iraq. Kennard's photo-montages of medals had ribbons made from frayed strips of the Stars and Stripes and the Union Jack, while the medallions were human faces.

the king introduced it into the royal standard as a supporter, but it was later replaced by the Scottish unicorn of the Stuarts, and Wales was not included in any of the Union Flag designs by heralds from the time of James I to that of Queen Anne and George III.[62] Traditionally, Welsh patriotism has not been expressed antagonistically – 'Land of My Fathers', for example, the Welsh national anthem written in 1856, celebrates 'poets and minstrels', 'brave warriors', and even 'the ancient language', but makes no mention of Welsh separatism, or even of St David, who fades from the cultural record from this point on.[63] But the arrival of the twentieth century encouraged Wales to begin to assert its identity within Britain and to reconsider its heraldic invisibility. An acknowledgement of the Welsh contribution to the Union was long overdue: Wales needed a more prominent position in the iconography of the United Kingdom.

Consequently, in an attempt to achieve greater national recognition, the Welsh petitioned the government in 1897, 1901, 1910, 1935, and 1945 to request that the Welsh dragon ('*Y Ddraig Goch*') be included in the royal arms. Each time they were refused because, in the words of the College of Arms, Wales had never been a kingdom: 'There is no such thing as a Welsh national flag.' The Garter Knight of Arms told the Home Office that, 'There is no more reason to add Wales to the King's style than there would be to add Mercia, Wessex or Northumbria or any other parts of England.'[64] Eventually, in 1953 – the coronation year – the palace offered a compromise in the shape of a new royal badge. The traditional dragon was redesigned, a crown was added, and the motto '*Y DDRAIG GOCH DDYRY CYCHWYN*' ('The red dragon leads the way'). The badge was for use in periods when there was no Prince of Wales; it was, however, ridiculed. The depiction of the dragon was derided for having its tail pointing downwards, and it was claimed that the motto was an unintentional double-entendre, originating from a verse in which a peasant farmer petitioned a neighbour for his bull, which he wanted for stud; the bull simply had to follow the way of his '*ddraig goch*'.

Official permission was still in any case required to fly this new Welsh standard, even on St David's Day, and so the popular Welsh dragon continued to be seen at rugby matches and in trinket shops. By 1958, a campaign had been launched to save it. The Gorsedd, a traditional gathering of Welsh bards, announced:

> We proclaim that the Red Dragon banner, as borne by Henry Tudor
> on Bosworth Field and as flown by Prince Cadwalador centuries
> earlier, is the only banner adopted by the Welsh people themselves
> over many years now as our national flag and that there is therefore
> no need to seek permission from any heraldic authority outside the
> Principality for the continuance of this usage. We entirely reject the
> badge granted in 1952–3 [as] too puny to signify anything.[65]

Wisely, the authorities conceded. Henry Brooke (Minister for Housing and Local Government, and Minister for Welsh Affairs) said in Parliament, 'I now have it in command from the Queen to say that Her Majesty has been pleased to direct that in future only the Red Dragon on a green and white flag and not the flag carrying the augmented Royal Badge shall be flown on Government buildings in Wales and, where appropriate, in London.'[66] The Red Dragon became official on 1 January 1960. In 1999, at the opening of the Welsh National Assembly by the Queen and Prince Charles, Buckingham Palace was persuaded to fly the Prince of Wales's flag (the four lions) alongside the royal standard of the Queen, which, as the most senior standard, should have been the sole flag flying.

As for the components of the Union Jack, the Scots have never balked at flying St Andrew's Cross, which even appeared on the Black Watch's armoured vehicles during the Second Gulf War. The saint's feast day, however, has been overshadowed by Hogmanay celebrations and Burns Night (25 January), although it is popular among Scots in America, Australia, India, and New Zealand. As for the ruddy lion, King George V issued a royal warrant in 1934 that allowed the standard to be used during the Silver Jubilee celebrations of 1935 in Scotland 'as a mark of loyalty to the Sovereign', but not to be flown from flagpoles or public buildings – it was solely for 'decorative ebullition', comparable today to its being displayed at football matches. By an act of 1679, the misuse of the royal arms actually remains a capital offence – as Denis Pamphilon, a St Albans linen merchant, discovered in 1978. Pamphilon was threatened with the death penalty by Scotland's Lyon Court for 'usurping' the red lion, which he had been printing on souvenir bedspreads and selling to Scottish football fans. He was fined £100 daily until he desisted. The Lyon Court then went on to admonish the Scottish National Party and Glasgow Rangers for using St Andrew's cross with the red lion.[67]

The cross of St Patrick has become increasingly significant throughout the twentieth century as an emblem that might be able to steer a course between political and religious factions. It has appeared in St Patrick's Day parades as a neutral Irish banner, and now forms part of the insignia of the reformed police service of Northern Ireland. It has also been adopted by the General Synod of the Church of Ireland, and churches may fly it on 'Holy Days and during the Octaves of Christmas, Easter, the Ascension of Our Lord and Pentecost, and on any other such day as may be recognised locally as the Dedication Day of the particular church building', thus avoiding the sectarian implications of raising the Union Flag, which is known to some republicans as the 'Butcher's Apron'.

The status of the Union Jack in Northern Ireland is, of course, particularly fraught. The government of Northern Ireland had introduced its own flag in 1924. This was an Anglicized version of the Ulster Flag, an ancient standard of the O'Neills that alluded to a widespread Irish legend that Ulster had been promised to the first man to lay his hand on the ground of the province – whereupon one warrior hacked off his hand and hurled it on to the land, throwing it over the heads of his comrades as they raced to claim the territory. The standard of the O'Neills, which dates from at least the sixteenth century, was yellow with a red cross surmounted by a white shield bearing the bloody hand. Following the declaration of the Irish Free State and partition in 1922, this design was reworked into a cross of St George, on which beneath a crown the red hand appeared on a six-pointed star, signifying the six counties. No use was made of the cross of St Patrick.

This Ulster banner was abandoned in 1973 when the Belfast Stormont Assembly was dissolved, and, since then, the Union Jack has been the only official flag in Northern Ireland. There have, however, been plenty of unofficial flags, among them the alternative Ulster flag (a British White Ensign bearing a central white shield and red hand), Orange Order flags (orange with purple stars, sometimes with St

George's cross in the canton), UVF flags (Ulster Volunteer Force: blue with St George's cross in the canton), the Starry Plough (a pale blue flag bearing the constellation, borne by republican paramilitary groups), and Fianna na hÉireann (IRA cadets: blue with a rising yellow sun in the bottom left). In Belfast, Protestant streets display Union Jacks, St Andrew crosses, and Israeli flags, whereas the Catholic areas have elaborate murals and fly Irish Tricolours and Palestinian flags.[68]

Despite (or perhaps because of) its incorporation of St Patrick, the Union Jack is perceived by republicans as partisan, and in the meantime the red hand has been appropriated by ultra-loyalist paramilitaries, much as the Union Jack itself was by neo-fascists in the 1970s. Indeed, in 2005 the BBC children's TV programme *Blue Peter* (itself named after a flag and characterized by badges) was embroiled in a row for suggesting the red hand be used as an emblem for aircraft livery representing 'the best of British'. The BBC immediately apologized for promoting sectarianism, but perhaps they apologized too soon. The iconography of the red hand is, in fact, subtle and complex, as both loyalists and nationalists identify with the symbol: loyalists see it representing the six counties of Northern Ireland, whereas nationalists perceive the nine counties of Old Ulster (three of which are now in the Republic). The red hand is also used as a symbol of a united Ireland, sometimes with a severed thumb to indicate the split between the North and the South. So this may actually be an emblem over which different factions agree. In any case, it remains in widespread use in Northern Ireland: the badge is worn by sports teams and the fire brigade and since 1951 has even been used in the Republic by Na Piarsaigh, a hurling team from Co. Cork.

Throughout this period there were also sporadic calls for St George's Day to be recognized, and for the cross of St George to be flown, but St George has not had the same success as his fellow saints have, or indeed as has the dragon, and celebrating St George's Day has suffered from fears of rising English neo-fascism. The observance of his feast day declined seriously after the war, although the flag continued to be flown from parish churches on particular occasions.* Aside from these glimpses, the flag of St George for many years fell from view until the extreme right appropriated St George much as it did the Union Jack.[69] In 1975, the neo-fascist League of St George was formed to revive Oswald Mosely's plan for a united Europe. It was a tiny and ineffective group that deserves no place in history, but as an ultra-right organization that adopted the cross of St George, the LSG has to some extent tarnished the emblem. Yet allowing such marginal organizations to dictate the meanings of national symbols merely plays into the hands of the neo-fascists themselves, making them appear to be considerably more powerful than they really are.

The name League of St George has, in any case, since been taken by a football website, and it is indeed to football that St Georgism owes its most recent revival. At Euro '96, English football supporters finally

---

* An Earl Marshal's Warrant of 9 February 1938 stipulates that the proper flag to be flown by any church in the Provinces of Canterbury and York is 'The Cross of St George and in the first quarter an escutcheon of the Arms of the See in which such Church is ecclesiastically situate [the diocesan arms]'. The expense attendant on this, however, means that the cross of St George is usually flown instead. The flying of such flags is not compulsory.

began to wear the colours of St George as opposed to the red-white-and-blue of the Union Jack, and a popular sense of Englishness as distinct from Britishness emerged. English nationalism had for too long over-lapped with British patriotism; at last some attempt was being made to distinguish the two. The English fans also realized that the Scots hated the English team with a rare vehemence (75 per cent of Scottish football fans would not support an English team; 40 per cent would prefer any other team to win), and they reluctantly began to reciprocate.[70] And coincidentally, a few weeks after Euro '96, the Church of England restored St George's Day to the status of a compulsory feast.

All of this led to a revival of St Georgism. The first St George's Day greetings cards were mass-produced in 1995 and currently sell about 50,000 every April. The *Sun* printed a cross of St George poster in April 1997, and the next year launched a campaign to revive the celebration of St George's Day. In 1998, the English Tourist Board ran a pro-gramme of events with the title 'St George Invades Britain'. At the 1998 World Cup, English football fans were again identified by the cross of St George. In 1999, the Royal Society of St George reversed its sixty-year decline in membership and the English Tourist Council (formerly Board) changed its logo to a flag of St George. Even the Christian name 'George' became almost five times as popular as it had been in the pre-vious decade, and it is the name under which Prince Charles intends to rule.[71] The revival has since continued, and by 2005 the English Folk Dance and Song Society were sponsoring St George pageants across the country by offering a £600 award for the celebration receiving the most coverage.

At the beginning of the twenty-first century, then, the different nations of the United Kingdom are all developing a sense of their respective identities, and of the symbolism that expresses those identities and how it can be combined into more elaborate devices, such as flags and coats of arms. Interestingly, it is just at this point that some radical redesigns have been proposed for the Union Jack itself.

In 2003, a group calling itself 'reFLAG' launched a campaign to 'modernize' the Union Jack. The suggestion was to add diagonal black stripes to the current design. The reason given was that this would represent black Britons: reFLAG's logic derived, somewhat paradoxically, from the neo-fascist chant, 'There ain't no black in the Union Jack', and aimed to rectify this apparent oversight – which, of course, completely misses the point.[72] The white in the Union Jack does not represent white people any more than the blue represents blue people or the red, red people: the colours are there to draw together three territories into a United Kingdom. To add black lines would infringe the laws of heraldry (perhaps a minor misdemeanour, but these laws did develop for very good reasons). It would destroy any sense of territorial integrity – which is, quite literally, the one thing that unites British citizens. And it would obliterate the saltire of St Andrew – and therefore Scotland – from the flag completely. It would also, incidentally, produce a flag that looked as if it had unsuccessfully tried to incorporate the cross of St Piran, patron of Cornwall – a white cross on black.* The reFLAG campaign was deservedly ridiculed (why not add pink for

---

* St Piran (Pirrin), the patron saint of miners, was adopted by the Cornish in the 1950s.

homosexuals, grey for the third age, and a variety of other hues?) and thankfully has since foundered.[73]

It is, however, striking that at precisely the same time, the Turner Prize-winning artist Chris Ofili redesigned the flag in a very similar way to create the *Union Black*, a piece inspired by the symbolic colours of the pan-African flag proposed by civil rights campaigner and founder of UNIA, Marcus Garvey, that was first unveiled in 1920.* This consisted of a horizontal tricolour in red, black, and green, in which red stood for blood, black for skin, and green for the fertile land of Africa. Hence Ofili, declaring that he 'wanted to make a flag for the African British people', replaced the white and blue of the Union Jack with black and green. The idea of tampering with the colours in this way was, it transpired, nothing new. In 1997, fellow artist Mark Wallinger flew a Union Jack in the colours of the Irish Tricolour over Brixton; the piece was titled *Oxymoron* – literally, 'pointedly stupid', and the writer and polemicist Stewart Home reported that Kenny Murphy-Roud had done the same thing with a piece called *Flag* in the 1980s in his decidedly more sectarian home town of Glasgow.

The design of the Union Jack obviously lends itself to recolouring for more commercial purposes as well. The cover of the Asian style magazine *Second Generation* displayed the pattern of the Union Jack in browns and yellows; Harrods advertised an Anglo-Italian festival with the flag in the colours of the Italian Tricolour; Marmite celebrated its hundredth anniversary with a Vivienne Westwood Union Jack in red,

---

* UNIA: Universal Negro Improvement and Conservation Association and African Communities League.

'Britain's Day' poster by James Montgomery Flagg. Britain and America are personified as Britannia and Uncle Sam, with national mascots the lion and the eagle in attendance (7 December 1918).

Postcard treating the Union Jack as the flag of British Empire: scenes and arms of (clockwise) India, Australia, New Zealand, and South Africa (c.1919).

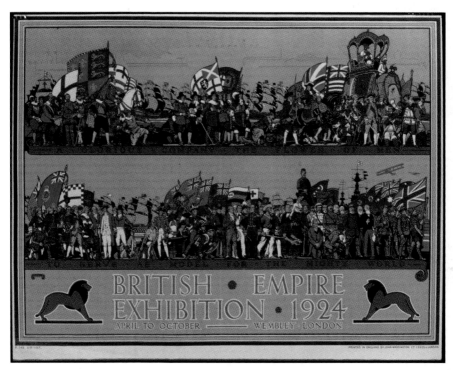

Poster for the British Empire Exhibition showing the history of Great Britain in flags (R.T. Cooper, 1924).

Africans shake hands: it was common for flags presented as gifts or stolen as trophies to be recycled into ceremonial robes (17 May 1941).

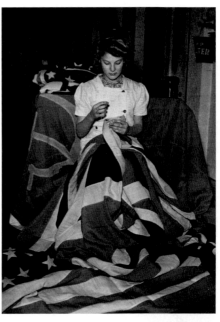

Sewing for victory: making flags in preparation for VE and VJ Days. In addition to the Union Jack, London was also decked with other Allied flags, such as the Stars and Stripes and the Hammer and Sickle (12 September 1944).

Women hand-printing woollen coronation banners (8 January 1953). The Parrack family factory in Rochford, Essex, produced ten miles of Union Jacks, Ensigns, and Royal Standards for the event.

The Jam pay homage to sixties Mod band, The Who, who helped to turn the red-white-and-blue into a fashion icon (12 August 1978).

Sebastian Coe after winning the Olympic 1500m final, Los Angeles (11 August 1984). Great Britain has always competed in the Olympics as a single nation – but will it continue to do so in 2012?

Ginger Spice at the Brit Awards during the height of Britpop (24 February 1997).

'Brightening Up London': the climax of this publicity campaign for mobile phones was wrapping Buckingham Palace in a gigantic illuminated Union Jack in time for Christmas Eve (23 December 2003).

Post-devolution Scotland goes to war under the silver saltire and the ruddy lion: the Black Watch on Operation Bracken, southern Iraq (27 October 2004).

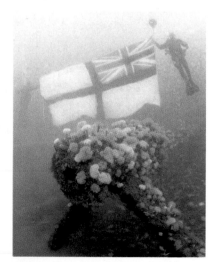

Britain's largest war grave: the Royal Oak, sunk by a German submarine in Scapa Flow, 14 October 1939. Navy divers annually honour the crew by changing the White Ensign at the stern of the vessel (7 February 2001).

black, and yellow; and even the logo of Karrimor, suppliers of outdoor clothing and equipment, is based on the Union Jack, as if the emblem is a traveller's talisman, carried to the least hospitable places on the globe in imitation of the flags planted by pioneering explorers and moun- taineers to claim territory and stake their conquests. In contrast, in 2002 the National Union of Students and Union of Jewish Students had an advertising firm tastelessly redesign the Union Jack into a swastika for an otherwise laudable poster campaign to stamp out campus racism.

The only justifiable argument for the redesign of the Union Jack is if the territories it represents change. And yet the flag remained the same, even with Irish independence. In 1937, the Irish Free State established in 1922 became Éire, and in 1949 it became a full republic wholly inde- pendent of both the United Kingdom and the Commonwealth. Northern Ireland remained a union province, but could no longer con- sider itself a separate kingdom. Technically, it should not therefore be afforded a separate status on the flag, any more than the principality of Wales is separately recognized. In other words, the red saltire of St Patrick should have been removed from the Union Jack back in 1937, and the flag should have reverted to the first Union design.[74] Perhaps if Éire had adopted St Patrick's cross as its own national flag, the red saltire would have been removed from the Union Jack. But that was never likely. The republicans continue to hoist the Tricolour – indeed, this banner had such significance that, in the 1960s, the Irish govern- ment petitioned British Prime Minister Harold Wilson for the return of the original Tricolour that had flown over the Post Office during the Easter Rising of 1916, and which had since been kept in London's Imperial War Museum. It was eventually returned.

In direct contrast, the Ulster Independence Movement has proposed the Ulster National Flag, since adopted by Ulster Nation. This party seeks Northern Irish independence from both Dublin and London, yet stresses the mix of Irish and Scots in Ulster. Its flag is effectively derived from a Union Jack from which the cross of St George has been removed, leaving the combined saltires of St Patrick and St Andrew: the flag is therefore a fimbriated diagonal red cross on blue, featuring a yellow star and the ubiquitous red hand.

These attempts to rethink the Union Jack show the flag's profound relevance in the current political climate and national culture. It is, therefore, all the more surprising that there is so little legislation concerning the flying and administration of the flag, except in the armed forces and at sea. The Ministry of Defence offers some guidance for the military use of flags in *Flags of All Nations* (known as *BR20*), and there are garrulous instructions in navy manuals. Similarly, from the seventeenth century onwards, maritime laws governing what ensigns may be flown at sea have been scrupulously maintained, in order to ensure that merchant and civil vessels are not confused with Her Majesty's ships, and under the 1995 Merchant Shipping Act, it is a criminal offence for a private citizen to fly the Union Jack afloat. But no such regulations exist for citizens on land. Indeed, there are still no stipulations on the design and proportions of the Union Jack, or on correct flying regulations, and no specific administration by the government. Even the flag's name remains in doubt. The 'Rules for Hoisting Flags on Government Buildings' are administered by the Department of Culture, Media, and Sport (see page 329), and there is a list of nineteen official Union Flag days, from Remembrance Sunday to the Countess of Wessex's birthday, but there is no active discouragement – or encouragement, for that matter – to fly the flag at other times.[75] Indeed, public demand can lead to quite unconstitutional displays. To mourn the death of Diana, Princess of Wales, the Union Jack flew at half-mast over Buckingham Palace, despite Diana being a commoner who therefore had no right to a half-mast salute.*

This attitude – a familiar combination of avid reinterpretation and apathetic indifference – has characterized the history of the Union Jack for four hundred years. In times of national confidence, the government was content to let the flag fly on land, but since the Second World War, Britain has been in a perpetual, if leisurely, decline, and the deep reluctance to engage seriously with displays of public patriotism today, symbolized by the ambiguous status of the Union Jack, suggests a refusal to acknowledge the very real possibility that the Union might disintegrate.

---

* The Union Jack was also flown at half-mast from royal residencies after the terrorist attacks of 11 September and 7 July.

VIII CONCLUSION

There are too many colours.

The Union Jack's all right, selective,

Two basic colours and one negative,

Reasonable, avoids confusion.

(Of course I respect the red, white and blue)

Adrian Mitchell, 'Hear the Voice of the Critic' (1953–84)

THE DREAM OF union has permeated the history and the imagination of the British Isles for over two thousand years. It is a dream that lies in the legendary histories of the British Isles – in the founding myth of Brutus and in the romances of King Arthur – but it is also a dream that has a political reality in the unification of the Scottish and Pictish kingdoms, the English Heptarchy, England and Wales, the thrones of England and Scotland (and Ireland), the Commonwealth, and the Acts of Union of 1707 and 1801. This dream has been heralded by dragons and lions, by unicorns and harps, and by the braiding together of three crosses. The royal coats of arms and, much more significantly, the Union Jack have been the symbols of concord of the United Kingdom for the past two centuries.

Two centuries out of more than a thousand years is perhaps a surprisingly short tenure, but during that time the Union Jack was raised across the globe. It flies over substantial territories still: the national flags of Australia and New Zealand, for example, bear the Union Jack in the canton. Indeed, the flag seems hardly less ubiquitous than it was at the height of the Empire in the nineteenth century. There are at least five hundred official or semi-official flags characterized by the interlaced design; the English, Scottish, Welsh, and Irish regiments of the British Army all march together under the Union Jack in allegiance to the Queen; the flag is particularly prominent on national commemorations such as VE and VJ Day and on Remembrance Sunday; it is also enthusiastically waved at the Last Night of the Proms (a peculiarly gentle expression of imperial patriotism) and at sporting events where Great Britain competes as a single team, such as the Olympic Games. Neither has the design lost any of its allure as an iconic fashion item: the designer Paul Smith, for instance, has recently been playing with the pattern again, recalling that the very first thing that he sold when he opened his boutique in Nottingham in 1970 was a Union Jack handkerchief; in popular music, the flag continues to flourish as a way of evoking the style of Mods and punks, and it has also become identified with black British rappers such as Iceberg Slimm and Sway. Meanwhile, the flag continues to adorn all sorts of commodities – anything from wallets to fridges, from contact lenses to the latest Minis.

The prevalence of the flag in contemporary culture at every level and the enthusiasm with which it is regularly appropriated and reinvented is only possible because the Union Jack has never been a simple flag identifying a single nation; rather it represents a series of relationships between nations and the history of those relationships. Except on water, the flag is not governed by strict laws, and even maritime laws are only really enforced in international shipping. There are no stipulations regarding the size or shape of the Union Jack, or of its geometry or colouring; crucially, of course, there is no law against desecrating the flag. In America, by comparison, the national flag is sacrosanct and debate continues as to whether 'profanation of the flag' is protected by the First Amendment or whether certain forms of profanation, such as physical abuse, should be specifically outlawed. Even in Britain, pro-testers have been prosecuted for crimes such as stamping on the Stars and Stripes and in 2004 the musician Kid Rock was attacked by the American far right for daring to wear the US flag as a poncho. The matter has been discussed in Congress as recently as 2005.

Such draconian flag laws are in stark contrast to the treatment of the Union Jack; indeed, it is the liberality of British attitudes that has sus-tained the flag's wide and continuing popularity as a design icon. There are also more serious implications. The appeal of the flag to a broad cross-section of society means that it continues to be a symbol of unity. It might mean different things in different contexts, but that is precisely its strength, and anyone who flies the flag today must be aware that it is a sign whose meaning is contingent on immediate circumstances. The Union Jack is not an emblem that transcends time and place with an ideal vision of unity, but an object with a long and rich history that has carried different meanings at different times for different people. It is not one flag, but many; it unites in spite of itself. The Union Jack is, in other words, unparalleled as a symbol of diversity, and, in an increasingly fragmenting world, it reflects a multifarious community and presents the opportunity to rally to that diversity.

Consequently, the flag is something that Britons are able to share in the face of mounting threats to British unity.[1] The traditional forces that held Britain together – Protestantism, antipathy towards France and Europe, industrial capitalism, Empire, war, and love of liberty – no longer create any national momentum or even remain coherent.[2] Union with Ireland half-collapsed as long ago as 1922 with partition and the creation of Éire, and after the end of the Second World War and the fulfilment of Great Britain's destiny, many Britons thought of themselves less as British and more as Scottish, Irish, and Welsh. The Irish situation remains unresolved, but the recent founding of the Scottish Parliament and the Welsh National Assembly has indeed weakened the Union by devolving a certain amount of legislative power from Westminster. This balance of national interests is extremely delicate. The Labour Party – which has not had an English leader for over twenty years – is reliant on support from Scotland and Wales, but has afforded the countries greater autonomy as a way of damping further calls for independence. This compromise has created serious contradictions in legislative responsibilities, although ironically enough, when the Scottish Parliament attempted to put its own house in order in 2000 and fix the colour of the St Andrew saltire as azure, or sky-blue – for which they had been petitioning for decades – it was not immediately clear whether it had the authority to do so.*

---

* The Scottish Parliament and Welsh Assembly may legislate on local housing, health, and education, but both countries still return MPs to Westminster to vote

New Labour's strategy, then, is to combine the maintenance of British identity with the cultivation of Scottish and Welsh interests: hence the promotion of Tony Blair, in polemicist Tom Nairn's words, as a 'practically identikit *British* individual in the sense most acceptable to English sensibility'.[3] But Blair has also been careful not to allow much expression to English identity: in a speech in May 2001, he positioned Britain as essentially European, 'with ancient European roots stamped through and through, dating as far back as … the Roman invasion'.[4]

The English question does, however, have to be addressed. For three centuries, England submerged its identity into Britain, and consequently has perpetually confused the two. An English nationalist movement in the nineteenth century would hardly have assisted the good running of the Empire and the maintenance of the union with Scotland and, more critically, Ireland. This is in part because the UK is asymmetrical. The vast majority of British citizens are English: fifty million out of a total population of fifty-eight million are English by residence, and as England is the dominant economic and political partner in the union, it inevitably subsidizes the other nations. Scotland, for instance, receives almost £8bn a year.[5] And yet of all the Britons, the English are most unsure of their identity, most unclear about the distinction between Britain and England, Britishness and Englishness. What, after all, is English identity? Is it confined to imperial pints of warm, flat beer, driving on the left, fish'n'chips on a Friday night, and

on English housing, health, and education, as Tam Dalyell, Member for West Lothian, tirelessly points out. In the 2005 general election five Scottish National Party MPs were returned, and three Plaid Cymru.

pounds, shillings, and pence? Can any sense of English identity, like Scottish and Welsh culture, usefully disentangle itself from British identity?

Perhaps not. England has no national dress. Scottish and Welsh national dress may have been nineteenth-century inventions, but they remain one of the ways in which identities can be expressed within Britain and abroad. There is no English national anthem. The royal anthem should obviously be reserved for teams that, as in athletics, compete as Great Britain, and it should not double as an English anthem, as it is in rugby and football. 'Land of Hope and Glory' seems to be being adopted at sporting events such as the Commonwealth Games, but 'Jerusalem' is perhaps more appropriate, and was memorably sung at Trafalgar Square when the English cricket team won the Ashes in 2005. Both the Rugby Football Union and the Football Association have been lobbied for new anthems, but there are as yet no plans for change.[6] Neither is there much popular indigenous English folk culture. This was variously swept away by the Reformation and, later, by industrialization, and what little remains, such as mumming and morris dancing, seems to embarrass the English – a people who would be charmed to find such traditions anywhere else in the world.*

These emblematic absences within English identity – folk music, costume, holidays, and customs – seem to be the very things that define the other partners in the Union. Irish culture, for example, is celebrated

---

* Traditional English music is, however, currently being compellingly revived by Eliza Carthy, Seth Lakeman, and Jim Moray (among many others), although in terms of popular music, this constituency is still relatively small.

internationally for St Patrick's Day and *Riverdance*, while all over the world there are Irish theme pubs playing Irish folk music. Similarly, the Scots have Burns Night and kilts, and the Welsh their Eisteddfods and singing. There is nothing for the English. What defines them? Julian Barnes, in his novel *England, England* (1998), lists 'Fifty Quintessences of Englishness', which include such things as the national anthem, the BBC, Winston Churchill, and the Battle of Britain; the list is topped by the royal family and Big Ben and the Houses of Parliament, and the Union Jack is there too. But a moment's reflection will reveal that these are all, in fact, British icons.[7] The right-wing philosopher Professor Roger Scruton's lament *England: An Elegy* (2000) is somewhat darker, concluding, 'Any activity connected with the hierarchy and squirearchy of Old England is now likely to be persecuted or even criminalised: not only hunting and gentlemen's clubs, but uniforms, exclusive schools, old ceremonies, even the keeping of old customs and the display of the national flag.'[8] The cross of St George has, at least, been restored.

But the seeds are being laid for a revival of English patriotism. On 14 March 2005, in a speech following his first resignation from the Cabinet, former hard-line Home Secretary David Blunkett called for *A New England: An English Identity within Britain*. He was careful to distance himself from right wing, anti-European, anti-immigration policies – the politics of grievance – but looked forward to treating St George's Day as a celebration of English landscape, poetry, music, democracy, radicalism – and a quirky sense of humour. Blunkett declared the need to 'champion Englishness', as it has been expressed through 'history, culture, and civic values', demanding that 'a more honest account of the distinctive English tradition and English history' be told: 'The challenge is to recast Englishness and English identity, exploring its place within the Union and its relationship with Europe and the wider world.'[9]

It is easy to dismiss this with Samuel Johnson's assertion that 'Patriotism is the last refuge of a scoundrel.'[10] In fact, this favourite rejoinder is a complete misappropriation, and Johnson was referring specifically to the radical 'Patriot' opposition of his period and those who put self-interest before king and country. Blunkett's comments, although admittedly made while he was on the back benches, are intriguing coming from a government that has worked almost ceaselessly to undermine and/or ignore English identity. They also develop his earlier remarks on British identity made in 2002, which famously suggested that, in the interests of an integrated society, British Asian families should speak English at home. What is notable about Blunkett on England, however, for all the implied Whiggism in his perception that history is a form of liberal progress, is that he recognizes the political, social, and cultural ground on which New Englishness can be expressed – and is careful to contain that ground within the wider concept of the union of Great Britain.

The celebration of landscape, poetry, music, democracy, radicalism, and humour is, however, hardly likely to distinguish what is specifically English from what is more generally British. Much of the English experience has been shared with the Scots, the Irish, and the Welsh, and then subsumed in defining Britain and the British Empire. Despite Darcus Howe's assertion that 'Englishness is invariably white and nationalistic', being English has not been a question of nationality in the past, and the whole history of the English people is one of pragmatic compromise and democratic consensus: a nation at once capacious and hybrid.[11] In the absence of *Riverdance* or Robert Burns, the English have William Shakespeare, whose plays offer an almost encyclopaedic account of the human condition and provide a thriving intellectual tourist industry that supports theatres across the world. These plays are not in the least dogmatic: in their very nature they are undecidable – character and action are forged in contingency and compromise, and they are therefore endlessly adaptable in their infinite variety. In this, Shakespeare's work reflects the English temperament: Shakespeare does not provide the English with a philosophy, or an identity, but with the idea of adaptability. Likewise, Shakespeare's raw material, the English language, has also become global through its flexibility. The English philosophical tradition too is characterized by pragmatism, and even the British armed forces have a reputation for improvisation. But the most significant aspect of English culture to be extended across the globe derives from its political temper. The English parliamentary system creates governments of contingency and compromise rather than of ideology and dogma, and through the British Empire, English unionism has extended parliamentary democracy throughout the world. Shakespeare, the English language, parliamentary democracy: these aspects of Englishness have permeated the global imagination in profound ways, and they have become so much part of the structure of our own and other peoples' perceptions and ways of thinking that they are almost invisible. They have effectively become universal human property.

But it is not enough to be able to recognize this elusive, fugitive English identity, or even to celebrate it by displaying the cross of St George on car number plates. Englishness is a way of living rather than a set of rigid principles – and specifically a way of living in Britain today. One could even go so far as to say that the future of British identity lies in adapting the resources of the English, much as it has done in the past. Englishness, in other words, is the key component of Britishness.

Disbanding the Union is simply not feasible. Scotland, Northern Ireland, and Wales could not exist as minnow states wholly independent of England: whether they like it or not, they would be unable to escape from the economy, infrastructure, population, history, and culture that has been shared with England for hundreds of years. Likewise, England needs to accept a responsibility towards its Celtic satellites. Despite this, commentators as different as Roger Scruton and the socialist and songwriter Billy Bragg have rejected the larger identity of Britain and advocated a return to English values. For Scruton, the problem with Britain is that it is defined primarily by law and that the constitution is only of use to immigrants from former colonies (which seems useful enough), while for Bragg, Britain is 'just an economic union that's passed its sell-by date' – a line from his anti-Jubilee anthem 'Take Down the Union Jack' (2002).[12]

Rather than taking down the Union Jack, the Union Jack is actually one way of flying the cross of St George. The Union Jack is an international flag, representing four nations and defining them in their relationships to each other. It is also, moreover, a global flag: the flag of the British Empire. The Nationality Act of 1948 was drafted in response to the post-war labour shortage: all subjects of the crown were made Britons and were therefore eligible for emigration to the motherland. British identity extended to every corner of the United Kingdom and Commonwealth (UKC), and the Act therefore created 'naturalized

British subjects'. Clearly, the idea of Britain is much more than just an institutional and administrative exercise for such citizens, and traditionally the relationship of immigrants to the country has been to Britain, rather than to England, Scotland, or Wales. By and large, non-white immigrant communities have in consequence tended to recognize that being British is a cohesive and unifying concept beyond immediate issues of laws and citizenship, and so have had a greater allegiance and a patriotic loyalty to Britain than the separatist Scots, Irish, or Welsh. The very absence of many British emblems of national identity – things that make up the tapestry of everyday experience such as dress, cuisine, music, and annual festivals – is perceived to be a positive advantage in forming communities that are able to celebrate activities taken from immigrant homelands within a British context, and which may in turn contribute to the diversity of British identity. Hence in 1998, Diwali, the Hindu festival of light, was celebrated on Radio 4's long-running soap *The Archers*, and in 2001 the then Foreign Secretary, Robin Cook, announced that chicken tikka masala was the national dish of Great Britain.[13]

Britain must certainly embrace this racial and national diversity, but it is easy to over-emphasize it. According to the 2001 census, the total number of Asians, Bangladeshi, Afro-Caribbean, and Chinese immigrants make up less than 8 per cent of the British population: individually, these groups are tiny minorities. While recognizing the contribution of such communities to British identity, it is essential not to lose sight of what the Scottish, Irish, Welsh, and, most importantly, the English contribution should be to Britain. The English voice cannot continue to be ignored or suppressed. Why cannot the English define themselves as such on official documentation? Why are they not afforded the same devolved rights as the Scottish and the Welsh? Labour governments, it transpires, have only had a majority three times in England in the post-war period, and in the 2005 election, although more voters in England actually voted Conservative, many more Labour candidates were returned. Scottish majorities for Labour or the Liberals were themselves of course three times rewarded with Conservative governments in Westminster, but the Scots at least now have their own Parliament, just as the Welsh have their Assembly. This limited devolution was made possible, ironically, because these nations were able to maintain a sense of their own identity and culture within that of Great Britain in a spirit of dual nationalism – which is what the English now need to develop: they are both English and British.

There could be no better flag to map the ebb and flow of identity and of multiple identities, of nationality, of dual nationality, and of plural nationalities than the Union Jack. It can be read as a symbolic chart of different lands and different peoples, and of the ways they found to live together. It reminds us that there is not one, but a series of united kingdoms, made up since Roman times of invaders, visitors, immigrants, and refugees to the British Isles. It is also a miniature history of this archipelago, as well as being an historical artefact itself – a medieval relic, generated by the art of heraldry. It has travelled widely: at war and in peace, for trade and defence, to the most distant shores and most remote reaches of the earth. It has been raised to protect the liberties of British citizens around the world, has stood up against some of the most tyrannical assaults on human rights, and has mourned its fallen heroes.

The Union Jack has memories lying in its folds and history wrapped in its furls. What are its future destinations? Where will it be struck? Three occasions are certain: 2006 is the four-hundredth anniversary of the first raising of the Great Flag of Union; 2007 is the three-hundredth anniversary of the Act of Union with Scotland; and in 2012, the Olympic Games will come to the United Kingdom. An old flag will fly over these events, a scrap of linen that has flown many, many times before, an emblem as much for Britain in the twenty-first century as it was when it was first hoisted. It will fly in many different variations, and it will continue to fly, streaming across the skies, floating over the ether, carried to the planets, and even to the stars: an emblem of unity, conciliation, and renewal – the Union Jack.

EARLY TEXTS OF 'RULE, BRITANNIA' AND 'GOD SAVE THE KING'

RULE, BRITANNIA

(James Thomson, 1740, set to music by Thomas Arne, 1753;
from David Mallet, *Alfred the Great, an Oratorio* (1754), 32–3)

ALFRED   When *BRITAIN* first, at Heav'n's Command,

Arose from out the azure Main;

This was the Charter of the Land,

And guardian Angels sung this Strain:

Rule, *BRITANNIA*, rule the Waves;

BRITONS never will be Slaves.

ELTRUDA   The Nations, not so blest as Thee,

Must, in their Turns, to Tyrants fall:

While thou shalt flourish great and free,

The Dread and Envy of them all,

                     Rule, *&c.*

ALFRED   Thee, haughty Tyrants ne'er shall tame;

All their Attempts to bend thee down,

Will but arouse thy gen'rous Flame;

But work their Woe and thy Renown.

Rule, *&c*.

Eʟᴛʀᴜᴅᴀ, and grand Chorus

The Muses, still with Freedom found,

Shall to thy happy Coast repair:

Blest Isle! with matchless Beauty crown'd,

And manly Hearts to guard the Fair.

Rule, *Bʀɪᴛᴀɴɴɪᴀ*, rule the Waves;

Bʀɪᴛᴏɴs never will be Slaves.

Gᴏᴅ Sᴀᴠᴇ ᴛʜᴇ Kɪɴɢ

(James Oswald, *c.*1740; set to music by Henry Carey; from
The Aviary: or, Magazine of British Melody (*c.*1750), 181–2)

Gᴏᴅ save great George our King,

Long live our noble King,

God save the King;

Send him victorious,

Happy and glorious,

Long to reign over us,

God save the King.

O Lord our God arise,

Scatter his Enemies

And make them fall;
Confound their Politicks,
Frustrate their knavish Tricks,
On him our Hopes we fix,
    God save us all.

Thy choicest Gifts in store,
On George be pleas'd to pour;
    Long may he reign;
May he defend our Laws,
And ever give us Cause,
To say with Heart and Voice,
    God save the King.

Oh! grant that Marshal Wade
May, by thy mighty Aid,
    Victory bring;
May he Sedition hush,
And like a Torrent rush,
Rebellious Scots to crush,
    God save the King.

Confound tall Jemmy's Plot,
Pope, French, and Spanish Knot,
    Confound them all;
Villains notorious,
Their Fears inglorious,

Never shall conquer us,
    Confound them all.

O Lord look down, and save
Thy Servant George, the brave,
    Our noble King;
Protect our Church and State,
And make true Britons hate
Priests with bald-headed Pates,
    Of the French King.

Oh! now some People say,
Young Charles is run away,
    Over to France;
'Cause he was sore afraid,
Of valiant Marshal Wade,
For if that he had staid,
    He'd stood no Chance.

Since this good News we bring,
Britons rejoice, and sing
    God save the King;
And the royal Family,
O may they multiply,
Sing till the Day we die,
    God save the King.

Let's drink a Health to them,

Fill your Glass to the Brim,

    God save the King;

Heavens grant the Wars to cease,

That trading may encrease,

Unite in Love and Peace,

    God save the King.

CHRONOLOGY OF ENGLISH, SCOTTISH, AND BRITISH MONARCHS

ENGLISH MONARCHS: YEARS RULED

These tables are guides only: dates and nomenclature, particularly pre-Conquest, are disputed. After Offa, there was no overlord of the English kings for ninety years. Mercia remained the dominant power in England until the death of Beornwulf. Thereafter, Wessex was in the ascendant under Ecgberht, who became overlord in 828. Ecgberht laid the foundations for a permanent unity, which was eventually achieved by Alfred, who became overlord in 886. The symbol † indicates kings of Mercia, and ‡ kings of Wessex.

Offa (King of Mercia, 757; English overlord, 774)	774–96
Ecgfrith†	796
Cenwulf†	796–821
Ceolwulf†	821–3
Beornwulf†	823–5
Ecgberht‡	825–39
Æthelwulf‡	839–55/8
Æthelbald‡	855/8–60
Æthelberht‡	860–6
Æthelred I‡	866–71

Alfred the Great (King of the English, 886)‡	871–99
Edward I, the Elder	899–924
Athelstan	924–39
Edmund I, the Magnificent	939–46
Eadred	946–55
Eadwig All-Fair	955–9
Edgar the Peacemaker/Pacific	959–75
Edward II, the Martyr	975–9
Æthelred II, the Unready	979–1013
[Sweyn II of Denmark	1013–14]
Æthelred II [restored]	1014–16
Edmund II, Ironside	1016
Canute I, the Great	1016–35
Harold I, Harefoot	1035–40
Canute II (Hardicanute)	1040–2
Edward III, the Confessor	1042–66
Harold II	1066
[numbering restarts]	
William I, the Conqueror	1066–87
William II, Rufus	1087–1100
Henry I	1100–35
Stephen, Count of Blois	1135–54
Henry II	1154–89
Richard I, the Lionheart/*Coeur de Lion*	1189–99
John	1199–1216
Henry III	1216–72
Edward I	1272–1307
Edward II	1307–27
Edward III	1327–77

Richard II	1377–99
Henry IV	1399–1413
Henry V	1413–22
Henry VI	1422–61
Edward IV	1461–83
Edward V	1483
Richard III	1483–5
Henry VII	1485–1509
Henry VIII	1509–47
Edward VI	1547–53
Jane	1553
Mary I	1553–8
Elizabeth I	1558–1603

SCOTTISH MONARCHS: YEARS RULED

Kenneth MacAlpin	844–59
Donald I	859–63
Constantine I	863–77
Ædh Swiftfoot	877–8
Eocha and Cric	878–89
Donald II	889–900
Constantine II	900–942
Malcolm I	942–54
Indulph	954–62
Dubh	962–7
Cuilean	967–71
Kenneth II	971–95
Constantine III	995–7

Kenneth III	997–1005
Malcolm II	1005–34
Duncan I, the Gracious	1034–40
Macbeth	1040–57
Lulach	1057–8
Malcolm III, Ceannmor (Great Head)	1058–93
Donald Bane	1093–4
Duncan II	1094
Donald Bane [restored]	1094–7
Edgar	1097–1107
Alexander I, the Fierce	1107–24
David I, the Saint of Scotland	1124–53
Malcolm IV, the Maiden	1153–65
William I, the Lion	1165–1214
Alexander II	1214–49
Alexander III	1249–86
Margaret, Maid of Norway	1286–90
[Disputed succession	1290–92]
John Balliol	1292–6
[Edward I of England	1296–1306]
Robert I, the Bruce	1306–29
David II	1329–71
Robert II	1371–90
Robert III	1390–1406
James I	1406–37
James II	1437–60
James III	1460–88
James IV	1488–1513
James V	1513–42

Mary	1542–67
James VI	1567–1625

BRITISH MONARCHS: YEARS RULED

James I (VI of Scotland)	1603–25
Charles I	1625–49
[Commonwealth	1649–60
Oliver Cromwell, Lord Protector	1653–8
Richard Cromwell, Lord Protector	1658–9]
Charles II	1660–85
James II (VII of Scotland)	1685–8
William III and II and Mary II	1689–94
William III and II	1689–1702
Anne	1702–14
George I	1714–27
George II	1727–60
George III	1760–1820
George IV	1820–30
William IV	1830–7
Victoria	1837–1901
Edward VII	1901–10
George V	1910–36
Edward VIII	1936
George VI	1936–52
Elizabeth II	1952–

DIMENSIONS OF
THE UNION JACK

The Union Flag shall be Azure, the Crosses Saltire of St Andrew and St Patrick, Quarterly per saltire, counterchanged Argent and Gules, the latter fimbriated of the second, surmounted by the Cross of St George of the third, fimbriated as the Saltire.

In the *Memorandum relative to the Origin of the Union Flag in its Present Form* (1801), the admiralty worked out a 'Table of Proportions, adapted for a Flag 15 feet by 7 $\frac{1}{2}$ feet', which follows the narrow fimbriation bordering the cross of St George:

					ft.	in.	
The + of	St George	.	.	$\frac{1}{5}$	1	6	
	Two borders of $\frac{1}{5}$ each			$\frac{2}{15}$	1	0	together $\frac{1}{3}$ ... $\frac{1}{3}$

The × of	St Patrick	.	.	$\frac{1}{15}$	0	6	
	Its border	.	.	$\frac{1}{30}$	0	6	together $\frac{1}{10}$ ... $\frac{1}{5}$
	St Andrew	.	.	$\frac{1}{10}$	0	9	

(Fox-Davies, 615)

RULES FOR HOISTING FLAGS ON GOVERNMENT BUILDINGS

THE FOLLOWING REGULATIONS are circulated by Her Majesty's Command to the Government Offices concerned.

DATES ON WHICH FLAGS ARE TO BE FLOWN

The dates named on the accompanying Schedule [see page 330].

The Department for Culture, Media and Sport will inform you of any other occasions where Her Majesty has given a special command.

HOW THE UNION FLAG SHOULD BE FLOWN

The broader diagonal white stripe should be at the top left hand side of the flag nearest the flagpole.

PROVINCIAL BUILDINGS

The Schedule applies to Provincial as well as to London buildings (*please see notes 1 and 4*). Where it has been the practice to fly the flag daily, as in the case of some Custom Houses, this may continue.

DEFINITION OF A GOVERNMENT BUILDING

A Government building for the purposes of flag flying is a building that is owned by the Crown or where the majority of occupants are civil servants.

OCCASIONS ON WHICH THE UNION FLAG IS TO BE FLOWN AT HALF MAST (HALF MAST MEANS THE FLAG IS FLOWN TWO-THIRDS UP BETWEEN THE TOP AND BOTTOM OF THE FLAGSTAFF)

a) from the announcement of the death of The Sovereign, except on Proclamation Day, when they are flown at full mast from 11am to sunset;

b) the funeral of members of the Royal Family, subject to special commands from Her Majesty in each case;

c) the funerals of foreign Rulers, subject to special commands from Her Majesty in each case;

d) the funerals of Prime Ministers and ex-Prime Ministers of the United Kingdom, subject to special commands from Her Majesty in each case;

e) the Department for Culture, Media and Sport will inform you of any other occasions where Her Majesty has given a special command.

RULES WHEN DAYS FOR FLYING COINCIDE WITH DAYS FOR FLYING FLAGS AT HALF MAST

To be flown at full mast

a) although a member of the Royal Family, or a near relative of the Royal Family, may be lying dead, unless special commands are received from Her Majesty to the contrary;

b) although it may be the day of the funeral of a foreign Ruler.

If the body of a very distinguished subject is lying at a Government Office the flag may fly at half mast on that office until the body has left (provided it is a day on which the flag would fly) and then the flag is to be hoisted right up. On all other public buildings the flag will fly as usual.

January 2004

DAYS FOR HOISTING FLAGS ON GOVERNMENT BUILDINGS
From 8am till sunset

20 January	Birthday of The Countess of Wessex
6 February	Her Majesty's Accession
19 February	Birthday of The Duke of York
1 March	St David's Day (in Wales only, *see note 1*)
8 March	Commonwealth Day (second Monday in March)
10 March	Birthday of The Earl of Wessex
21 April	Birthday of Her Majesty The Queen
23 April	St George's Day (in England only, *see note 1*)
9 May	Europe Day (*see note 5*)
2 June	Coronation Day
10 June	Birthday of The Duke of Edinburgh
12 June	Official Celebration of Her Majesty's Birthday
15 August	Birthday of The Princess Royal
14 November	Remembrance Day (second Sunday, *see note 3*)
14 November	Birthday of The Prince of Wales
20 November	Her Majesty's Wedding Day
30 November	St Andrew's Day (in Scotland only, *see note 1*)

Also

The day of the opening of a Session of the Houses of Parliament by Her Majesty (*see note 4*)

Also

The day of the prorogation of a Session of the Houses of Parliament by Her Majesty (*see note 4*)

Notes

1. Where a building has two or more flagstaffs the appropriate National flag may be flown in addition to the Union flag but not in a superior position

2. Date to be confirmed

3. Flags should be flown at full mast all day

4. Flags should be flown on this day even if Her Majesty does not perform the ceremony in person. Flags should only be flown in the Greater London area

5. The Union flag should fly alongside the European flag. On Government buildings that only have one flagpole, the Union flag should take precedence

6. If The Queen is to be present in a building, you should get in touch with the Department for Culture, Media and Sport, Architecture and Historic Environment Division

[The days for hoisting flags in Northern Ireland are slightly different.]

March 2004

NOTES

REFERENCES ARE GIVEN as briefly as possible, usually by name of author or editor and page number. Where confusion might arise, short titles are also given. Where no page number appears, the reference is to an online archive, such as the *Oxford Dictionary of National Biography*, or to one of the newspaper databases. A list of all works cited can be found in the bibliography that follows the notes.

ABBREVIATIONS

BL   British Library
Bodl.   Bodleian Library
NLS   National Library of Scotland
NQ   *Notes and Queries*
ODNB   *Oxford Dictionary of National Biography* (online)
OED   *Oxford English Dictionary* (online)

PREFACE
1 Orwell, 533.
2 First suggested in 1975 by J. G. A.
   Pocock and since taken up by
   others including Simon Partridge
   in his British Council lecture
   (2000).
3 Cannon (ed.), 349.
4 Samuel, 208ff.

CHAPTER 1
1 *Caesar's Commentaries on the Gallic
   and Civil Wars* (1851), 113 (Book V,
   Chapter 14).
2 Caplan (ed.), 37, 69; Camden,
   Britannia (1610), 115.
3 Camden, *Remains*, 227.
4 Smiles, 130–31.
5 Camden, *Britannia* (1695), xxxv

(italics reversed):

Solinus tells us, That they painted themselves with certain marks, which *Tertullian* calls *Britonum stigmata*. *He says farther*, The Country was partly possess'd by Barbarians; with the shapes of several beasts, artfully cut out in the bodies of them in their youth, so that these prints in their flesh might grow and increase as their bodies did. Nor is there any thing reckon'd a sign of more patience among these Barbarian Nations, than to make such deep scars in their limbs, as may receive a great deal of this dye.

6 Galatians, 6:17.

7 Caesar's expeditions in 55 and 54 BC were reconnaissance sorties.

8 'De signis', Book XVIII, Chapter 3: Griffiths, *Dragon*, 19.

9 Arrianus, *Tactica*: Griffiths, *Dragon*, 17.

10 *Ammianus Marcellinus*, I, 245 (Book XVI, Chapter 10, vii).

11 Simon James: 'The undoubted similarities and relations between them are best explained in terms of parallel development of many societies in intimate contact, rather than of radiation from a recent single common origin' (Pryor, 9).

12 Geoffrey of Monmouth, VIII, 14–15, 17.

13 Simpson, *Dragons*, 30.

14 Wood, *England*, 29–30; Barber, *King Arthur*, 4 (disputing the authorship of Nennius).

15 Wood, *England*, 30; Barber, *King Arthur*, 8.

16 Barber, *Legends*, 16. Geoffrey of Monmouth was also responsible for (or at least a popularizer of) the Brutus myth that Britain had been founded by the grandson of Aeneas and that London was the New Troy.

17 Barber, *Legends*, 39.

18 Revelation, 13:11–13. This is the Beast of 666, but note that the great dragon of Revelation 12 attempts to deluge the world in *water* spewed from its mouth.

19 Griffiths, *Dragon*, 21–4.

20 *Stories of the Martyrs*, Book II, Chapter 2, 34–6: Griffiths, *Dragon*, 18.

21 Simpson, *Dragons*, 29.

22 *Anglo-Saxon Chronicles*, 54.

23 From Henry of Huntingdon's twelfth-century account, which is where the Uther Pendragon association originates: Griffiths, *Dragon*, 20.

24 *Anglo-Saxon Chronicles*, 3. The *Chronicles* identify *Angelcynn* ('the English race') and *Engla land* ('land of the English') (xxxii).

25 Boutell, 206. John Selden notes in *Titles of Honor* (1614), that 'In that Heptarchie of our Saxons, usually six of the Kings were but as subjects to the supreme' (*OED*).

26 Bede, 75. They also made their entry into Canterbury with this

27 King Canute (Cnut) had a magical
flag which was white until battle
commenced, whereupon a raven
appeared, either cawing in
triumph or despondent in defeat
(Perrin, *British Flags*, 31).

28 Prince Charles's parents do share a
common ancestor in Queen
Victoria.

29 Sellar and Yeatman, 19; *Anglo-
Saxon Chronicles*, 80–81.

30 *Anglo-Saxon Chronicles*, 104.

31 *Chronicon*: Kumar, 42.

32 Harrison, *Anglo-Saxon Thegn*, 48;
Paterson, 125.

33 Hereditary arms may have
originated much earlier with the
families descended from
Charlemagne: see Woodcock and
Robinson (eds.).

34 Cannon and Griffiths, 91. Camden
notes that Henry I's shield and
boots were decorated with golden
lions (*Remains*, 229).

35 Roger de Hoveden claimed that
Robert Trussebut had the
hereditary right to bear the
standard (Perrin, *British Flags*, 33).

36 Cannon and Griffiths, 112;
Bartlett, plate after 148.

37 'Roll of Caerlaverock': *Siege of
Carlaverock*. 'Heraldry is therein,
for the first time, presented to us as
a science' (*Debrett's Peerage...*,
513).

38 Innes of Learney, 102.

39 Hector Boece, *Scotorum Historia*,
tr. John Bellenden, Book I,
Chapter 7: Harvey, *Scottish Flags*,
9.

40 Ormrod, Plate 2; Harvey, *Scottish
Flags*, 11.

41 '*Regale vexillum quod a similitudine
draconis figurata facile agnoscetur*':
McMillan and Stewart, 7; Perrin,
British Flags, 49.

42 Camden, *Remains*, 369–70.

43 It was probably Sir Walter Scott
who first used this phrase to
describe the contention between
the houses of Lancaster and York
in his novel *Anne of Geierstein*
(1829).

44 Listed by Boutell, 207–22.

45 Boutell, 174; Copinger lists 285
(17).

46 Camden, *Remains*, 230.

47 *Siege of Carlaverock*: see Denholm-
Young, 112.

48 Cannon and Griffiths, 254.

49 See Copinger, 248–9.

50 Froissart, 308 (Book I, Chapter
125); Boardman, 51ff.

51 Paterson, 13.

52 Camden, *Remains*, 371.

53 Froissart, 161 (Book I, Chapter
159).

54 Likewise standards – eight yards
long for a king, four for a knight –
but there is no consistency in these
recommendations (Franklyn, 186;
Woodward, 305; Copinger, 247).

55 Chandler and Beckett (eds.), 2.
(Note: bannerolls were silk
banners displayed at funerals and

described lineage in heraldic
pedigrees.)
56 James, 159.
57 Boutell, 166; Ormrod, Plate 5.
58 Carroll, 197.
59 Froissart, 165 (Book I, Chapter
 159).
60 Gillingham, 38.
61 Boardman, 172.
62 Leviticus, 11:29–30.
63 Paterson, 32. The English had
 themselves been slaughtered by
 Welsh archers earlier in the year at
 the Battle of Pilleth.
64 Raphael Holinshed, *The Chronicles
 of England, Scotlande, and Irelande*
 (1587): Shakespeare, ed.
 Humphreys, 171.
65 Holinshed: Shakespeare, ed.
 Humphreys, 175.
66 According to Adam of Usk,
 Douglas declared, 'Have I not slain
 two King Henries … with mine
 own hand? 'Tis an evil hour for us
 that a third yet lives to be our
 victor.'
67 Adam of Usk, 83, 253.
68 Adam of Usk, 83, 253.
69 Boardman, 157–8.
70 Perrin, *British Flags*, 34.
71 Barber, *Legends*, 68; see also Sir
 Galahad in Malory II, 236–40
 (Chapter 11).

CHAPTER 11
1 Green, *Union Jack*, 1.
2 'Padstow May Song', Gundry, 14.
3 Voraigne, I, 238.

4 Riches, 34–5; Cannon.
5 James, 5.
6 Riches, 17.
7 Summerson.
8 Barber, *Knight*, 28.
9 Boulton, 12.
10 Voraigne, I, 242.
11 The most complete surviving cycle
 is at St Neot's in Cornwall.
12 Riches, 34–5.
13 Froissart, 68 (Book I, Chapter 27).
14 Summerson.
15 Pryor, 36.
16 Perrin, *British Flags*, 34.
17 Riches, xiii.
18 Sisam (eds.), 384.
19 Barber, *King Arthur*, plate 12;
 Riches, 19–20.
20 Riches, 103.
21 Thomas of Chobham:
 Summerson.
22 Woodward, I, 305.
23 Harvey, *Scottish Flags*, 20.
24 Kumar, 83.
25 Kumar, 84.
26 James, 113.
27 Camden, *Remains*, 10.
28 Froissart, 76 (Book I, Chapter 31).
29 Summerson. Green gives the
 Wardrobe Accounts for 1345–9
 (*Union Jack*, 2). Note that from the
 1330s, ships were being named
 after saints.
30 Froissart (Book I, Chapter 50), 102.
31 Ormrod, 188; Griffiths, 'Later
 Middle Ages', 254.
32 Perrin, *British Flags*, 37.
33 Summerson.

34 Speed, 687 (quoting Polydore Vergil): Harvey, *Scottish Flags*, 20.

35 Perrin, *British Flags*, 43–4; Summerson.

36 Froissart, 382–3 (Book IV, Chapter 81).

37 Franklyn, 186–7.

38 James, 89.

39 Boulton, 17–18, 14, 7–8.

40 Barber, *Knight*, 339. The FSKSG appear to have worn black mantles, and carried a red shield with a white cross; their seal was of St George slaying the dragon (Boulton, 17–45).

41 Froissart claimed that in 1344, Edward founded the 'Knights of the Blue Garter': 'the most gallant knights in the land', up to forty in number (128 (Book I, Chapter 100)).

42 Barber, *Knight*, 343ff.

43 See Boulton, 96–166.

44 Boulton, 348–55.

45 Green, *Union Jack*, 2–4.

46 BL, Harl. MSS 1309, fo. 34: Green, *Union Jack*, 3. Perrin argues that the ordinance was issued after and in response to the Scottish order (*British Flags*).

47 Nicolas, 'Battle of Agincourt', 107: Harvey, *Scottish Flags*, 5.

48 Walsingham, 27: Boardman, 213.

49 Summerson.

50 BL, Lansdowne MS 285: Twiss, I, 456; Perrin, *British Flags*, 41.

51 Green, *Union Jack*, 2.

52 Davies (ed.), 185.

53 Hardyng: Summerson.

54 Griffiths, 'Later Middle Ages', 255.

55 Griffiths, 'Later Middle Ages', 256.

56 Summerson.

57 Scruton, 1.

58 Hutton, 55.

59 Hutton, 27.

60 Summerson.

61 Hutton, 98, 208.

62 Perrin, *British Flags*, 45–6.

63 Riches, 115.

64 Camden, *Remains*, 7.

CHAPTER III

1 Boece, Book X, Chapter 5: Harvey, *Scottish Flags*, 3. In John Bellenden's translation (1536) of Hector Boece (*c.* 1520), who worked from a now lost source (*c.* 1165), this is erroneously given as the eve of a battle with the Saxons at East Lothian in 832, led by Athelstan – not to be confused with King Athelstan, who led the English at the Battle of Brunanburh in 937.

2 His biographer Ursula Hall points out that 'in no early or medieval text is there any reference to Andrew's being put to death on a special X-shaped cross' (*ODNB*).

3 Woodward, II, 309.

4 *Anglo-Saxon Chronicles*, 109.

5 Harvey, *Scottish Flags*, 4.

6 Hall, *ODNB*.

7 McMillan and Stewart, 13.

8 Wallace later became a figure of the British resistance to the Norman

yoke: see Colin Kidd, 'Sentiment, Race and Revival: Scottish Identities in the Aftermath of Enlightenment', in Brockliss and Eastwood (eds.), 121.

9 Hall, *ODNB*.

10 Froissart, 30 (Book I, Chapter 17); Child 161, stanzas 47–8; Paterson, 3.

11 *Acts of the Parliament of Scotland*, I, 191: Perrin, *British Flags*, 47.

12 Boulton, 371.

13 McMillan and Stewart, 19.

14 Hall, *ODNB*.

15 The Aberdeen breviary of Bishop Elphinstone: Hall, *ODNB*.

16 McMillan and Stewart, 27.

17 Aeneas Sylvius Piccolimini: Paterson, 75.

18 Paterson, 67.

19 Griffiths, 'Later Middle Ages', 192.

20 Neville, 152.

21 See William Dunbar's 'The Thrissill and the Rois'.

22 See Major.

23 Stancliffe.

24 McCullough (ed.), 55.

25 McCullough (ed.), 77.

26 McCullough (ed.), 77.

27 Numbers, 1:52 and throughout. There is also a striking passage in The Song of Solomon, 6:4, 'Thou art beautiful, my love, as Tirzah, comely as Jerusalem, terrible as an army with banners.'

28 McCullough (ed.), 113.

29 McCullough (ed.), 116.

30 Ferguson, *Empire*, 55ff.

31 Perrin, *British Flags*, 51.

32 Perrin, *British Flags*, 52.

33 *Neptune François* (1693) describes the 'Ierse Irlondois' as the red diagonal on white, and the standard is confirmed in *De Doorliughtige Weerld* (1700): see G. A. Hayes-McCoy, *A History of Irish Flags from Earliest Times* (Academy Press, Dublin, 1979).

34 Weight, 703.

35 According to the BBC, Wales should no longer be described as a 'principality' (Paxman, viii).

36 McGann (ed.), 635.

37 *Anglo-Saxon Chronicles*, 12 (records that three German tribes arrived: the Saxons, Angles, and Jutes).

38 Pryor, 143–4, 152ff., 224, 234, 240.

39 Kumar, 71.

40 Gerald of Wales, 274.

41 Evans, 'St David'.

42 Bartlett, 150.

43 Pierre de Langtoft: Bartlett, 160–61.

44 Cannon (ed.), 962.

45 Gerald of Wales described the skill of the Welsh archers (Chandler and Beckett (eds.), 9).

46 Bartlett, 201.

47 Minot, 'The Bataile of Halidon Hyll', 34.

48 Froissart, 149 (Book I, chapter 129); Barber, *Knight*, 234.

49 Bartlett, 177.

50 Griffiths, 'Later Middle Ages', 224.

51 Griffiths, 'Later Middle Ages', 223.

52 Cannon (ed.), 944.

53 Colley, 13.

54 Siddons, *passim*.

CHAPTER IV

1 Proclamation of Accession made 24 March 1603: *Stuart Royal Proclamations*, I, 14.

2 On her deathbed, being asked to nominate her successor, Elizabeth declared, 'I told you my seat had been the seat of kings and I will have no rascal to succeed me. Who should succeed me but a king?' This was taken to mean her cousin, James VI.

3 Kishlansky, 64; *Scarce and Valuable Tracts*, I, 148–59 (Speech to Houses of Parliament, 19 March 1603).

4 Atwood, iv: Stat.1, Jas.1, C.1 (James's first proclamation, 20 October 1604; *OED*).

5 Scarce and *Valuable Tracts*, I, 171.

6 Cornwallis, C1r.

7 Cornwallis, C2v.

8 Gordon, 44: Levack, 4. Gordon (or Gordoun) also argued that division was satanic destructiveness.

9 Daiches, 17.

10 Thomas, 418.

11 Bacon, *Letters*, III, 194: Thomas, 417–18.

12 Camden, *Remains*, 185.

13 Campion.

14 Drummond, 'The River of Ferth Fasting', 182.

15 Spenser, *Faerie Queene*, III, iii, 48: 'So shall the Briton bloud their crowne againe reclame'.

16 There are also brief remarks in the 'Notes' to Michael Drayton's *Barrons Wars* (1603) and Francis Bacon's *Advancement of Learning* (1605); likewise in less well-known works such as Francis Godwin's *A Catalogue of the Bishops of England…* (1601) and Matthew Sutcliffe, *The Subuersion of Robert Parsons his Confused and Worthlesse Work, entitled, A Treatise of Three Conuersions of England from Paganisme to Christian Religion* (1606); and there are a handful of mentions (ten) in Sir William Segar's *Honor Military, and Ciuill contained in foure bookes* (1602), concerning chivalry and the Order of the Garter.

17 Luke 16:22, the parable of Dives and Lazarus, has 'Abraham's bosom' as heaven; for 'When Arthur first in court began', see Percy's *Reliques*, I, IX.

18 The Arthurian thread in the texture is confirmed by a later remark by Shallow: 'I remember at Mile-End Green, when I lay at Clement's Inn – I was then Sir Dagonet in Arthur's show…' (*Henry IV (Part 2)*, III, ii, 277–8). According to Malory, Sir Dagonet was the fool in King Arthur's court, and 'The Auncient Order, Society, & Vnitie Laudable, of Prince Arthure, and his knightly Armory of the Round Table' practiced archery on Mile-End

Green. Richard Mulcaster, first headmaster of Merchant Taylors' School, whose pupils included Spenser, describes the society in *Positions... for the Training up of Children* (1581).

19 Brian Levack argues regarding the creation of 'Great Britain', 'The only evidence we have of its use, except in diplomatic communications and in official Scottish documents, comes from the letters of a few self-conscious unionists and the works of a number of poets, scholars, and dramatists' (Levack, 190); Thomas, 428.

20 Cannon (ed.), 351.

21 See pro-union works by Sir Thomas Craig, *De Unione Regnorum Tractatus* (1605), *A Treatise on the Union of the British Realms*, and L. Loyd, *The Jubile of Britane* (1607).

22 NLS, MS 2517, fo. 67v.

23 Boutell, 255.

24 *Stuart Royal Proclamations*, I, 135–6 (no. 64).

25 *Register of the Privy Council of Scotland*, VII, ed. David Masson (1885), 498–9.

26 Balfour's *Annals for 1606: Register of the Privy Council of Scotland*, VII, 499n.

27 Stewart, 8; see *Ensigns, Colours or Flags*, 17.

28 Hugh Lee, 23 March–2 April 1607, in *Calendar of Manuscripts of... the Marquis of Salisbury*, XIX, 72. See also Pepys, 27 June 1662.

29 Paterson, 215.

30 Bacon, *A Briefe Discovrse, tovching the Happie Vnion of... England, and Scotland* (1603) (Bacon's *Works*, VI, 464): Thomas, 390.

31 *Stuart Royal Proclamations*, II, 418n.

32 Perrin, *British Flags*, 58.

33 Perrin, *British Flags*, 59. The earliest use of 'jack' to describe a flag also came from Pennington on 3 July 1633, in directions for pirate patrols (Perrin, *British Flags*, 61).

34 *Stuart Royal Proclamations*, II, 417–18 (no. 181).

35 Perrin (*British Flags*) dates it to 1625.

36 Stancliffe.

37 I, i, 153–4.

38 Helm, 7: Summerson.

39 Clarendon, 249 (Chapter 35).

40 Ashley, 93.

41 See Ashley, 170.

42 Exodus 20:4.

43 There is a Holler etching of this in John Vicar's *Sight of the Transactions of these Latter Yeares* (London, 1646): Ashley, 67.

44 Hutton, 208. On 8 June 1647, all feast days were abolished (*Acts and Ordinances of the Interregnum*, I, 954).

45 Perrin, *British Flags*, 62–3; Summerson.

46 A sequel to the ballad 'St George for England', attributed to one

John Grubb, included the line,
'Like plowmen, when they hew
their way / Thro' stubborn rump
of beef', alluding to the Rump
Parliament (Percy's *Reliques*, IX,
xv).

47 *Calendar of State
Papers... 1649–1650*, 14.

48 'The flag to be borne by the
admiral, vice-admiral, and rear-
admiral to be the one now
presented, viz., the arms of
England and Ireland in two
escutcheons, on a red flag within a
compartment, or' (*Calendar of State
Papers... 1649–1650*, 28).

49 Daiches, 28.

50 BL, Harl. MS, 1460; see McMillan
and Stewart, 42–4. Abroad,
Scottish brigades often carried the
saltire on a green field.

51 Stewart, 12.

52 *Interesting Tracts relating to...
Jamaica*, 273.

53 Green, *Union Jack*, 9, 12.

54 Pepys, II, 136–7.

55 James II, *Memoirs*, 17.

56 James II, *Memoirs*, 152, 156, 200.

57 The *Proclamation* is printed in
black letter and roman fount. See
also *The Royal Charter of
Confirmation...*, 162.

58 *Our Jack*, 8.

59 Lowick, A2v (italics reversed).

60 Hutton, 230.

61 Hewitt.

62 Smiles, 159–60.

63 Dresser, 29.

64 Hewitt.

65 Camden, *Britannia* (1610), 119. See
also Speed, 167.

66 Dresser, 32.

67 McMillan and Stewart, 21; Hewitt.

CHAPTER V

1 Defoe, *Union*, 32.

2 'Jack' was a cant term for a Jacobite:
see Jonathan Swift, 'A Quibbling
Elegy on the Worshipful Judge
Boat': 'With ev'ry *Wind* he *sail'd*,
and well could *tack*: / Had many
Pendents, but abhor'd a *Jack*'
(*Works*, II, 331).

3 Defoe, *Union*, 46–9.

4 Ferguson, *Empire*, 40; Dilke, 525

5 Nairn, 93.

6 Kishlansky, 326–9.

7 Chamberlen, 248.

8 Defoe, *Union*, 'On the Carrying On
of the Treaty in Scotland', 17.

9 Defoe, *Union*, 'On the Carrying
On...', 18.

10 Nairn, 94 (Lockhart went on to
advocate a dissolution of the
Union); Defoe, *Union*, 'On the
Carrying On...', 44, and 'An
Abstract of the Proceedings on the
Treaty of Union', 196.

11 Kumar, 136.

12 *Articles of the Treaty for an Union
between England and Scotland...*, 1.

13 *Articles of the Treaty for an Union
between England and Scotland...*,
'The Minutes and Proceedings of
the Lords Commissioners', 52, 55.

14 Perrin, *British Flags*, 71 (there is no

record of any alternatives they might have proposed); Green, *Union Jack*, 10.

15 *OED*.

16 Stewart, 14.

17 See Justice, endpaper.

18 Scott, 304–5; 'Mons Meg' was an antique cannon.

19 Nairn, 12.

20 Nairn, 132.

21 Nairn, 108; Kishlansky, Chapter 13.

22 Piggott, 8. The Society of Ancient Britons, for instance, was a group of Welshmen who met in London.

23 Scruton, 2.

24 See Brewer; George Grenville was by this time prime minister.

25 Tooke, 8.

26 Langford, 327; Kidd, *Subverting*, 205.

27 Colley, 116.

28 Sambrook, 53; see Brooks and Faulkner (eds.), 11.

29 Mallet, *Alfred the Great*, 32 (italics reversed); for early text, see pages 317–8.

30 Thomson, xiv.

31 *Merry Musician*, I, 198–201.

32 *The Aviary*, 181 (song 396).

33 *Collection of Old Ballads*, III, 192 (also known as 'When This Old Cap Was New').

34 Colley, 44.

35 *Jacobite Songs and Ballads*, 143.

36 *Pig's Meat* (August/September, 1793), I, iv, 42. Spence also satirized 'Rule, Britannia' as 'The Progress of Liberty' – an anthem that American radicals had also reworked as 'A New Liberty Song'.

37 Znamierowski, 80.

38 Paris, 25.

39 Colley, 123.

40 See Asplin.

41 See, for example, the residence of Lt. Thomas Bowling in Smollett's *Roderick Random* (1748), 238 (II, 42); and 'John Brazier, Victualler' in Willoughby's *Nottingham Directory*.

42 Bailey; the author was a Seventh-Day Baptist.

43 Defoe, *Great Law…*, 20 (Defoe first used the image in his thinly veiled satire, *The Consolidator*, 150).

44 Colley, 260.

45 *Loyal Volunteers*, XLVIII.

46 *Annual Register* (1799), 77.

47 See Benjamin West's iconic painting *The Death of General Wolfe* (1770).

48 Stancliffe gives 1762, Cronin and Adair 1766.

49 James, 289.

50 Colley, 136.

51 *The Remembrancer*, 342.

52 Guthrie, I, frontispiece and 'Explanation'.

53 Hewitt.

54 See also Thomson's 'Summer', ll. 1580–1619.

55 Robert Williams Buchanan wrote a satirical attack on the figure in

'Tommie Atkins': see Brooks and Faulkner (eds.), 312–13.

56 *Humorous and Diverting Dialogues*, 17.

57 *Naval Songster*, 7.

58 *Naval Songster*, 8.

59 See Chamberlayne, II, 52.

60 See Molloy, 189 – these ordinances date back to 1 May 1666.

61 See Chambers, *Cyclopædia*, II, 'Signals'; for more detail on signals, see *General History of Sieges and Battles*, VI, 20–40.

62 See *Signal-Book for the Ships of War*, 58, and Perrin, *Nelson's Signals*.

63 Jones, *Compleat History*, 489–90; Sir George Rooke was Admiral of the Fleet, later succeeded by Sir Cloudesley Shovell.

64 Cooke, I, 145; Simes, I, 201.

65 Palliser, 5.

66 Burchett, xxix: 'besides the Colours borne by Merchant Ships, they are allowed to wear a Pendant, together with a red Jack, with the Union Jack described in a Canton at the upper Corner thereof next the Staff.' The long tapering pendant had St George's cross at the top and was striped red, white, and blue from top to bottom. See also Cowley, 59.

67 See, for example, *Laws, Ordinances, and Institutions of the Admiralty*, II, 342; *Regulations and Instructions Relating to His Majesty's Service at Sea*, 13; and Mountaine, 73–4.

68 *Ensigns, Colours or Flags*, 15–16.

69 Dalrymple, 54.

70 Byron, 76 (repr. in Brosses; a version was also pirated, 'By a Midshipman', which is slightly cruder in tone).

71 Cook, 35; see *Beauties of Nature and Art Displayed*, XI, 112, and XIII, 159.

72 Smith, *New Voyage*, 119 (repr. in *New General Collection of Voyages and Travels*, II, 579).

73 Hunter, 377–8, 386.

74 Drury, 224.

75 *The Meeting of Britannia and Citizen François* (1 January 1803 – to commemorate Peace of Amiens) recognizes the recent union with Ireland with a representation of the second Union Flag.

76 Several other jacks seem to have been inspired by the characteristic spider design of the Union Jack, such as those of Bulgaria, Estonia, Latvia, the Netherlands, Norway, Russia, and Sweden.

77 Ogden, II, 43.

78 Published posthumously as 'EPIGRAM CCXLVI' in Bishop, II, 340–41; subtitled *'Suaviter nunc est'* ('considering how sweet it is at present').

79 Hillsborough, 4–5.

80 *Answer to the late Proposal for Uniting the Kingdoms*, 6.

81 James, 248.

82 *Union Magazine* (January 1801), 52: *OED*.

83 *Statutes...from the Thirty-Ninth Year of the Reign of King George the Third...*, XIV, 359.

84 Vint, I, 590; De Quincey, I, 163; Green, *Union Jack*, 16.

85 *Mariner's Mirror* (April 1952): described on *Flags of the World* website.

86 See Vint, I, 590.

87 Franklyn, 183–4.

88 *Saint George and Saint Patrick*, 23, 26. There was not a great deal of celebratory unionist writing published in 1801; an exception is J. Bisset, *The Peace Offering* (1801), which includes verses and songs on the Irish Union.

89 *Saint George and Saint Patrick*, 20. This may also allude to one of the scandals of 1800, such as the birth of Princess Sophia's son, Thomas Garth.

90 Pye, *Alfred*, 149–50. Flags characterize the imagination too: 'Though on the lips was Death's pale ensign spread, / Though from the cheek the blooming rose was fled, / Though on the liquid radiance of the eyes, / The sable lash a silken curtain lies...' (VI, 233–6; 219).

91 Camden, *Remains*, 228.

92 Pye, 51; see also 'The mingling ensigns wanton in the wind' (IV, 106; 116).

93 Pye, 235 ('Second Prophecy of the future Fortune of Alfred, and of the British Islands').

94 Brooks and Faulkner (eds.), 128.

95 Brooks and Faulkner (eds.), 129. There has been some vexillological debate about the 'meteor flag', considering whether it is an ensign or not. During the eighteenth century, the Red Squadron was the first squadron in the Royal Navy, of which the 'Budge Flag' was a variation flown by privateers, and the British Army carried a very similar flag on campaign. The reference to the meteor is derived from Milton's description of the diabolical standard of the fallen angel Azazel, based on the royal standard of Charles, as opposed to the 'holy memorials' of the heavenly host (V, 593), which are derived from the flags of the Commonwealth:
Who forthwith from the
glittering staff unfurled
The imperial ensign, which full
high advanced
Shone like a meteor streaming to
the wind
With gems and golden lustre
rich imblazed,
Seraphic arms and trophies...
(*Paradise Lost*, I, 535–9)
The nineteenth-century antiquary Emanuel Green claims that the Union Jack is the 'meteor flag' (1).

96 *Hansard* (1805), 365.

97 Harvey, 217; Anderson, 146. Even in 1775, General Howe had rallied the British Army before Bunker

Hill with the words, 'I do not in the least doubt you will behave like Englishmen' (James, 280).

98 Paxman, 243; it was signalled in four minutes, running up twelve separate hoists (Perrin, *Nelson's Signals*, 31).

CHAPTER VI

1 Ferguson, *Empire*, 241.

2 Seeley, 10.

3 Hemans, 7.

4 James, 279.

5 Cowdell, 99–100.

6 Colley, 227.

7 Griffith: Hughes.

8 Bodl. Firth b.25(219) [n.d.]; Bodl. Harding B 11(1227); Bodl. Harding B 11(4313); Bodl. Johnson Ballads 2983–4; Bodl. Harding B 11(466)–(467); Bodl. Harding B 15(109b); Bodl. Harding B 11(1736); Bodl. Firth c.16(65); Bodl. Firth c.16(67) [all mid-nineteenth century].

9 Grant, II, 122.

10 Monkman. See also Butler, 'At Half Mast' (31): 'Aye, trail that banner in the dust / That's braved a thousand years; / For You – who Freedom's sacred form / Has drowned in blood and tears.'

11 Bodl. Harding B 25(289–290) [1819–44]; Bodl. 2806 c.13(324) [n.d.]; Bodl. Harding B 11(396); Bodl. Johnson Ballads 1794–6 [c.1840].

12 Bodl. Harding B 16(292d) [n.d.].

13 *The Times* (18 September 2004), 2w.

14 *Union Jack* (5 February 1880), I. VI, 81.

15 *The Union Jack. Library of High-Class Fiction*, 1, 16.

16 Paris, 71–3.

17 *Cassell's*, II, 8.

18 Frost, 30.

19 For example, there were marches written by Arthur Sowerby (1890) and C. W. Bennett (Boston, *c.* 1910).

20 Bodl. Johnson Ballads 2375. Redman forgets to include the cross of St Patrick in his account.

21 The author and mountaineer Albert Smith's skit *Christopher Tadpole* (1848) includes a comic scene that climaxes, 'Quite unexpectedly they all produced union-jack pocket handkerchiefs, at the same moment', XXIV, 220: *OED*.

22 Dickens, *Dickens' Journalism*, 'Bound for the Great Salt Lake', 250.

23 Sturt: 'Some young ladies of the colony … had worked a silken union to present to Mr. Eyre' (I, 20); Yonge: 'Harry used to write his name all over his [blotting paper] – see – and draw Union-Jacks on it' (I, Chapter 19): *OED*.

24 Dickens, *Great Expectations*, 206 (Chapter 6).

25 Dickens, *Great Expectations*, 206, 292 (Chapter 37).

26 *OED*; the phrase was resurrected by the *New Statesman* (27 March 1997). See also *Daily Chronicle* (2 December 1901): 'Men who no doubt call themselves patriotic Union-Jackites and Big Englanders'.

27 *Ruddigore* (1887), II, 82ff.

28 *Regulations and Ordinances of the Army* (1844), 48: *OED*.

29 See, for example, *Royal Navy Directive*, 26 February 1914.

30 James, 287.

31 Colley, 163–4.

32 Stancliffe.

33 Hill, 47.

34 *Freeman's Journal* (18 March 1857): Hill, 48 (Stancliffe).

35 See Cronin and Adair.

36 Paris, 56–7.

37 Colley, 216.

38 Ruskin, *Fors Clavigera*, IV, 1–15 (Letter xxxvii, January 1874) [Vol. XVIII]; see also *The Stones of Venice*, III, 205–9 (Appendix 2) [Vol. IX]; and 'Guild of St George', XXX, 287–306.

39 Crane, 494; Ward, 31.

40 Elgar and Wensley, iv.

41 Jennings, 3–4: Summerson.

42 Summerson.

43 Baden-Powell, 358, 214.

44 Simpson, *Camelot, passim*; Bryden, *passim*.

45 Fitchett, XV, 390; see Parker, Chapter 5.

46 Mallet, *Alfred the Great*, 49 (V, v).

47 Austin, 49 (II, iii).

48 Brooks and Faulkner (eds.), 255.

49 Matthews and Manley, 15.

50 Bloxam, 16–17.

51 Bloxam, 17, 15, 27.

52 Brontë, 341 (Chapter 2q); Wilde, 138 (Chapter 15).

53 See World Museum, Liverpool.

54 Green, *Union Jack*, 15; Perrin discusses the fimbriation and reduction in size of St Patrick (*British Flags*, 72; see page 328).

55 Green, *Union Jack*, 19.

56 Bodl. Firth b.28(14c) [1840–66]; Bodl. Firth c.16(402) [1858–85]; Bodl. Firth c.26(247) [mid-nineteenth century]; Bodl. Harding B 16(294a) [1858–85]. The ballad attacks the flags of the French and the Russians before concluding:
And long may the brave old banner wave on high,
    Over mountains, river and sea,
As a beacon to friends, and terror to foes,
    Of our country so happy and free.
And if there's a despot who dares to defy,
    Those glorious colours that ever will fly,
They'll find that an Englishman knows how to die,
In defence of the Flag of Old England.

57 Brooks and Faulkner (eds.), 170.

58 Weight, 10; Baden-Powell, 358.

59 *A New Song on the Turko-Russian*

War, Bodl. Harding B 12(253) [1877].

60 *The New Rome: Poems and Ballads of Our Empire* (1899): Brooks and Faulkner (eds.), 314.

61 Buchanan, 331.

62 18 April 1900: Brooks and Faulkner (eds.), 325.

63 'Havelock', *London Illustrated News*: Paris, 40.

64 Paris, 42.

65 The Lucknow Union Jack is currently in the British in India Museum, Nelson, Lancashire.

66 Crosland, 'To the True-Born Briton (After Peace Night)', 5.

67 *NQ* (16 June 1900), 478.

68 *NQ* (9 June 1900), 457–8.

69 Green, *Union Jack*, 20. The *NQ Supplement* adds complications concerning diplomatic officers, and so forth.

70 Baden-Powell, 291.

71 Fox-Davies, 478.

72 Bloxam, 3.

73 Baden-Powell, 292.

74 Fox-Davies, 361.

75 There was a simultaneous debate in NQ.

76 20 October 1902 (PRO HO 144/602/B22911): Flags of the World website.

77 *Hansard* (1902), CXIII, Col. 476.

78 *Hansard* (1908), CXCII, 579: Stewart, 24.

79 Ferguson, *Castle Gay*, 160, 164. See also:

Show thereon a lion rampant,

On a flag of yellow hue,
With St. Andrew's Cross triumphant,
    Blazing on a field of blue.

80 Cuthbertson, 'Britannia Lacessita', 7.

81 Hewitt.

82 BL, Add. MSS, 1879cc3, fo. 7.

83 BL, Add. MSS, 1879cc3, fo. 3.

84 BL, Add. MSS, 1879cc3, fo. 4; also Harrison, *Union Flag*.

85 BL, Add. MSS, 1879cc3, fo. 4.

86 Trippel, endnotes, xiv.

87 Inserted into Trippel, NLS.

Chapter VII

1 Trippel, 109.

2 Trippel, 43.

3 Johnston-Smith, *Union Jack Lyrics*, 9.

4 Johnston-Smith, *The Union Jack*, 15.

5 Curchard, 8–9, 28–9; Stevenson and Troubridge.

6 Baden-Powell, xxxvii. The Girl Guides were formed in 1910.

7 Ferguson, *Pity of War*, 176.

8 In *Pity of War*, Ferguson argues that comradeship was more important than regimental or national loyalty (446).

9 *The Times* (12 November 1918), 10.

10 Ferguson, *Empire*, 306; Miles, 427.

11 The Scots were keenest – by 1915 over a quarter of eligible men had volunteered and the Scottish casualty rate was only exceeded by that of the Turks and the Serbs. Only 11 per cent of Irish enlisted,

and after 1916 even that number dropped in the south (Ferguson, *Pity of War*, 446).

12 Churchill, 208.

13 Coogan, 611.

14 Paxman, 72.

15 Weight, 49–50; O'Donoghue, *passim*.

16 Weight, 56.

17 Weight, 26–7.

18 Ferguson, *Empire*, 348.

19 James, 674.

20 *New Statesman*: Miles, 439.

21 Weight, 103.

22 'Union Jack flies over Berlin', *The Times* (7 July 1945), 4; raising the Hammer and Sickle over the Reichstag on 2 May is the more familiar image.

23 *The Times* (16 August 1945), 1.

24 *Hansard* (1933), cclxxix, 1324.

25 Eliot, 55.

26 Samuel, 88–9; Wood, *England*, plate 15.

27 Weight, 199; Samuel, 185.

28 Weight, 199, 195.

29 Hobsbawm, 222n.

30 Paris, 226.

31 Weight, 230.

32 Weight, 300.

33 Quoted by Weight, 359.

34 Weight, 392.

35 Green, *Days*, 63 (Pearce Marchbank, graphic designer).

36 Nuttall, 121–2.

37 Giuliano, 51–2.

38 *Disc Weekly* (17 July 1965), 6.

39 Kureishi and Savage (eds.), 239

(Nick Jones). See also: 'It is re-representing something the public is familiar with, in a different form. Like clothes. Union Jacks are supposed to be flown, we have a jacket made of one' (*Melody Maker* (3 July 1965), 11).

40 *Disc Weekly* (1 October 1966), 20.

41 Melly, 148.

42 Hebdige, 104.

43 Kureishi and Savage (eds.), 239 (Angela Carter), 319.

44 Green, *Days*, 63 (Marchbank).

45 Based on Davey, 80.

46 *Fabulous 208* (1969), 38.

47 *Telegraph Magazine*, April 1966 (Sheila Macivor): *Telegraph Magazine* (4 September 2004), 15.

48 Weight, 462.

49 Wolstenholme, 118.

50 *The Times* (26 November 1953): Weight, 259.

51 Weight, 464.

52 Weight, 511.

53 Hebdige, 150, n. 16.

54 Savage, 255.

55 Vermorel, 205.

56 Sabin, 209–10.

57 Note that members of the Clash also wore Union Jacks.

58 Davey, 11.

59 *2000AD*, 1084 (25 February–10 March 1998).

60 Joan Bull was created by cartoonist David Low, most famous for Colonel Blimp.

61 Cawthorne, 259.

62 This leads Richard Weight to note,

somewhat archly, that 'in a sense, therefore, it was the Scots and Germans, and not the English, who erased the Welsh from the British mind' (281).

63 Evans, 'St David'.

64 Weight, 283, 284.

65 Weight, 285.

66 Boutell, 259.

67 Cawthorne, 11–12.

68 Miles, 446.

69 Fox-Davies, 362n.

70 Weight, 711.

71 Paxman, 21; Weight, 713.

72 The line 'Ain't no Black in de Union Jack' also appears in Zephaniah, 'Self Defence', 76.

73 This campaign was parodied by Mick Hume in *The Times* (16 June 2003), who discussed adding green, orange, pink, grey, and so forth (T2, 2).

74 Captain Malcolm Farrow, RN, recommends setting up a Union Flag Committee to investigate this and other anomalies.

75 The flag days have recently been questioned by Labour MP Tom Watson (West Bromwich East), (*Independent on Sunday* (9 May 2004), 10). Among his proposals are making 6 June, the anniversary of D-Day, a flag day. Currently in England secular public buildings are only permitted to fly the English flag alongside the Union Jack on St George's Day.

CHAPTER VIII

1 Trevor-Roper, 100.

2 Jones, *English Nation*, 23.

3 Nairn, 317.

4 Jones, *English Nation*, 354.

5 Heffer, 50–1.

6 Campbell. Other suggestions include 'Rule, Britannia', which is obviously a British anthem, and 'Land of Hope and Glory', which is actually an Empire anthem.

7 Is Barnes possibly being ironic? I say 'possibly' because of the strange absence in this novel of black and Asian people.

8 Scruton, 247.

9 Blunkett, 7.

10 Boswell, II, 348 (7 April 1775).

11 Weight, 716.

12 Billy Bragg's attempts to top the charts failed to capture the popular imagination (the single reached No. 22). Strangely, among his criticisms was the complaint that Britain does not have a patron saint.

13 Tariq Modood: 'While Pakistanis in Bradford have been coming to terms with an understanding of themselves as British, it is some Scots and Irish – both within and outside their territorial nations – who are in denial about being British, who see one national identity as incompatible with another', 21.

BIBLIOGRAPHY

PLACE OF PUBLICATION and date only are given for pre-1800 works and for journals; post-1800 works have place, publisher, and date. Unless otherwise stated, place of publication is London; if no publisher is given, the text is on the web. Works with no stated author appear alphabetically by the first significant word in the title. In the interests of allowing for rapid cross-referencing with notes, the only bibliographical distinctions made are between records and official publications, published books, and major online resources; manuscript call numbers are given in the notes, as are references to anonymous songs and ballads.

RECORDS AND OFFICIAL PUBLICATIONS

Acts and Ordinances of the Interregnum, 1642–1660, ed. C. H. Firth and R. S. Rait (Stationery Office, 1911)

Annual Register

The Articles of the Treaty for an Union between England and Scotland, Agreed on by the Commissioners of both Kingdoms, on the Twenty Second of July, 1706 (1707)

Calendar of Manuscripts of the Most Honourable the Marquis of Salisbury, K. G., preserved at Hatfield House, 22 vols. (Historical Manuscript Commission, 1883–1971)

Calendar of State Papers, Domestic Series, 1649–1650, ed. Mary Anne Everett
Green, 13 vols. (Longman and Co., 1875–86)

*Debrett's Peerage, Baronetage, Knightage, and Companionage: with Her Majesty's
Royal Warrant Holders* (Cambridge: Chadwyck-Healey, 199–)

*The Ensigns, Colours or Flags of the Ships at Sea (c.*1750)

A Handy Book of Company and Battalion Drill, (Bemrose and Sons, *c.*1870).

Interesting Tracts relating to the Island of Jamaica (St Jago de la Vega, 1780)

*The Laws, Ordinances, and Institutions of the Admiralty of Great Britain, Civil and
Military*, 2 vols. (1746; also 1766, etc.)

*Loyal Volunteers of London & Environs, Infantry & Cavalry, in their Respective
Uniforms* (1799)

Our Jack (Eyre and Spottiswoode [Government, Legal, and General
Publishers], *c.* 1897)

The Register of the Privy Council of Scotland, 14 vols. (Edinburgh: Privy
Council, 1877–99)

*Regulations and Instructions Relating to His Majesty's Service at Sea. Established
by His Majesty in Council*, seventh edn (1747; also 1767, etc.)

Regulations and Ordinances of the Army (Bemrose and Sons, 1844)

A Roll of Arms of the Reign of Edward the Second, ed. N. H. Nicolas (Pickering,
1828)

*The Royal Charter of Confirmation granted by His Most Excellent Majesty King
James II to the Trinity-House of Deptford-Strond; for the Government and
Increase of the Navigation of England, and the Relief of Poor Mariners, their
Widows, and Orphans, &c.* (1763)

Signal-Book for the Ships of War. Day and Fog (1796)

*The Statutes At Large, from the Thirty-Ninth Year of the Reign of King George the
Third, to the End of the Fifth and Concluding Session of the Eighteenth and Last*

Parliament of Great Britain, held in the Forty-First Year of the Reign of George the Third, 14 vols. (1786–1800)

Stuart Royal Proclamations, 2 vols.: I, ed. James Larkin and Paul Hughes (Oxford: Oxford University Press, 1973); II, ed. James Larkin (Oxford: Oxford University Press, 1983)

PUBLISHED BOOKS

Ackroyd, Peter, *Albion: The Origins of the English Imagination* (Chatto and Windus, 2002)

Adam of Usk, *Chronicon Adæ de Usk, A.D. 1377–1421*, ed. and tr. Edward Maunde Thompson (Oxford: Oxford University Press, 1904)

Ammianus Marcellinus, tr. John Rolfe, 3 vols., Loeb Classical Library (Heinemann, 1950)

Anderson, Benedict, *Imagined Communities: Reflections on the Origin and Spread of Nationalism* (London and New York: Verso, 1991)

The Anglo-Saxon Chronicles, tr. and ed. Michael Swanton (Phoenix, 2000)

An Answer to the late Proposal for Uniting the Kingdoms of Great Britain and Ireland (Dublin, 1751)

Ashley, Maurice, *The English Civil War* (Gloucester: Alan Sutton, 1990)

Asplin, William, *The Impertinence and Imposture of Modern Antiquaries Display'd* (1740)

Atwood, William, *The Superiority and Direct Dominion of the Imperial Crown* (1705)

Austin, Alfred, *England's Darling* (Macmillan and Co., 1896)

The Aviary: or, Magazine of British Melody. Consisting of A Collection of One Thousand Four Hundred and Seventeen Songs, 2nd edn (c.1750)

Bacon, Francis, *The Letters and the Life of Francis Bacon*, ed. James Spedding, 7 vols. (Longman, 1861–74)

Baden-Powell, Robert, *Scouting for Boys* (1908), ed. Elleke Boehmer (Oxford: Oxford University Press, 2004)

Bailey, Nathan, *The Universal Etymological Dictionary* (1727)

Barber, Richard, *King Arthur: Hero and Legend* (Woodbridge: Boydell, 1993)

—*The Knight and Chivalry* (Woodbridge: Boydell, 2000)

—*Legends of King Arthur* (Woodbridge: Boydell, 2001)

Barber, Richard, and Barker, Juliet, *Tournaments: Jousts, Chivalry and Pageants in the Middle Ages* (Woodbridge: Boydell, 2000)

Barclay, Alexander, *The Life of St George*, ed. William Nelson, Early English Text Society (Oxford University Press, 1955)

Barnes, Julian, *England, England* (Picador, 1998)

Barraclough, E. M. C., and Crampton, William, *Flags of the World* (Warne, 1981)

Bartlett, W. B., *The Taming of the Dragon: Edward I and the Conquest of Wales* (Stroud: Sutton, 2003)

Beauties of Nature and Art Displayed, in a Tour through the World, 2nd edn, 13 vols. (1774–5)

Bede's Ecclesiastical History of the English People, ed. Bertram Colgrave and R. A. B. Mynors (Oxford: Oxford University Press, 1992)

Begent, Peter, and Chesshyre, Hubert, *The Most Noble Order of the Garter: 650 Years* (Spink, 1999)

Bishop, Samuel, *The Poetical Works*, 2 vols. (1796)

Bisset, J., *The Peace Offering* (Birmingham: privately printed, 1801)

Blake, Robert (ed.), *The English Word: History, Character, and People* (New York: Harry N. Abrams, 1982)

Blind Harry, *Hary's Wallace*, ed. Matthew P. McDiarmid, 2 vols., Scottish Text
Society (Edinburgh and London: Blackwood and Sons, 1968–9)

Bloxam, M., *The History and Heraldry of the Union Jack and of the Royal Coat of
Arms of Great Britain* (Exeter: Southwoods, *c.* 1928)

Blunkett, David, *A New England: An English Identity within Britain* (Institute
for Public Policy Research, 2005)

Boardman, A. W., *Hotspur: Henry Percy, Medieval Rebel* (Stroud: Sutton, 2003)

Boswell, James, *Boswell's Life of Johnson*, ed. George Birkbeck Hill, rev. L. F.
Powell, 6 vols. (Oxford: Clarendon Press, 1934–50)

Boulton, D'A. J. D., *The Monarchical Orders of Knighthood in Later Medieval
Europe, 1325–1520* (Woodbridge: Boydell, 2000)

Boutell, Charles, *Boutell's Heraldry*, rev. J. P. Brooke-Little (Warne, 1978)

Brewer, John, *Party Ideology and Popular Politics at the Accession of George III*
(Cambridge: Cambridge University Press, 1976)

Brockliss, Laurence, and Eastwood, David (eds.), *A Union of Multiple Identities:
The British Isles, c. 1750–c. 1850* (Manchester: Manchester University Press,
1997)

Brontë, Charlotte, *Villette*, ed. Margaret Smith and Herbert Rosengarten
(Oxford: Oxford University Press, 1984)

Brooks, Chris, and Faulkner, Peter (eds.), *The White Man's Burdens: An
Anthology of British Poetry of the Empire* (Exeter: University of Exeter Press,
1996)

Brosses, Charles de, *Terra Australis Cognita: or, Voyages to the Terra Australis, or
Southern Hemisphere, during the Sixteenth, Seventeenth, and Eighteenth
Centuries*, 3 vols. (Edinburgh, 1766–8)

Browne, Felicia Dorothea [afterwards Hemans], *England and Spain: Or, Valour
and Patriotism* (Cadell and Davies, 1808)

Bryden, Inga, *Reinventing King Arthur: The Arthurian Legends in Victorian Culture* (Aldershot: Ashgate, 2005)

Buchanan, Robert Williams, *Complete Poetical Works*, 2 vols. (Chatto and Windus, 1901)

Burchett, Josiah, *A Complete History of the Most Remarkable Transactions at Sea, from the earliest accounts of time to the conclusion of the last war with France* (1720)

Butler, Martin, *Patriotic and Personal Poems* (Fredericton, *c*.1898)

Butler, Samuel, *Hudibras: In Three Parts* (1710)

Byron, John, *A Journal of a Voyage round the World, in His Majesty's Ship the Dolphin, commanded by the Honourable Commodore Byron... By an Officer on Board the said Ship* (1767)

Caesar, Gaius Julius, *Caesar's Commentaries on the Gallic and Civil Wars*, ed. and tr. W. A. Macdevitt (Bohn, 1851)

Camden, William, *Britannia* (1610)

—*Britannia*, rev. and tr. Edmund Gibson (1695)

—*Remains Concerning Britain* (1674)

Campbell, Denis, 'National Anthem faces Red Card', *Observer*, 5 March 2000

Campion, Thomas, *The Discription of a Maske, presented before the Kinges Maiestie at White-Hall, on Twelfth Night last, in honour of the Lord Hayes, and his Bride, Daughter and Heire to the Honourable, the Lord Dennye, their marriage hauing been the same day at court solemnized* (1607)

Cannon, John (ed.), *The Oxford Companion to British History* (Oxford: Oxford University Press, 1997)

Cannon, John, and Griffiths, Ralph, *The Oxford Illustrated History of the British Monarchy* (Oxford and New York: Oxford University Press, 1998)

Cannon, Jon, unpublished paper

Caplan, Jane (ed.), *Written on the Body: The Tattoo in European and American History* (Reaktion, 2000)

Carr, H. Gresham (ed.), *Flags of the World* (Warne and Co., 1953)

'Lewis Carroll' [Charles Lutwidge Dodgson], *Through the Looking Glass* (London and Glasgow: Blackie and Son, *c*.1950)

Cass, Eddie, and Roud, Steve, *Room, Room, Ladies and Gentlemen: An Introduction to the English Mummers' Play* (EFDSS, 2002)

Cassell's Union Jack Series (Cassell and Co., 1893–4)

Cawthorne, Nigel, *The Strange Laws of Old England* (Portrait, 2004)

Chamberlayne, John, *Magnæ Britanniæ Notitia: or, The Present State of Great Britain*, 31st edn, 2 pts (1735)

Chamberlen, Paul, *An Impartial History of the Life and Reign of our Most Gracious Sovereign Queen Anne* (1738)

Chambers, Ephraim, *Cyclopædia: or, an Universal Dictionary of Arts and Sciences*, 2 vols. (1738)

Chandler, David, and Beckett, Ian (eds.), *The Oxford History of the British Army* (Oxford: Oxford University Press, 1994)

Chick, Leonard, Roth, Charles, and Snyder, Ted, *My Dream of the Union Jack* (Ted Snyder, 1909)

Child, Francis James (ed.), *The English and Scottish Popular Ballads*, 5 vols. (New York: Folklore Press, 1957) [ballads given by number rather than page]

Churchill, Winston, *Into Battle*, ed. Randolph Churchill (Cassell, 1941)

Clarendon, Edward Hyde, First Earl of, *Selections from The History of the Rebellion and The Life of Himself*, ed. G. Huehns (Oxford: Oxford University Press, 1978)

A Collection of Old Ballads Corrected from the Best and Most Ancient Copies Extant, 3 vols. (1723–5)

Colley, Linda, *Britons: Forging the Nation 1707–1837* (New Haven and London: Yale University Press, 1992)

Collis, John, *Celts: Origins, Myths and Inventions* (Stroud: Tempus, 2003)

Coogan, Tim Pat, *Eamon de Valera: The Man Who Was Ireland* (New York: Barnes & Noble, 2001)

Cook, James, *Captain Cook's Second Voyage Round the World, in the Years MDCCLXXII, LXXIII, LXXIV, LXXV* (1776)

Cooke, Edward, *A Voyage to the South Sea, and Round the World, perform'd in the Years 1708, 1709, 1710, and 1711*, 2 vols. (1712)

Copinger, W. A., *Heraldry Simplified: An Easy Introduction to the Science and Complete Body of Armory* (Manchester: Manchester University Press, 1910)

Cornwallis, William, *The Miracvlovs and Happie Vnion of England and Scotland* (Edinburgh, 1604)

Cowdell, Thomas Daniel, *The Nova Scotia Minstrel, Written on a Tour from North America to Great Britain and Ireland; with Suitable Reflections and Moral Songs Adapted to Popular Airs* (Dublin: printed for the author, 1817)

Cowley, John, *The Sailor's Companion, and Merchantman's Convoy* (1740)

Cowper, William, *The Task, A Poem* (1785)

Crane, Walter, *An Artist's Reminiscences* (Methuen and Co., 1907)

Crofts, Cecil, *ABC of the Union Jack* (Gale and Polden, *c*. 1915)

Cronin, Mike, and Adair, Daryl, *The Wearing of the Green: A History of St Patrick's Day* (London and New York: Routledge, 2002)

Crosland, T. W. H., *Outlook Odes* (Unicorn, 1902)

Crystal, David, *The Stories of English* (Penguin, 2005)

Curchard, Madame Henri, *The Union Jack and other Battle Songs & Poems* (Paisley: Alexander Gardner, 1915)

Cuthbertson, James Lister, *Barwon Ballads and School Verses* (Melbourne and London: Melville and Mullen, 1912)

Daiches, David, *Scotland and the Union* (John Murray, 1977)

Dalrymple, Alexander, *A Collection of Voyages chiefly in the Southern Atlantick Ocean. Published from Original M.S.S.* (1775)

Daniel, Samuel, *Complete Works in Verse and Prose of Samuel Daniel*, 5 vols., ed. A. B. Grosart (privately printed, 1885)

Davey, Kevin, *English Imaginaries: Six Studies in Anglo-British Modernity* (Lawrence and Wishart, 1999)

Davies, R. T. (ed.), *Medieval English Lyrics: A Critical Anthology* (Faber, 1966)

De Quincey, Thomas, *Collected Writings*, ed. David Masson, 14 vols. (A. and C. Black, 1896–7)

Defoe, Daniel, *The Consolidator: or, Memoirs of Sundry Transactions from the World in the Moon* (1705)

—*The Great Law of Subordination Consider'd; or, The Insolence and Unsufferable Behaviour of Servants in England duly enquir'd into* (1724)

—*History of the Union of Great Britain* (Edinburgh, 1709)

—*The True-Born Englishman. A Satyr* (1701)

Denholm-Young, N., *History and Heraldry: A Study of the Historical Value of Rolls of Arms* (Oxford: Clarendon Press, 1965)

Dickens, Charles, *Dickens' Journalism: 'The Uncommercial Traveller' and Other Papers, 1859–70*, ed. Michael Slater and John Drew (Dent, 2000)

—*Great Expectations*, ed. Charlotte Mitchell (Harmondsworth: Penguin 1996)

Dickinson, H. T., *Caricatures and the Constitution 1760–1832* (Cambridge: Chadwyck-Healey, 1986)

Dilke, Charles, *Greater Britain: A Record of Travel in English-Speaking Countries*, 8th edn (Macmillan, 1885)

Dresser, Madge, 'Britannia', in Samuel (ed.), *Patriotism*, 26–49

Drummond, William, *The Poems of William Drummond, of Hawthornden*, (1791)

Drury, Robert, *The Pleasant, and Surprizing Adventures of Mr. Robert Drury, during his Fifteen Years Captivity on the Island of Madagascar* (1743)

Duffy, Michael, *The Englishman and the Foreigner* (Cambridge: Chadwyck-Healey, 1986)

Elgar Edward, and Wensley, Shapcott, *The Banner of St George: A Ballad for Chorus and Orchestra* (Novello and Co., *c.* 1900)

Eliot, T. S., *Notes Towards the Definition of Culture* (Faber, 1973)

Evans, George, *Heraldry in Britain* (Foyle, 1953)

Evans, J. Wyn, 'St David', *ODNB*

Ferguson, Dugald, *Castle Gay and Other Poems* (Dunedin: Stone & Co., 1912)

Ferguson, Niall, *Empire: How Britain Made the Modern World* (Penguin, 2004)

—*The Pity of War* (Harmondsworth: Penguin, 1998)

Fitchett, John, *King Alfred: A Poem*, ed. R. Roscoe (privately printed, 1841)

Fox-Davies, A. C., *A Complete Guide to Heraldry*, rev. J. P. Brooke-Little (Nelson, 1969)

Franklyn, Julian, *Shield and Crest: An Account of the Art and Science of Heraldry* (MacGibbon and Kee, 1967)

Froissart's Chronicles, tr. and ed. John Jolliffe (Harmondsworth: Penguin, 1967)

Frost, W. Lane, *The Birth of the Union Jack: A Patriotic Opera for Children* (Curwen and Sons, *c.* 1900)

Gayre of Gayre and Nigg, Lt.-Col. George Robert, *Heraldic Standards, and Other Ensigns* (Edinburgh and London: Oliver and Boyd, 1959)

A General History of Sieges and Battles, by Sea and Land, 12 vols. (1762)

Geoffrey of Monmouth, *The History of the Kings of Britain (Historia regnum Britanniae)*, tr. and ed. Lewis Thorpe (Harmondsworth: Penguin, 1976)

Gerald of Wales, *The Journey through Wales, and The Description of Wales*, tr. Lewis Thorpe (Harmondsworth: Penguin, 1978)

Gibbon, Edmund, *The History of the Decline and Fall of the Roman Empire*, 8 vols., ed. Betty Radice (Folio, 1985)

Gilbert, Sir W. S., and Sullivan, Sir Arthur, *Ruddigore: or, The Witch's Curse*, ed. George Lowell Tracy (Chappell, 1887)

Gillingham, John, *The Wars of the Roses: Peace and Conflict in 15th Century England* (Phoenix, 1981)

Gilroy, Paul, *There Ain't No Black in the Union Jack* (Routledge, 1992)

Giuliano, Geoffrey, *Behind Blue Eyes: The Life of Pete Townshend* (Dutton, 1996)

Gordon, John, *Enotikon* [Uniter]*, or a Sermon of the Union of Great Brittannie in Antiquitie of Language, Name, Religion and Kingdome* (1604)

Grant, Anne, *Eighteen Hundred and Thirteen* (Longman, Hurst, Rees, Orme, and Brown, 1814)

Green, Emanuel, *The Union Jack* (Exeter: William Pollard and Co., 1891), reprinted from *Archaeological Journal* 98 (December 1891), 295–314

Green, Jonathon, *Days in the Life: Voices from the English Underground, 1961–71* (Pimlico, 1998)

Griffith, Owen, *Mynydd Parys* (Caernarfon: Gwasg Genedlaethol Gymreig, c.1898)

Griffiths, Bill, *Meet the Dragon: An Introduction to Beowulf's Adversary* (Heart of Albion, n.d.)

Griffiths, Ralph, 'The Later Middle Ages', in Morgan, 192–256

Gundry, Inglis, *Canow Kernow: Songs and Dances of Cornwall* (St Ives: Federation of Old Cornwall Societies, 1966)

Guthrie, William, *General History of Scotland, from the Earliest Accounts to the Present Time*, 10 vols. (1767)

Hall, Ursula, 'St Andrew', *ODNB*

—*St Andrew and Scotland* (St Andrews: St Andrews University Library, 1994)

Hannay, R. K., *St Andrew of Scotland* (Edinburgh and London: Moray Press, 1934)

Harris, Paul, *The Story of Scotland's Flag* (Lang Sine, 1992)

Harrison, A. P., *The Union Flag of Great Britain* (Soho: A. P. Harrison, *c.*1859)

Harrison, Mark, *Anglo-Saxon Thegn: AD 449–1066* (Osprey, 1993)

Harvey, A. D., *Britain in the Early Nineteenth Century* (Batsford, 1978)

Harvey, C. Cleland, *The Scottish Flags: Notes on the History of S. Andrew's Banner and the Royal Arms* (Glasgow: St Andrew Society, *c.* 1914)

Hastings, Adrian, *The Construction of Nationhood: Ethnicity, Religion and Nationalism* (Cambridge: Cambridge University Press, 1997)

Hebdige, Dick, *Subculture: The Meaning of Style* (Routledge, 1979)

Heffer, Simon, *Nor Shall My Sword: The Reinvention of England* (Weidenfeld and Nicolson, 1999)

Helm, Alex, *The English Mummers' Play* (Woodbridge: Brewer [Folklore Society], 1981)

Hemans, *see* Browne

Hewett, Nora, Home, Beatrice, and Leale, Enid, *Flags, Places, and Songs of Britain* (A. & C. Black, 1938)

Hewitt, Virginia, 'Britannia', *ODNB*

Hill, J. R., 'National Festivals, the State and "Protestant Ascendancy" in Ireland, 1790–1829', *Irish Historical Studies* 24 (1984–5), 30–51

Hillsborough, Wills, Marquess of Downshire, *A Proposal for Uniting the Kingdoms of Great Britain and Ireland* (1751)

Hobsbawm, Eric, *Industry and Empire: From 1750 to the Present Day* (Harmondsworth: Penguin, 1999)

Hughes, E. Wyn, *Looking Back: Anglesey Life in Bygone Days* (*c*.1992)

Humorous and Diverting Dialogues (1755)

Hunter, John, *An Historical Journal of the Transactions at Port Jackson and Norfolk Island, with the Discoveries which have been made in New South Wales* (1793)

Hutton, Ronald, *The Rise and Fall of Merry England: The Ritual Year 1400–1700* (Oxford: Oxford University Press, 1994)

Innes of Learney, Sir Thomas, *Scots Heraldry*, 2nd edn, rev. Malcolm Innes (London and Edinburgh: Johnsonton and Bacon, 1978)

An Introduction to Heraldry (Brook and King, 1823)

Jacobite Songs and Ballads, ed. Gilbert S. MacQuoid (Walter Scott, 1888)

James II, *Memoirs of the English Affairs, Chiefly Naval, from the Year 1660, to 1673* (1729)

James, Lawrence, *Warrior Race: A History of the British at War* (Little, Brown, 2001)

Jennings, Hargrave, *St George: A Miniature Romance* (privately printed, 1853)

Johnston-Smith, Frederick James, *The Union Jack, What it Is and What it Means* (Portsmouth: Holbrook and Son, 1914)

—*Union Jack Lyrics and a Foreword concerning the Flag* (Erskine Macdonald, 1914, repr. 1915, 1916)

Jones, David, *A Compleat History of Europe: or, A View of the Affairs thereof, Civil and Military, for the Year, 1704*, 2nd edn (1710)

Jones, Edwin, *The English Nation: The Great Myth* (Stroud: Sutton, 1998)

Justice, Alexander, *A General Treatise of the Dominion of the Sea* (*c.*1709)

Kidd, Colin, *British Identities Before Nationalism: Ethnicity and Nationhood in the Atlantic World, 1600–1800* (Cambridge: Cambridge University Press, 1999)

—*Subverting Scotland's Past: Scottish Whig Historians and the Creation of an Anglo-British Identity, 1689–c.1830* (Cambridge: Cambridge University Press, 1993)

—'Sentiment, Race and Revival: Scottish Identities in the Aftermath of Enlightenment', in Brockliss and Eastwood (eds.), 110–26

Kipling, Rudyard, *The Collected Poems*, ed. R. T. Jones (Ware: Wordsworth, 2001)

Kishlansky, Mark, *A Monarchy Transformed: Britain 1603–1714* (Harmondsworth: Penguin, 1996)

Kumar, Krishan, *The Making of English National Identity* (Cambridge: Cambridge University Press, 2003)

Kureishi, Hanif, and Savage, Jon (eds.), *The Faber Book of Pop* (Faber, 2002)

Langford, Paul, *A Polite and Commercial People: England 1727–1783* (Oxford: Clarendon Press, 1989)

Leonard, Mark, *Britain™* (Demos, 1997)

Levack, Brian, *The Formation of the British State: England, Scotland, and the Union, 1603–1707* (Oxford: Clarendon Press, 1987)

Lionarons, Joyce Tally, *The Medieval Dragon: The Nature of the Beast in Germanic Literature* (Hisarlik, 1998)

Lipton, Dan, and Thurban, T. W., *My Girl's a Union Jack Girl* (Francis, Day and Hunter, *c.* 1914)

Longmate, Norman, *Island Fortress: The Defence of Great Britain, 1603–1945* (Hutchinson, 1991)

Lowick, Thomas, *The History of the Life & Martyrdom of St. George, the Titular Patron of England* (1664)

McCormick, Bridget, *Perceptions of St Patrick in Eighteenth-Century Ireland* (Dublin: Four Courts, 2000)

McCullough, David Willis (ed.), *Wars of the Irish Kings* (New York: History Book Club, 2000)

McGann, Jerome (ed.), *The New Oxford Book of Romantic Period Verse* (Oxford and New York: Oxford University Press, 1994)

McMillan, William, and Stewart, John, *The Story of the Scottish Flag* (Glasgow: Hugh Hopkins, 1925)

Magnusson, Magnus, *The Vikings* (Stroud: Tempus, 2000)

Major, John, *A History of Greater Britain, as well England as Scotland, compiled from the Ancient Authorities*, tr. Archibald Constable (Edinburgh, 1892)

Mallet, David, *Alfred: A Masque* (1751)

—*Alfred the Great, an Oratorio* (1754)

Malory, Thomas, *Le Morte Darthur*, ed. William Caxton, A. W. Pollard, and Edward Strachey, 2 vols. (Macmillan, 1903)

Marvin, Carolyn and Ingle, David W., *Blood Sacrifice and the Nation: Totem Rituals and the American Flag* (Cambridge: Cambridge University Press, 1999)

Matthews, Vivian, and Manley, Alice, *Little Red Robin: Or, The Dey* [sic] *and the Knight. Original Burlesque Extravaganza* (Lloyd's Register Printing House, 1900)

Melly, George, *Revolt into Style: The Pop Arts in the 50s and 60s* (Oxford: Oxford University Press, 1989)

The Merry Musician; or, A Cure for the Spleen, 4 vols. (1716–33)

Miles, David, *The Tribes of Britain* (Weidenfeld and Nicolson, 2005)

Miller, John, *Religion in the Popular Prints 1600–1832* (Cambridge: Chadwyck-Healey, 1986)

Minot, Laurence, *The Poems of Laurence Minot 1333–1352*, ed. Richard H. Osberg (Michigan: Medieval Institute Publications, 1996)

Mitchell, Adrian, *Heart on the Left: Poems 1953–1984* (Newcastle upon Tyne: Bloodaxe Books, 1997)

Modood, Tariq, 'Defined by Some Distinctly Hyphenated Britishness', *Times Higher Education Supplement* (3 September 2004), 20–21

Molloy, Charles, *De Jure Maritimo et Navali: or, A Treatise of Affairs Maritime and of Commerce*, 7th edn (1722)

Monkman, Thomas Jefferson, *Lyrics: Marine and Rural* (Simpkin, Marshall and Co., 1885)

Morgan, Kenneth O., *The Oxford History of Britain* (Oxford: Oxford University Press, 1988)

Mountaine, William, *The Seaman's Vade-Mecum, and Defensive War by Sea* (1744)

Nairn, Tom, *After Britain: New Labour and the Return of Scotland* (Granta, 2001)

The Naval Songster, or Jack Tar's Chest of Conviviality (c. 1798)

Neville, Cynthia J., *Violence, Custom and Law: The Anglo-Scottish Border Lands in the Later Middle Ages* (Edinburgh: Edinburgh University Press, 1998)

A New General Collection of Voyages and Travels, 4 vols. (1745–7)

Nisbet, Alexander, *A System of Heraldry Speculative and Practical: with the True Art of the Blazon, according to the most approved Heralds in Europe*, 2 vols. (Edinburgh, 1722)

Norris, Una, *The Flag of the Free* (National Union of Conservative and Unionist Associations, c. 1928)

Nuttall, Jeff, *Bomb Culture* (Paladin, 1970)

O'Donoghue, David, *Hitler's Irish Voices: The Story of German Radio's Wartime Irish Service* (Belfast: Beyond the Pale, 1998)

Ogden, James, *The Revolution. An Epic Poem in 12 Books* (1790)

The Orkneyinga Saga: The History of the Earls of Orkney, tr. and ed. Hermann Pàlsson and Paul Edwards (Harmondsworth: Penguin, 1981)

Ormrod, W. M., *The Reign of Edward III* (Stroud: Tempus, 2000)

Orwell, George, *Down and Out in Paris and London*, *The Road to Wigan Pier*, *Homage to Catalonia*, *Essays and Journalism* [single volume] (Secker and Warburg, 1981)

Palliser, Hugh, *An Authentic and Impartial Copy of the Trial of Sir Hugh Palliser, Admiral of the Blue ... by a Person who attended during the Whole Trial* (Portsmouth, 1779)

Paris, Michael, *Warrior Nation: Images of War in British Popular Culture, 1850–2000* (Reaktion, 2000)

Partridge, Simon, 'The British-Irish Council: The Trans-Islands Symbolic and Political Possibilities', *Report on England* (2000)

Paterson, Raymond Campbell, *My Wound is Deep: A History of the Later Anglo-Scots Wars 1380–1560* (Edinburgh: John Donald, 1997)

Parker, Joanne, *'England's Darling': The Victorian Cult of King Alfred the Great* (Manchester: Manchester University Press, 2007 forthcoming)

Paxman, Jeremy, *The English: A Portrait of a People* (Harmondsworth: Penguin, 1999)

Pepys, Samuel, *The Diary of Samuel Pepys*, ed. Robert Latham and William Matthews, 11 vols. (E. Bell & Sons, 1970–83)

Percy, Thomas, *Reliques of Ancient English Poetry*, ed. Nick Groom (Exeter: Exeter University Press, 2006) [ballads given by book and number rather than page]

Perrin, W. G., *British Flags: Their Early History, and their Development at Sea; with an Account of the Origin of the Flag as a National Device* (Cambridge: Cambridge University Press, 1922)

—*Nelson's Signals. The Evolution of the Signal Flags* (HMSO, *c.*1908)

Philips, John, *Cyder, A Poem in Two Books* (1708), ed. John Goodridge and J. C. Pellicer (Cheltenhem: Cyder Press, 2001)

Pig's Meat: or, Lessons for the Swinish Multitude, 3 vols. (1793–5)

Piggott, Stuart, *William Stukeley: An Eighteenth-Century Antiquary* (New York: Thames and Hudson, 1985)

Pocock, J. G. A., 'British History: A Plea for a New Subject', *Journal of Modern History* 47 (1975), 601–24

Pryor, Francis, *Britain AD: A Quest for Arthur, England and the Anglo-Saxons* (HarperCollins, 2004)

Pye, Henry, *Alfred, An Epic Poem, in Six Books* (Bulmer and Co., 1801)

The Remembrancer, or Impartial Repository of Public Events (1776)

Riches, Samantha, *St George: Hero, Martyr and Myth* (Stroud: Sutton, 2000)

Russell, Conrad, *The Causes of the English Civil War* (Oxford: Clarendon Press, 1990)

Ruskin, John, *Complete Works*, 30 vols. (New York: Thomas Crowell, *c.*1900)

Sabin, Roger, '"I Won't Let that Dago By": Rethinking Punk and Racism', in Sabin (ed.), 199–218.

Sabin, Roger (ed.), *Punk Rock: So What? The Cultural Legacy of Punk* (London and New York: Routledge, 1999)

Saint George and Saint Patrick: or, The Rival Saintesses (Dublin, 1800)

St John Hope, W. H., 'The National Flag', *NQ* (30 June 1900), supplement

Sambrook, James, *James Thomson, 1700–1748. A Life* (Oxford: Clarendon Press, 1991)

Samuel, Raphael, *Island Stories: Unravelling Britain* (Verso, 1998)

Samuel, Raphael (ed.), *Patriotism: The Making and Unmaking of British National Identity*, 4 vols. (Routledge, 1989)

Savage, Jon, *England's Dreaming: Sex Pistols and Punk Rock* (Faber, 1991)

Scarce and Valuable Tracts, A Second Collection, 4 vols. (1750)

Scott, Sir Walter, *Waverley Novels*, 25 vols.: Vol. IV, *Rob Roy* (Edinburgh: A. & C. Black, 1870)

Scruton, Roger, *England: An Elegy* (Chatto and Windus, 2000)

Seeley, Sir John, *The Expansion of England* (Macmillan, 1883)

Sellar, W. C., and Yeatman, R. J., *1066 and All That* (Methuen, 1930)

Shakespeare, William, *The First Part of King Henry IV*, ed. A. R. Humphreys, Arden Shakespeare (Methuen, 1960)

—*The Second Part of King Henry IV*, ed. A. R. Humphreys, Arden Shakespeare (Methuen, 1966)

—*King Henry V*, ed. T. W. Craik, Arden Shakespeare (Routledge, 1996)

—*King John*, ed. E. A. J. Honigmann, Arden Shakespeare (Methuen, 1981)

—*The Riverside Shakespeare* [Complete Works], ed. G. Blakemore Evans, *et al*. (Boston: Houghton Mifflin, 1974)

Siddons, Michael Powell, *The Development of Welsh Heraldry*, 2 vols. (Aberystwyth: National Library of Wales, 1991)

The Siege of Carlaverock, ed. and tr. Nicholas Harris Nicolas (Nichols and Son, 1828)

Simes, Thomas, *A Portable Military Library*, 4 vols. (1782)

Simpson, Jacqueline, *British Dragons* (Ware: Wordsworth Folk Lore Society, 2001)

Simpson, Roger, *Camelot Regained: The Arthurian Revival and Tennyson, 1800–1849* (Cambridge: Brewer, 1990)

Sisam, Celia and Kenneth (eds.), *The Oxford Book of Medieval English Verse* (Oxford: Clarendon Press, 1970)

Skeat, Walter, 'The Flag', *NQ* (9 June 1900), 457–8

Smiles, Samuel, *The Image of Antiquity: Ancient Briton and the Romantic Imagination* (New Haven and London: Yale University Press, 1994)

Smith, Albert, *The Struggles and Adventures of Christopher Tadpole at Home and Abroad* (Bentley, 1847)

Smith, Whitney, *Flags through the Ages and across the World* (New York and London: McGraw-Hill, 1976)

Smith, William, *A New Voyage to Guinea* (1744)

Smollett, Tobias, *The Adventures of Roderick Random*, ed. Paul-Gabriel Boucé (Oxford: Oxford University Press, 1979)

Smyth, Alfred P., *The Medieval Life of King Alfred the Great: A Translation and Commentary on the Text Attributed to Asser* (Houndmills: Palgrave, 2002)

Speed, John, *The History of Great Britain under the Conquests of the Romans, Saxons, Danes and Normans with the Successions, Lives, Acts and Issues of the English Monarchs from Julius Caesar to King James* (1611)

Spenser, Edmund, *The Faerie Queene*, ed. A. C. Hamilton (London and New York: Longman, 1977)

Stancliffe, Clare, 'St Patrick', *ODNB*

Stevenson, Robert, and Troubridge, Amy, *The Union Jack. Song for Girl Guides* (Weekes and Co., 1917)

Stewart, John A., *The Union Flag: Its History and Design* (Glasgow and
    Edinburgh: The Scottish Patriotic Society and The St Andrew Society,
    1909)

Sturdy, David, *Alfred the Great* (Constable, 1995)

Sturt, Charles, *Narrative of an Expedition into Central Australia performed under
    the autonomy of Her Majesty's Government during the years 1844, 5 and 6*
    (T. and W. Boone, 1849)

Summerson, Henry, 'St George', *ODNB*

Swift, Jonathan, *The Works of J. S, D.D, D.S.P.D.*, 4 vols. (Dublin, 1735)

Thomas, Keith, *Religion and the Decline of Magic* (Weidenfeld and Nicolson,
    1971)

Thomson, James, *The Complete Poetical Works*, ed. J. Logie Robertson (Oxford
    University Press, 1908)

Tooke, John Horne, *The Petition of an Englishman* (1765)

Trevor-Roper, Hugh (Lord Dacre), 'The Unity of the Kingdom: War and
    Peace with Wales, Scotland, and Ireland', in Robert Blake (ed.), 100–110

Trippel, Major H. F., *The Flag (Daily Mail* [Union Jack Club], *c.* 1908)

Twiss, Sir Travers, *Monumenta Juridica: The Black Book of the Admiralty*, 4 vols.
    (London: Rerum Britannicarum medii ævi Scriptores, 1871–5)

The Union Jack, ed. W. H. G. Kingston and George Alfred Henty (1880–83)

The Union Jack. Library of High-Class Fiction (1894–1933)

The Union Jack Bazaar Cookery Book, compiled Mrs Arthur Hill (Dudley:
    Herald Press, *c.*1910)

Vermorel, Fred and Judy, *Sex Pistols: The Inside Story* (Omnibus, 1987)

Vint, John, *A Concise System of Modern Geography*, 2 vols. (Newcastle upon
    Tyne: Vint and Anderson, 1800–8)

Voraigne, Jacobus de, *The Golden Legend: Readings on the Saints*, tr. William
  Granger Ryan, 2 vols. (Princeton: Princeton University Press, 1993)

Walsingham, Thomas, *The St Albans Chronicle: 1406–20*, ed. V. H. Galbraith
  (Oxford: Clarendon Press, 1927)

Ward, Paul, *Red Flag and Union Jack: Englishness, Patriotism and the British
  Left, 1881–1924* (Royal Historical Society Studies in History, 1998)

Richard Weight, Patriots: *National Identity in Britain, 1940–2000* (Macmillan,
  2002)

Wilde, Oscar, *Complete Works* (Collins, 1980)

Willoughby, Edward, *The Nottingham Directory, containing the Name,
  Profession, and Residence, of every principal Inhabitant* (Nottingham, 1799)

Winter, Eliza, *The Making of Our Union Jack: 1707–1801* (Ontario: privately
  printed, 1911)

Wolstenholme, Kenneth, *They Think It's All Over…: Memories of the Greatest
  Day in English Football* (Robson, 1998)

Wood, Michael, *In Search of the Dark Ages* (New York: Checkmark, 2001)

—*In Search of England: Journeys into the English Past* (Harmondsworth:
  Penguin, 1999)

Woodcock, Thomas, and Robinson, John Martin (eds.), *Oxford Guide to
  Heraldry*, (Oxford: Oxford University Press, 1988)

Woodward, John, *A Treatise on Heraldry British and Foreign*, 2 vols. (Edinburgh
  and London: W. and A. K. Johnson, 1896)

Yonge, Charlotte, *The Daisy Chain; or, Aspirations. A Family Chronicle* (John
  Parker and Son, 1856)

Zephaniah, Benjamin, *Propa Propaganda* (Newcastle upon Tyne: Bloodaxe
  Books, 1996)

Znamierowski, Alfred, *The World Encyclopedia of Flags: The Definitive Guide to International Flags, Banners, Standards and Ensigns* (Lorenz, 1999)

Significant online resources

British Council (http://www.britishcouncil.org/studies/england/report_6.htm)

Burke's Peerage (www.burkes-peerage.net)

Department for Culture, Media and Sport, Architecture and Historic Environment Division (http://www.culture.gov.uk/NR/rdonlyres/B924215A-93CE-4648-9BAD-F2CE4AE26F9A/0/Flagflyingrules20041.pdf)

Flags of the World (http://flagspot.net/flags/)

Union Flag Committee (http://www.flagwire.com/display_article.asp?id=6638)

ACKNOWLEDGEMENTS

THIS PROJECT BEGAN in conversation with Toby Mundy and Angus MacKinnon, and I am extremely grateful both to them and to all at Atlantic for their continued support and enthusiasm; Angus deserves particular thanks for his rigorous and exacting editing. Early drafts were read by Nick Champion and Joanne Parker, who provided keen criticism and corrected errors, and Annie Blinkhorn was especially helpful. Information, insights, and encouragement were provided by Patricia Bihlmaier, Ben Bourdillon, Beverley Campion, Jon Cannon, Chris Chapman, Brian Edwards, John Goodridge, John Halliwell, Mel Kersey, Matthew Kilburn, Wendy Lymer, Michael Nath, Henry Nelson, Jen Ogilvie, and Pangur Ban. I would also like to thank the staff and librarians of the Bodleian Library, British Library, London Library, National Library of Scotland, University of Bristol Library, and the archives responsible for the visual images.

My ideas benefited considerably from conference discussions at '(Re)creating Arthur', King Alfred's College, Winchester, 3–6 August 2004; 'Celtic Romanticism and Gothic Revisionism', Universities of Bristol and Otago, 15–16 January, 2005; the British Association for Romantic Studies Annual Conference 2005, University of Newcastle, 28–31 July 2005; and 'Flying the Flag: Critical Perspectives on Symbolism and Identity', Cultural Complexity in the New Norway,

University of Oslo, 24–5 November 2005. At this latter event it was a pleasure to meet Richard Jenkins and Thomas Hylland Eriksen, and Dominic Bryan, Anne Eriksen, Ole Kristian Grimnes, Neil Jarman, Jonathan Leib, Orvar Löfgren, Manuel Madriaga, Carolyn Marvin, and Iver Neumann. The University of Bristol Arts Faculty Research Fund was generous with funding that allowed me to attend these events, and to visit libraries across Britain.

Finally, thanks are due to the unerring attention of my agent David Godwin and his team, to my friends at the Ox, the Devy, and the King's, to my family, and to Joanne.

NG
South Zeal
St Blaise, 2006

INDEX